I0192553

WAR DEPARTMENT

OFFICE OF THE QUARTERMASTER-GENERAL

MANUAL OF PACK TRANSPORTATION

QUARTERMASTER CORPS

BY

MR. H. W. DALY

Chief Packer

UNDER DIRECTION OF THE QUARTERMASTER-GENERAL
U. S. ARMY

Fredonia Books
Amsterdam, The Netherlands

Manual of Pack Transportation

by
Henry W. Daly

ISBN: 1-58963-453-5

Reprinted from the 1917 edition

Fredonia Books
Amsterdam, The Netherlands
http://www.fredoniabooks.com

In order to make original editions of historical works available to scholars at an economical price, this facsimile of the original edition of 1917 is reproduced from the best available copy and has been digitally enhanced to improve legibility, but the text remains unaltered to retain historical authenticity.

WAR DEPARTMENT,
OFFICE OF THE CHIEF OF STAFF,
Washington, December 21, 1916.

The following Manual of Pack Transportion, revised 1916, is published for the information and guidance of all concerned.

By order of the Secretary of War:

H. L. SCOTT,
Major General, Chief of Staff.

CONTENTS.

Chapter IV.

War Department,
Office of the Quartermaster-General,
Washington, July 17, 1908.

Sir: I have the honor to forward herewith manuscript copy of a manual entitled "Pack Transportation, Q. M. D.," with 93 illustrations.

Under direction of this office, Mr. H. W. Daly, chief packer of the army, has prepared this work, which was later sent to Col. H. L. Scott, Superintendent of the Military Academy, who has had a wide experience with pack trains, and who, at the request of the Quartermaster-General, undertook the work of revision of this manuscript.

It is recommended that this work be published in an edition of 1,000 copies, 250 in cloth and 750 in paper binding. So far as this office has been able to ascertain, this manual contains the most complete history and detailed explanation of the art of packing that has yet been published and is, of its kind, it is believed, unique. It is considered that it will be of great value to the army at large and a valuable addition to the literature heretofore published upon this subject.

In transmitting this manuscript for publication this office desires to record its appreciative thanks to Colonel Scott and Mr. Daly for their efforts, which, it is confidently believed, in the form of this publication, will be valued by the army at large.

Very respectfully,

J. B. Aleshire,
Quartermaster-General, U. S. Army.

To the Secretary of War.

PREFACE.

The writer of this manual, Mr. Henry W. Daly, chief packmaster, Quartermaster's Department, U. S. Army, is the last of the old-time packers, the last of those who grew up with the pack service under Gen. George Crook, some of whom have followed "the bell" from the British line far down into old Mexico, and later in Alaska, Cuba, China, and the Philippines. Of them all he stands foremost as the most observant, the one who has added most to the efficiency of the pack service, and one who has placed the mounted service under lasting obligations to him—

First. By discovering the causes of the various "bunches" that arise on the mule's body.

Second. In discovering a simple remedy which reduces these "bunches" before they break down and suppurate.

Third. By his various inventions described in these pages.

Fourth. Finally, by placing the results of his experience in written form, so as to be preserved for the use of others.

From time to time, on account of the expense and difficulty of application, efforts have been made without success to substitute some other system of packing for the aparejo and the diamond hitch. In testing these systems there is always one fundamental and vital question to be asked, viz, does the substitute permit the rapid and easy alteration of the bearing surface promptly to reduce the "bunches" which arise from many causes and which, if not promptly reduced, speedily render the animal unserviceable. If the substitute does not adequately meet this test (which so far has only been met by the aparejo) it must be rejected. There are many other important advantages possessed by the aparejo over other systems, as will appear in the study of this book.

The value of the pack train has not lessened since the days of the Indian campaigns. Rapid and prolonged marches (impossible for wagons) are not yet out of date. It is just as necessary now to arrive on the field with food, ammunition, and medical supplies as it ever was. The usefulness of the pack train in carrying ammunition to supply the firing line where wagons can not go is not disputed by anyone. It behooves, therefore, all officers of the mobile force to understand the management of the pack train in all its branches, remembering that the "throwing of the diamond" is but a small part of the art, and one that is easily and quickly learned; that in the adjustment of the interior of the aparejo lies success or failure in the conservation of the back of the animal; that the train must be kept hard, lean, muscular, and docile by constant exercise carrying loads, and that by so doing mounted officers will be able to keep the accomplishment of their plans and the success of their undertakings in their own hands. I urge upon all persons in authority that they cherish the pack train and the packer, and see to it that proper trains are always ready in time of need, which time will come at the very beginning of any war on land.

H. L. SCOTT,
Colonel, U. S. Army,
Superintendent U. S. Military Academy.

WEST POINT, N. Y., *December 10, 1907.*

In the present book it is designed to give a general history of pack transportation, its employment in European and Asiatic countries, and its introduction into and development in the army of the United States, including a description of the various pack saddles, their comparative usefulness, and the latest improvements.

In the school system of packing the detailed instruction of an individual packer is first considered; then the more general instructions applicable to the service of a pack train is provided for. A brief discussion of marches and loads is included, with carefully prepared tables, showing practicable marches, loads, and rates of travel, etc., for a well-organized pack train.

A few notes on feeding, watering, traveling, etc., are included, as also a glossary of terms.

H. W. D.

FORT LEAVENWORTH, KANS., *June, 1907.*

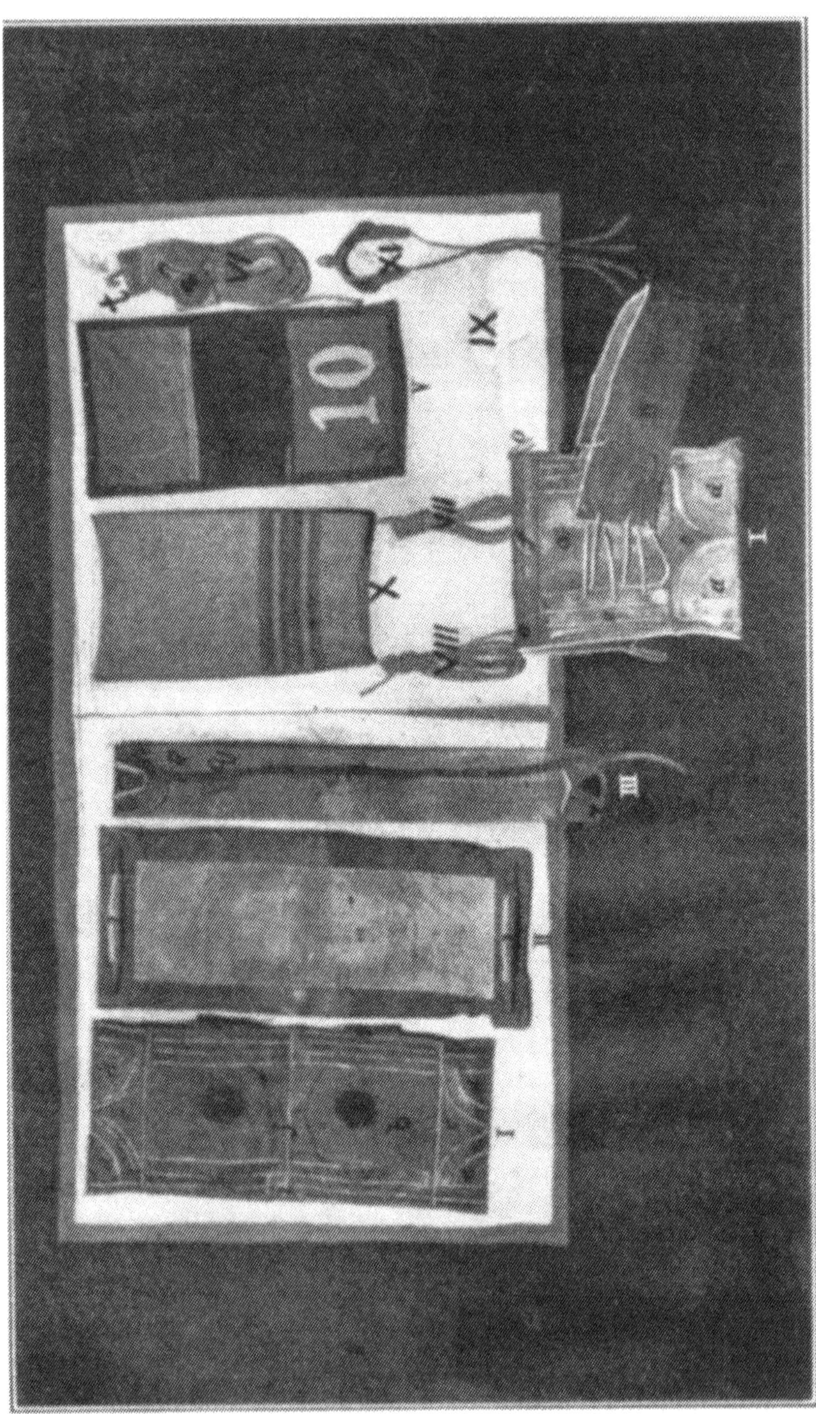

PACK TRANSPORTATION.

GENERAL HISTORY.

Primitive man in seeking a mode of transportation other than that of the personal burthen naturally utilized the most docile and tractable of the available animal kingdom. The elephant, camel, llama, ox, horse, mule, burro, reindeer, and dog, all by natural selection, have paid tribute to assist him in his travels.

There resulted necessarily pack saddles of various designs adapted to the conformation of the animal employed.

When man in an inventive mood introduced the "wheel" and developed this wheel transportation progressively by animal draft, steam, and electrical power, the employment of pack animals as the only means of rapid transportation had been relieved to a considerable extent; yet the occasion has and will oftentimes be necessary to cut loose from railroad and animal draft, when time, celerity, and freedom of movement becomes a prime factor in the success of an undertaking, especially in the zone of active operations.

The "crosstree" or sawbuck and the "aparejo" are used by civilized man, and it is a question which antedates the other.

The crosstree may be said to be universal, as it has been in use in European and Asiatic countries for centuries. It is believed that the Romans carried it into Gaul (France) and Britain in the conquest of these countries under Julius Cæsar. The French and the British carried it into Canada and the United States in the settlement of those territories.

In the mountainous portions of the British Isles and Switzerland there may be still seen the original method of carrying marketable supplies in "wicker" baskets fitted over the forks of the saddle and strapped to the donkey by the cincha and tightening strap. It is not unusual for the baskets to be unequally loaded, and often the loads are balanced by the addition of a billet of wood or a few stones. I have seen a sack of wheat en route to the mill balanced by a large stone in the opposite basket; also, en route to market, all hobbled and alive, a pig balancing a goat and a bunch of chickens.

In Canada, United States, Mexico, and South America they use "panniers" (French for basket) or pouches, made of canvas or leather which fit over the forks of the saddle and are strapped to the animal with cincha and tightening strap. In the above-named countries organized "burro" pack trains equipped with these panniers are employed to pack the ore from the mines to the stamp mills.

The system of "slinging and lashing" the load by means of ropes was seldom employed in the government service because of a lack of pad protection for the animal's body. However, the system was used by Gen. R. S. Mackenzie after the civil war in his Indian campaigns against the Kiowas and Comanches in the Southwest. The individual trapper, miner, and prospector packed with this system his few wants, consisting of his grub stake and mining tools.

The aparejo (pronounced "ap-pa-ray-ho"), a pack saddle, is believed to be of Arabian origin, the Arabs being a nomadic and pastoral people, employing the camel, horse, burro and its cross descendant, the mule, indigenous to Asiatic countries. The origin of the aparejo dates back to the employment of these animals as beasts of burden from remotest ages.

The aparejo was introduced into Spain by the Moors (see footnote) on the conquest of that country in the eighth century, and on the discovery of the western continent (America) the Spaniards carried it into South America and Mexico. Irving in his Conquest of Granada[a] records that Isabella of Spain, in 1486, organized, equipped, and maintained pack trains for the conquest of Granada, aggregating 14,000 mules and burros, which carried supplies and munitions of war for her army of 13,000 cavalry and 40,000 infantry. In the retinue of many nobles of note (Don Inigo Lopez de Mendoza, Duke of Infantado)[b] the sumpter (pack) mules had housings similar to those of the cavalry, of rich cloth embroidered with gold, and others of brocade with halters of silk, while the bridles, headpieces, and all the harnessings glittered with silver. An imitation of this feudal custom was made in the United States Government service prior to the Spanish-American war, 1898, when the "arrieros" (packers) would spend odd hours of loving toil upon the "grupera" and "corona" (crupper and saddle cloth), working the representation of some animal, bird, insignia, or legend with silken thread of various colors; the saddle, stock or cowboy, costing, when "full rigged," from $75 to $100, with its full skirting, sweaters, toe fenders fitting over the stirrups, from 12 to 18 inches long, and cantinas (saddle pockets) over cantle and pommel, the pommel being provided with the customary horn or cap (cabeza de silla), a necessary holdfast when throwing the lasso and various other uses known to western men. The whole beautifully stamped or engraved by hand, was trimmed with beaten silver dollars (Mexican), cut, and chased in various designs to suit the "arriero;" the bridle in similar manner with bit and spurs (Spanish) chased and inlaid with silver and gold, the spurs having a bunch of tiny spangles which were made to tinkle in the strut of the packer, who would thus affect the garb of his Spanish brother, wearing high-heeled top boots, with silken banda (sash) wrapped two or three times around the waist, embroidered shirt front, and conical sombrero (Mexican hat) with silver snake around the crown, the under side of brim being trimmed with silver braid.

NOTE.—Prior to the expulsion of the Moors the Moriscos of Spain practically controlled all the inland (pack) transportation. Many of their merchants became very wealthy and contributed very largely to the revenues of the Spanish Crown. Overtaxation, the improvidence of the Spanish princes, and the expulsion of these frugal and industrious people may be said to have led to the decline of Spain as a world power.

Such was the holiday costume of the packer of thirty-five or forty years ago, when, mounted on his favorite mule, he would sing some

[a] Irving, Conquest of Granada, chap. LXX, p. 383.
[b] Conquest of Granada, p. 225.

Spanish ditty when visiting friends in some near-by hamlet; a man who never turned his back on a foe or forsook a friend in moments of peril, honest and honorable in all his dealings with his fellow-men, kind to animals in his care, with a love for his calling, and thoroughly imbued with an "esprit de corps" for the pack service.

On the discovery of gold in California the adaptability of the pack mule for carrying supplies into the mining camps, not accessible by wagons, was readily recognized by the Americans. The mule and aparejo were in constant demand, and the employment of pack trains became a source of profit to many individuals.

In Mexico, on the road from Vera Cruz to the City of Mexico, a stone-paved road (Calzada), laid out by Cortez, and nearly 300 miles long, I have seen before the advent of the railroad, in 1873, pack trains loaded with coffee, sugar, and spices. These packs were made up to weigh from 100 to 125 pounds each, and were wrapped in coarse matting made from the fiber of the agave and other indigenous plants.

Rates for freighting, ranging from 30 to 75 cents per ton per mile, or for the service of the animal for the trip from $18 to $25, compared favorably with the rates charged after the discovery of gold in California, when pack trains, controlled by Americans, dotted the hills, carrying provisions, furniture, mining supplies, etc., to the mining towns in Oregon, Washington, Idaho, Montana, Nevada, and California.

In the early fifties and sixties on the trail from The Dalles to Umatilla Landing, Walla Walla, Lewiston, Kootenay, Salmon River, Frazer River, etc., could be heard from hill to hill the tinkle of the pack-train "bell horse." The "bell" was ordinarily a sheep bell attached by a strap to the neck of the horse. The latter is termed the "bellhorse," and is alluded to as the "bell," in such expressions as "lead the bell," "stop the bell," etc.

The service rendered by civilian aparejo pack trains employed by Gen. George Crook, after the close of the civil war, in operations against the hostile Paiutes, Shoshones, and Bannocks in Nevada, Oregon, and Idaho was so satisfactory that he caused the purchase of three of these trains by our Government, so that General Crook may well be called the "father" of modern pack service in the United States Army.

On the assignment of General Crook to the Department of Arizona, these trains were transferred with him and others organized for the campaign against the hostile Apaches, known as the "Tonto Basin war," 1871–1875. These trains were under the supervision of Thomas Moore as chief packer and Dave Mears, assistant chief packer, and the names of Hank and Yank, Jim O'Neil, Harry Haws, Chileno John, Frank Monack, Sam Bowman, the two Crooks ("Long" and "Short" Jim), Bill Knight, Nat Noble, Charley Hopkins, Bill Duklin, Manuel Lopez, and Lem Pyatt are inseparably connected with those campaigns.

In 1875 a number of these trains were transferred to the Department of the Platte, taking station at Camp Carlin, Cheyenne, Wyo., under Maj. J. V. Furey, depot quartermaster, and still others organized for the expedition of 1876, known as the "Sioux campaign." These trains were likewise under the supervision of Thomas Moore, as chief packer, and Dave Mears, assistant chief packer; and the names of

Dick Closter (better known as "Uncle Dick"), Johnny Patrick, Ed. Delaney, John Jaycox, Frank Houston, Pat Nolan, Tom McCaulif, Tom Mason, and Dave Young, packmasters, were inseparably connected with the "Sioux campaigns."

The success of General Crook in being able to cut loose from his wagon transportation, rendering his command thoroughly mobile by the aid of pack trains, led to their further employment by other officers of the Army, viz, Generals Mackenzie, Howard, Terry, Custer, and Miles, in the subjugation of the hostile tribes, notably the warlike Sioux, Cheyennes, Nez Perces, and Arapahoes in the Northwest, the fleet and vindictive Kiowas and Comanches through the Middle West, and last, but not least, the wily, slippery, and bloodthirsty Apache tribes who overran Arizona, New Mexico, and Texas.

Through all the arduous field service necessitated by campaigns against these various tribes, the pack mule has borne its part, and now may be regarded as thoroughly identified with our Army as an essential means of transportation.

As instancing a case in which pack animals have been employed for continuous work, the Geronimo campaign, lasting from May, 1885, to September, 1886, may be mentioned. Several pack trains followed the troops, taking part in the various operations. These trains were continuously on the move, traveling through the Territories of New Mexico and Arizona, and through the States of Sonora and Chihuahua in old Mexico, crossing the Sierra Madre Mountains at their highest and most precipitous part, from Opata in Sonora to Casas Grandes in Chihuahua. Through such a country any other form of transportation would have been utterly impracticable.

The mules carried loads averaging 250 pounds; the average day's march was 30 miles, except when climbing mountains, when about 15 miles per day was the rule. The mules subsisted entirely on the grasses found in the country, and when the campaign was over were returned to their posts in good condition.

As embodying some of the results of this experience with these trains for years, the present book aims to provide a system of instruction in the duties of a packer and in the service of a pack train.

H. W. Daly,
Chief Packer, Quartermaster's Department,
United States Army.

EVOLUTION OF THE APAREJO.

The aparejos used by the Mexicans [a] may be divided into two classes, having special uses—the first made of matting, from the fiber of the agave or similar fibrous plants growing in abundance in Mexico; the second of leather, of Mexican tan and finish. The first is used extensively by what we term in the United States "truck" farmers, who may be seen in the small hours of the morning approaching the hamlet, town, or city, driving before them a few donkeys laden with grass, wood, live or dressed pigs, goats, chickens, and various commodities under charge of a single native; the second in packing merchandise, mining material, and product of the mines; for this latter purpose the

[a] See Mexican prototype of the American aparejo, without sticks. The writer is indebted to Col. H. L. Scott, U. S. Army, Superintendent United States Military Academy, West Point, N. Y., for this view.

mule takes the place of the donkey. The aparejo in both cases, to protect the animal's body, is filled with dried grass. The aparejo cincha was provided with wooden stiffeners at each end; at one end the latigo is secured by means of leather thongs over the stiffener; at opposite end the wood is shaped to have a depression at center to receive the folds of the latigo in cinching the aparejo. All ropes were made of rawhide carefully prepared and plaited, and a wooden hook was provided on end of lash-rope cincha. In the spring of 1878 I saw both of these forms of aparejos in use in the State of Coahuila, Mexico, and wooden hooks were used in our service to some extent until the fall of 1886.

In 1867 Pack Master Richard Closter, better known as "Uncle Dick," stated his first attempt in ribbing the aparejo was for the purpose only of causing the aparejo to stand on its boots, the better to protect the rigging while in camp from the inclemencies of the weather, the usual method being to make as many rows of the rigging as a wagon sheet would cover, the series of rows helping as a brace to hold them on their boots; and to distinguish each aparejo, a design usually of the cactus was provided on the corona.

In the early morning the animals were brought in from the herd ground, rounded up, and either caught singly or tied to a picket line, in preparation for the day's travel.

The arrangement of the aparejos in an orderly manner (see fig. 108) by this provision gave opportunity to feed the animals on the rigging by spreading sections of canvas thereon, the night herders keeping watch on the animals while feeding to prevent their wasting the grain, which was an item of considerable expense in those days (1850–1870) and not always available. The method of feeding on the rigging taught the animals to come up to the rigging in patient expectation of the evening meal. This led to teaching the animals to come up to the rigging for grooming and in preparation for the day's travel.

At first but two sticks on each side were employed to stiffen the aparejo, one at front and one at rear; these reached but midway between the boots and center stitch line of the aparejo. Later sticks of full length were used for the same purpose, but not with any expectation of assisting the aparejo to hold a weighty load away from the withers and backbone of the animal.

After each day's travel it was noted on taking off the aparejo that the animal's backbone and withers were free of moisture, especially at front and rear, showing that the aparejo did not bear on that part of the body. This led to inserting an additional stick in rear of the "collar" known in those days by the term "crux," or cross, from the fact that that portion of the aparejo fitted over the cross on the withers of the mule and burro; later on from two to four additional sticks were inserted on each side between the collar and carrier pieces or rear of the aparejo, with the view only of saving the backbone and withers, which for twenty years following the discovery of gold in California were usually a mass of sores; the fact that the sticks supported the weight of the load was considered an absurd proposition, and at the present writing is not clearly understood by all pack masters. The fact is that the boots of the aparejo standing clear from contact with the animal's body the cincha, in compressing the aparejo on the body of the mule, gives to the aparejo the form of an arch, the cincha forming the base on which the boots of the aparejo rest. If the aparejo is of sufficient length, it will be noticed that in cinching, the aparejo is lifted by the cincha until the proper base line is formed from the center of the animal's belly each way. If the aparejo is too short or too long, its lifting power is lost, as is also the case when there is not sufficient padding in the boots, which should not be permitted to hug the body of the mule (a serious defect in the English pack saddle). The weight of the load being practically what is termed a dead weight, the lift or spring of the sticks is lost in the travel of the animal.

As pack trains were numerous in the early days (1850–1870) on the Pacific coast and in the Territories of the Northwest, the information spread rapidly from train to train and a system of ribbing the aparejo from front to rear became general. Each owner of a pack outfit, known as the "padrone," adopted a method of his own as his understanding of conditions prompted.

The eagerness to save the animal's backbone caused many pack masters to rib the aparejo too stiff—that is, by using sticks of too large diameter, giving rise to many body bunches and belly sores; and to save the loins from what are termed "kidney sores" sticks of too small diameter were employed, without regard to proportion from front to rear, causing the aparejo to flare out at front, giving opportunity for the aparejo to work forward and causing sore tails. To relieve this condition the reverse method of ribbing was used, with no better results.

The conformation of the mule was not considered in those days in ribbing the aparejo. The California mule being a cross between the burro and cayuse (pony), with large and deep belly, short in stature, was a great climber and hardy packer.

This conformation of mule afforded ample cause for sore tails, the difference in girth back of the elbow and at point of greatest swell of the barrel or belly varying from 8 to 16 inches. As ribbing by the mule's conformation as a guide was neither understood or attempted, mules of the above description always had sore tails, developing a double lip or growth above and below the sore. The mule having the reverse of this conformation—that is, of greater or equal girth back of the elbow as at center of barrel—will never have a sore tail, but mules of this description are not suited for pack service.

The success attending the introduction of sticks of full length in protecting the backbone led to a general application of their uses; the "round" collar gave way to the "square" collar to give opportunity to supply more ribs to protect the withers.

In trial of the square collar (6 by 6 inches) it was found that the aparejo often pinched the withers, and an offset of 2 by 2 inches was provided; this provision opened the collar with satisfactory results. (See i, fig. 1.)

In 1886 Mr. Moore supervised the construction of 100 or more aparejos at the military prison, Fort Leavenworth, Kans., in which a second offset was provided, and resulted in contracting the collar in a manner similar to the action of the square collar. This led to the return of the first offset, which has been used ever since.

The saddlery company of Messrs. Main & Winchester, 216 Battery street, San Francisco, Cal., furnished the Government the first regular stitched (wax end) aparejo some time during the early seventies.

The old aparejo of Mexican manufacture was of whitish tan or rawhide color of long life, a few of these being still in use during

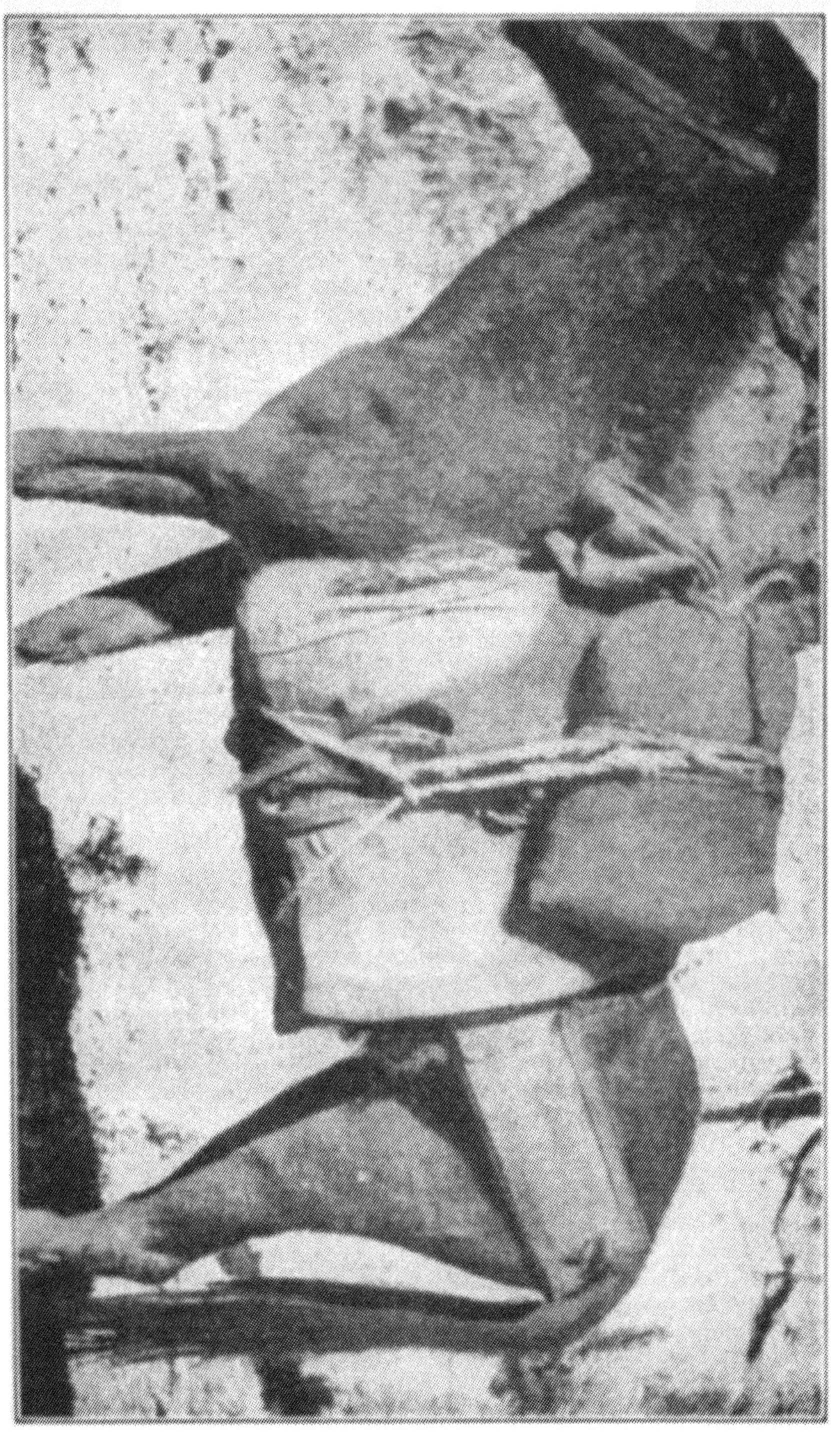

the Spanish-American war (1898). The leather was very heavy, a requisite to hold the hay or padding in position, and there were no facings on back or belly piece; a strip 12 inches long and from 3 to 6 inches wide was attached to the outside along the front edge, the inner edge provided with holes to lace the crupper; at rear a strip of leather about 3 by 6 inches was attached as a carrier piece and provided with holes to support the crupper by means of a short lace string, all sewing being done by whang and needle.

The crupper was made in sections termed "panels"—hence the name "panel crupper"—the center panel being usually provided with a surface covering of morocco or other fancy colored leather on which various designs or legends were stitched with silken threads of various colors, corresponding figures being provided on the corona or saddle pad.

The aparejos made by Main & Winchester were of light stock and in time became baggy. To overcome this defect, facings (reenforcings) of leather were employed on the "boots," back, and belly pieces of the aparejo, the backpiece having an additional reenforcing at its center, termed the "center facing." With all this reenforcing, the belly or body piece was too light and in short time became baggy, i. e., the belly piece stood away from the hay or padding, permitting the hay to fall from its proper position, a very serious defect.

The establishment of J. C. Johnson & Co., of San Francisco, turned out the best aparejos ever made for the United States Government. In the eighties some very good aparejos were supplied by a firm in Chicago. The initials stamped on the aparejos were, if I am not mistaken, "O. H. & Co." The Collins Saddlery Company, of Omaha, Nebr., also furnished some good aparejos in the eighties. Since that time St. Louis, Mo., controls the trade in pack equipment.

During the Geronimo campaign (1885) the Cheyenne pack trains, under charge of Mr. Thomas Moore, chief packer, were ordered to Fort Bowie, Ariz., and additional pack trains organized. Mr. Moore, in order to hasten the ribbing or "setting up" of the aparejos had a quantity of hickory slats or ribs made, about 1 inch wide and three-eighths of an inch thick throughout their entire length. No taper being provided on any of the sticks, necessarily the sticks bearing over the swell of the body received practically all of the pressure, causing terrible misery to the animal, and when loaded and turned loose the animal would immediately throw itself on the ground, when the snapping of the ribs (breaking) could be plainly heard, with a wail from the pack master of "There goes another one."

After the Geronimo campaign I was ordered to Cheyenne Depot (Camp Carlin), Cheyenne, Wyo., for station, under Capt. C. F. Humphrey, quartermaster, afterwards Quartermaster-General of the Army. Two pack trains were there organized, one under Pack Master Edward Delaney and one under myself, with Mr. Moore, chief packer.

In January, 1887, while setting up the aparejos, Mr. Moore had provided a quantity of those hickory slats for ribbing purposes; on my urging the necessity of their being tapered and tested before insertion, Mr. Moore stated why not use two or three slats and then two or three willow sticks, and alternate that way, with a view to weakening the ribbing, forgetting the fact that the slats would be hard to compress, while the fresh willows would readily yield to compression.

I had set up one aparejo with hickory slats, providing a suitable taper on each slat from front to rear, and testing each slat before inserting it in the aparejo. The results obtained were satisfactory. Mr. Moore, however, abandoned the hickory slats without sufficient reason.

It was the custom until 1880 to insert the "boot" sticks *after* ribbing the aparejo. This method on cinching the aparejo caused the sticks at center of boot to spread apart and override the sticks adjoining, and also forced the boot sticks upwardly by the action of the lash-rope cincha.

The insertion of the boot stick before ribbing held the boot from gathering or crumpling and gave a guide to measure the length of sticks between the center line and lower edge of boot stick, and prevented the displacing of the sticks at center of boot, as the boot stick offered resistance to action of the aparejo and lash-rope cincha.

The method of ribbing the aparejo by providing a gradual lessening of diameter to each stick from front to rear and from bottom toward top with as many sticks as the boot would contain, laid side by side, the butt ends resting on the flat surface of the boot stick, was not practiced until the spring of 1880. At first the custom was to alternate the butt end of stick between boot and center line (bottom and top).

I have also seen packers place a stick across the ribs close to the center stitch line, sometimes called the "eve," or comb, of the aparejo, and one or two midway, for the purpose, it was said, of keeping the sticks in position; in fixing for a bunch the cargador would locate the position of the bunch by observation, take out the hay, teaze it up, and replace it. This flattened or spread the bunch, which, if of medium size, always resulted in a steadfast; instead of cutting out the callous flesh and saving the mule further misery, it was permitted to spread, from a desire to hide the condition of the animal and as was usually the case, in not properly understanding how to arrange the hay or padding, and so prevent the bunch resulting into a steadfast.

It was about this time also (1880) that the practice of wetting the surface of the bunch (only) so as to locate its position on the aparejo was first introduced, by placing the aparejo on the mule, without corona or blanket or turning the crupper; and exactly over the position on the animal's body, where it rests, when cinched to the animal, and by rocking the aparejo with each hand the wet imprint was shown on the belly or body piece of the aparejo; then all the hay down to the sticks beneath the wet surface marked by the bunch was taken out without, in any manner, disturbing the rest of the bed of hay; on the next day's travel the bunch disappeared.

It was in the fall of 1883, while pack master of Lieutenant Gatewood's train at Fort Apache, that I discovered the cause of belly bunches and sore tails.

In 1884, General Crook stated that Mr. Moore, then chief packer, had said, "Pack animals were bound to become sore and there was no known way to avoid it."

The Geronimo campaign, lasting from May, 1885, to September, 1886, proved this statement to be a fallacy.

In the days of the "panel" crupper, the division of the crupper below the dock was a straight cut, provided with holes on either side for lacing. When the animal's tail became sore the lacing was tightened, with the object of drawing the dock of crupper downward from the animal's tail or dock, in each case affording no relief, but instead, causing soreness across the buttocks.

The latter trouble caused many pack masters to be constantly at work on the dock, adding more filling, some going so far as to provide a wooden stick to give it stiffness, without relief. (See sec. 9.)

When the withers and loins became sore, the aparejo was said to be "broken down;" hence the packer's objection to the use of the aparejo as a seat, an objection well taken, but not the direct cause. (See footnote.)

It was considered that tight cinching caused "belly bunches," and that unevenness in the filling or padding was alone responsible for body bunches.

For "body bunches" (a puffing up of the skin), the hay or padding was loosened up in the aparejo, with the expectation of giving relief, when perhaps a fault in one or more of the "ribs" may have been the direct cause of the "bunch." In the first instance, a loosening of the hay will not reduce a bunch; in the second instance, an improper rib or stick in the aparejo will always cause trouble. Both of these conditions must be removed to relieve the animal of its misery.

For "belly bunches" a gunny sack or other similar material was provided and folded in several thicknesses, so as to have a surface about 10 inches square, and held together by a few stitches; a hole was then cut at center, corresponding to the size of the bunch; the pad was then held over the affected part, the cincha of the aparejo holding pad to place and expecting to afford relief or reduce the bunch. The cause of the trouble not being removed, the use of the pad did not relieve it.

When the aparejo was improperly ribbed, by being too weak in front, the cinch of the aparejo worked forward, causing what are termed "cinch sores," retarding the travel of the animal, as well as throwing the load forward and eventually on the animal's neck if not attended to, and, if ribbed too weak, at rear, throwing the load over the animal's kidneys, preventing the animal from retaining its aparejo in proper position and carrying its load with comfort.

When the pack mule would leave the trail and lie down, endeavoring to relieve itself of its burden, it was said the animal could not stand tight cinching, and was not a suitable animal for pack service.

The misery shown by the dumb animal never appealed to the sense of the animal man.

For all these evils the proper "setting up" of the aparejo must be intelligently understood, and sore mules will be a thing of the past; or, in other words, there must be smooth bearing on the body of the animal covered by the aparejo and its cincha. (See secs. 4 to 7.)

NOTE.—The objection taken by packers to using the aparejo as a seat when in bivouac is because the weight of the body when seated on the aparejo compresses the ribs more than happens when the aparejo is on the animal.

EVOLUTION OF THE DIAMOND HITCH.

This form of hitch has its origin in the crosstree hitch. The early trappers of the Hudson Bay Company introduced the crosstree hitch among the Indians of the Northwest, and later the Americans gave to this hitch the name of the "squaw" hitch; along the Pacific coast, in sections where sheep raising has become an industry, it is known as the "sheepherder's" hitch, and by miners and prospectors as the "prospector's" hitch.

In the use of the aparejo, in forming the crosstree hitch (sec. 40) in bringing the loop of the running rope under the boot of the aparejo instead of around the "side" pack on each side, evolved the "double" hitch, and in not bringing a loop of the running rope under and forward of the standing rope—that is, forming the loop in rear of the standing rope—led to the formation of the "Oregon" diamond hitch (sec. 38), so named in being first practiced in that Territory before it became a State.

The practice of first throwing the lash rope cincha under the animal's belly to the off packer, in forming the regular diamond, in contrast to the crosstree and Oregon hitches, in which the lash rope is first thrown over the load and under the animal's belly by the near packer, may be said to date with the advent of the Americans after the discovery of gold in California, 1848–49. This I have heard disputed by some of the old-time packers of the early fifties, who stated the regular diamond was practiced by the Mexicans of California. However this may be, it may be stated the regular diamond hitch is used in the States bordering on the Rio Grande. In the Santa Rosa mines, State of Coahuila (Mexico), I have seen the diamond in use in 1878. In Mexico it has been the custom to use the crosstree and stirrup hitches, with the employment of the donkey, and aparejo made of matting; in the case of the stirrup hitch (sec. 41) a cincha 2 feet long, having a ring at each end, is employed; in forming the hitch the cincha is held under the animal's belly, using the ring on each end instead of forming the stirrup.

The double diamond hitch (sec. 33) was used in the days of freighting by civilian pack trains from The Dalles to the mining camps in the interior when barrels of flour, vinegar, pork, etc., had to be transported. This hitch had become a lost art in government service, due to a lack of necessity for its use, and is known to very few packers of the present day, the double hitch being erroneously called the "double diamond." (Sec. 34.)

The pole hitch has been erroneously called the "squaw" hitch; the fact that the Indians have never used the aparejo confirms this statement. It can not be used with the crosstree or riding saddle, as no portion of the rope in the formation of the hitch encircles the body of the animal. (Sec. 37.)

CHAPTER 1.

PACK SADDLES—DESCRIPTION AND USES.

THE APAREJO.

SECTION 1. The aparejo and its various accessories are called, collectively, "The aparejo complete" (fig. 1).

The aparejo complete includes the following:

Aparejo complete:
- Aparejo proper—
  1. Body of the aparejo.
  2. Aparejo cover, or sobre jalma.
  3. Aparejo cincha.
  4. Crupper, or grupera.
  5. Corona, or saddle pad.
- Accessories—
  6. Lash rope with cincha and hook.
  7. Sling rope.
  8. Lair ropes (two).
  9. Pack covers, or mantas (two).
  10. Pack blanket.

NOTE.—For convenience the packer divides the aparejo complete into two sections—the aparejo proper and the aparejo complete.

The first five items of the above form what is termed the "aparejo proper," and in the vernacular of the packer are referred to as the "rigging."

To explain: When in bivouac the aparejo (proper) is held apart from its accessories, i. e., the aparejos are arranged in an orderly manner, and the animals are taught to approach them and stand quietly, as if at attention. The accessories are employed in the make-up of commercial packages into what is termed "side" packs, and and are likewise arranged in an orderly manner adjacent to the rigging, and termed the "cargo."

The last item, the pack blanket, must be considered a part of its complete equipment, as its use supplies additional padding for the aparejo, the blanket being carried between the corona and aparejo, folded in such manner as to cover the corona, and is used as bedding by the packer, who, it should be remembered, is not permitted to supply personal bedding which impairs the carrying capacity of the train.

Three sizes of aparejos are provided, respectively 58, 60, and 62 inches in length, and uniformly 24 inches throughout their entire width.

A brief description follows of the parts included in the aparejo complete:

1. *The body of the aparejo* (I, fig. 1).—The principal leather parts are:

(*a*) Backpiece.
(*b*) Body piece.
(*c*) Boots, or end pieces.
(*d*) Boot facings.
(*e*) Front facing.
(*f*) Center facing.
(*g*) Carrier pieces.
(*h*) The welts.

NOTE.—See "Specifications for aparejos," section 130.

2. The aparejo cover (or sobre-jalma) (II, fig. 1) is made of No. 4 cotton duck. It is faced at sides and ends with leather, so as to give sufficient width to enable it to cover the aparejo. The ends are protected by wooden sticks or shoes, held in place by caps of leather, sewn over either end (L, II, fig. 1). These shoes serve to stiffen the ends of the aparejo cover and keep it from wrinkling and gathering. The cover is secured by thongs to the aparejo at the extremities of its middle or center line (*o*, L, fig. 1).

NOTE.—Sobre-Jalma, erroneously called sovereign hammer, soldier hammer, is a compound word of Arabic and Spanish used by the Morriscos of Spain, meaning "over cover;" sobre-jalma is a contraction of sobre-en-jalmas, meaning a covering for the harnessing, and applied to the aparejo or pack saddle, now called aparejo cover, or sobre-jalma, sobre-halma (or so-bre-hal-ma).

3. The aparejo cincha (III, fig. 1), is made of No. 4 cotton duck, doubled so as to have a width of 10 inches, and sewn along its center with two seams spaced 1 inch apart. At one end it is faced with leather (*m*, III, fig. 1); a $\frac{5}{16}$-inch iron rod being held in the fold of the facing, so as to be on the edge of the cincha. (Sec. 130.)

After this facing is in place three holes are punched through it to receive the lacing of the latigo, or cincha strap. The latigo (*n*, III, fig. 1), is from 6 to 7 feet long. In its attachment to the cincha it carries a ring, called the "rendering" ring, through which the latigo passes in tightening (*p*, III, fig. 1). Fifteen inches from this end of cincha a round piece of leather 3 inches in diameter is sewed on, and two holes punched through it; a leather thong is attached thereto, so as to leave a loop of 3 inches. This is called the "finger" loop, and is used to secure the end of the latigo strap after cinching (*q*, III, fig. 1).

The other end of the cincha carries a curved piece of gas pipe (*r*, III, fig. 1), flattened at each end, and provided with holes to receive rivets. It is secured to the canvas by a leather facing. This curved piece of pipe takes the place of an ordinary ring in the end of cincha.

When finished the cincha should be 8 inches longer than the aparejo with which it is to be used and ten inches longer for mountain battery service.

4. The crupper (IV, fig. 1) is made of heavy, black leather, about 78 inches long and 12 inches wide. At its middle part it is shaped down to fit under the animal's dock. The portion which fits under the dock is provided with a cover, called the "dock" piece. The dock piece is filled with padding, antelope hair being considered best

for the purpose, and is rounded (IV, fig. 1). The ends and upper edges are provided with holes for lacing the crupper to the front facings of back piece and to the carrier pieces, respectively. Leather thongs are employed for these lacings, and by means of these the crupper may be adjusted to the length of the animal.

5. The corona, or saddle pad (V, fig. 1), is made of three thicknesses of good blanket, with a center facing of similar material; at one edge at center of its length a semicircular stitch line is provided to indicate the front, or that portion fitting over the animal's withers, and a center stitch line to indicate the middle of the corona. In the center of one-half of its length a numeral to designate the number of the aparejo is placed on the upper or outward side of the corona, the under side being lined with light canvas, and the whole bound all around with suitable material.

In use the "canvas" side rests on the animal's back, and the corona is cleaned from day to day, a table knife being carried by cutting a horizontal slit between the two lines of stitching on the front facing of the aparejo for this purpose.

ACCESSORIES OF THE APAREJO.

6. *The lash rope with cincha and hook* (VI, fig. 1).—The lash rope is about 50 feet long, size nine-sixteenths or one-half inch, best hand-laid manila. At one end it has a loop or eye to receive the lacing of its cincha; the other end is well seized or wrapped to prevent unraveling. The cincha (VI, *s*, fig. 1) is made of light canvas, folded so as to have a width of 6 inches; at one end it has a facing of leather on both sides and is provided with five holes to carry lacing, by means of which it is attached to the loop or eye of the lash rope; the other end is faced with leather in similar manner, and a strong hook (VI, *t*, fig. 1) of metal or wood is supplied. When made, the cincha must not be more than 30 inches long.

7. The sling rope (VII, fig. 1) is about 30 feet long, size three-eighths inch, best hand-laid manila, well seized at each end. It is used for slinging the load preparatory to lashing.

8. The lair rope (VIII, fig. 1) is about 30 feet long, size three-eighths inch, best hand-laid manila; at one end a loop or eye is prepared; the other is securely seized. The free end is passed through the loop or eye, preparatory to "lairing up" the side packs—i. e., for securing the pack covers or mantas around the packs.

9. The pack cover or manta (IX, fig. 1) is made of 72-inch No. 4 cotton duck. When made, it is 6 feet square.

Each pack is ordinarily wrapped in a manta. Such as are liable to suffer damage or deterioration during transportation are always so protected.

10. The pack blanket (X, fig. 1) is similar to the issue (bed) blanket in use in the service; in the center of the blanket the initial letters, "U. S., Q. M. C., P. T.," are provided. The two last letters are to distinguish pack transportation blankets from others, so that they may be traced if lost or stolen. Each particular train has the serial number stamped on each blanket, as an additional guide to keep them together.

CROSS-TREE OR SAWBUCK.

SEC. 2. The cross-tree, as the term implies, consists of two saddle boards, shaped somewhat similar to the McClellan saddletree, connected at front and rear (pommel and cantle), by crosspieces shaped like the letter "X," termed the "cruz" (cross), or forks of the saddle, supplied with a breast strap, breeching, and quarter straps, holding cincha and latigo, or tightening strap, accompanied by a saddle pad or blanket.

For the carrying of supplies two methods are in use:

First (or original method). By the employment of wicker baskets, and panniers made of canvas or leather, constructed so as to fit over the forks of the saddle, and strapped to the animal by the aid of cincha and latigo.

Second. By the employment of "sling and lash" rope. (See secs. 39–40.) This latter method has a more general application, due to its relative lightness and cheapness, and is used by trappers, miners, prospectors, small hunting parties, and members of the Bureau of Forestry, etc. (See secs. 39 and 40 and figs. 54 to 57.)

THE "MOORE" PACK SADDLE.

SEC. 3. Description of this saddle is copied from pamphlet published by authority of the War Department, Washington, Government Printing Office, 1881. (Figs. 3, 4, 5.)

The pack saddle consists of the "saddle proper," two pads, corresponding with the pads of the aparejo, laced on either side of the saddle to the skirts and at the upper edges over the top; a crupper similar to the aparejo crupper, but lighter, laced to the rear edges of the saddle skirts; a corona, or pad, used under the saddle and next to the animal's back; a manta, or pack cover, two pieces of canvas 7 feet long and 22 inches wide, stitched together along their long edges; halter and strap; cincha of canvas 10 inches wide, and in length according to the size of the animal; "sling rope;" best hand-laid manila whale line, one-half inch, 20 to 30 feet long; "lash rope," with leather cincha, same as above, five-eighths inch, 42 feet long, and one blind to each five packs. (6, fig. 3.)

When the saddle is "full-rigged," as it is called, that is, supplied with sling straps and cargo cinch, the sling and lash ropes are dispensed with. (Fig. 4.)

After years of its use, under personal observation, the following defects have developed:

The crupper, being too short in length, when laced to the rear edges of the saddle skirts, leaves a space of from 4 to 12 inches, as determined by the conformation of the animal. Necessarily the action of the saddle and crupper are independent of each other, causing soreness by friction of the lacing, due to travel action of the animal.

When a "bunch" arises (a puffing up of the skin), caused by unevenness in the filling of the pads, or shape of the saddle boards lacking conformation to fit the varying flesh conditions of the animal's back, there is no provision in the make-up of the saddle to relieve the animal of its misery, and, necessarily, its constant use destroys the usefulness of the animal.

The "arch" irons at front and rear, connecting the saddle boards, occasionally spread apart, allowing the irons to rest on the animal's withers and backbone by compression of weight of load. The arch iron at front, being higher, prevents the employment of "top" loads and, I may add, all "box" loads, as the weight of load is thrown

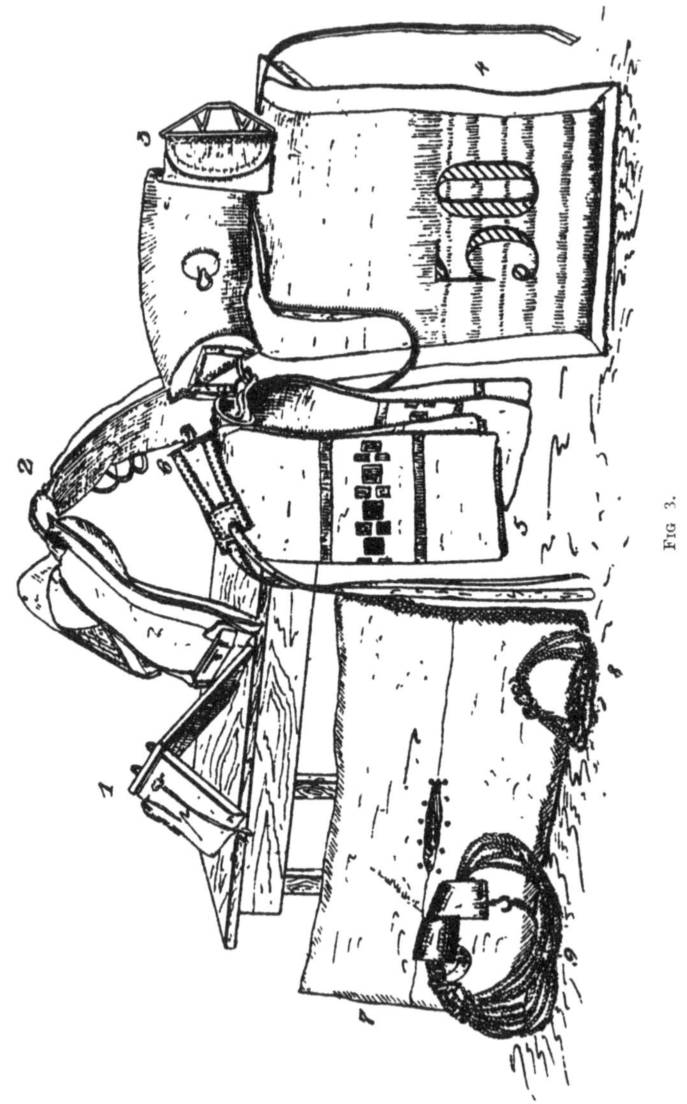

Fig 3.

to the rear over the animal's kidneys, causing soreness and kidney trouble. All packages of greater length than the width of the saddle rest on the animal's hips, causing soreness, due to the low and close fit of the saddle on the animal's body.

In the application of the "diamond" hitch the rope slips off the corners at ends of pads, due to lack of sufficient stiffness, as well as allowing the cincha to work forward, interfering with the travel of the animal, and causing a soreness at elbow or forearm, termed cinch sore.

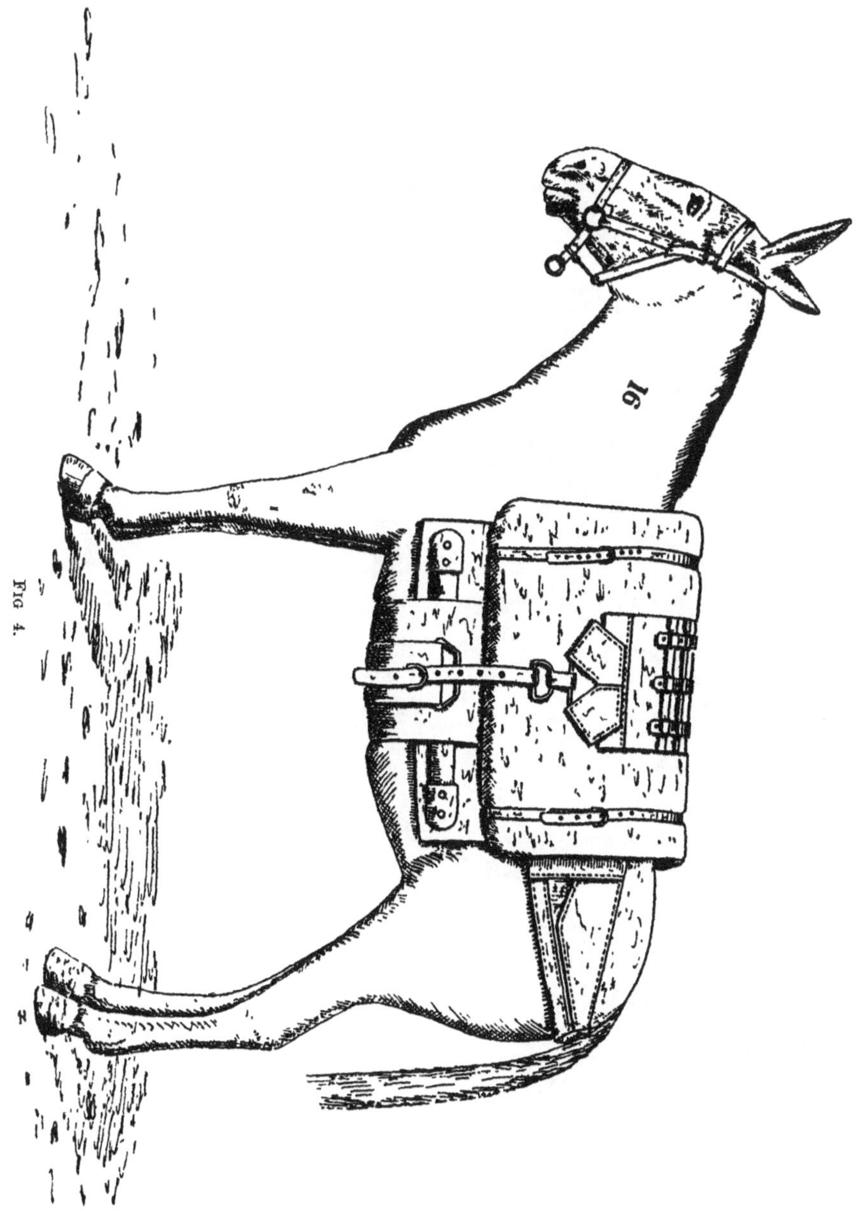

FIG 4.

The employment of "sling straps" and cargo cinch with the saddle, termed "full-rigged," was early dispensed with as unsuited to securing commercial packages. (Fig. 4.)

In the annual report of Maj. Gen. Leonard Wood, commanding the Department of Cuba, Habana, Cuba, June 30, 1901, "report of the chief quartermaster of the department," page 13, says:

Under date of June 4, 1901, the department commander ordered a competitive trial at Camp R. S. MacKenzie, Cuba, to determine the relative merits of the aparejo

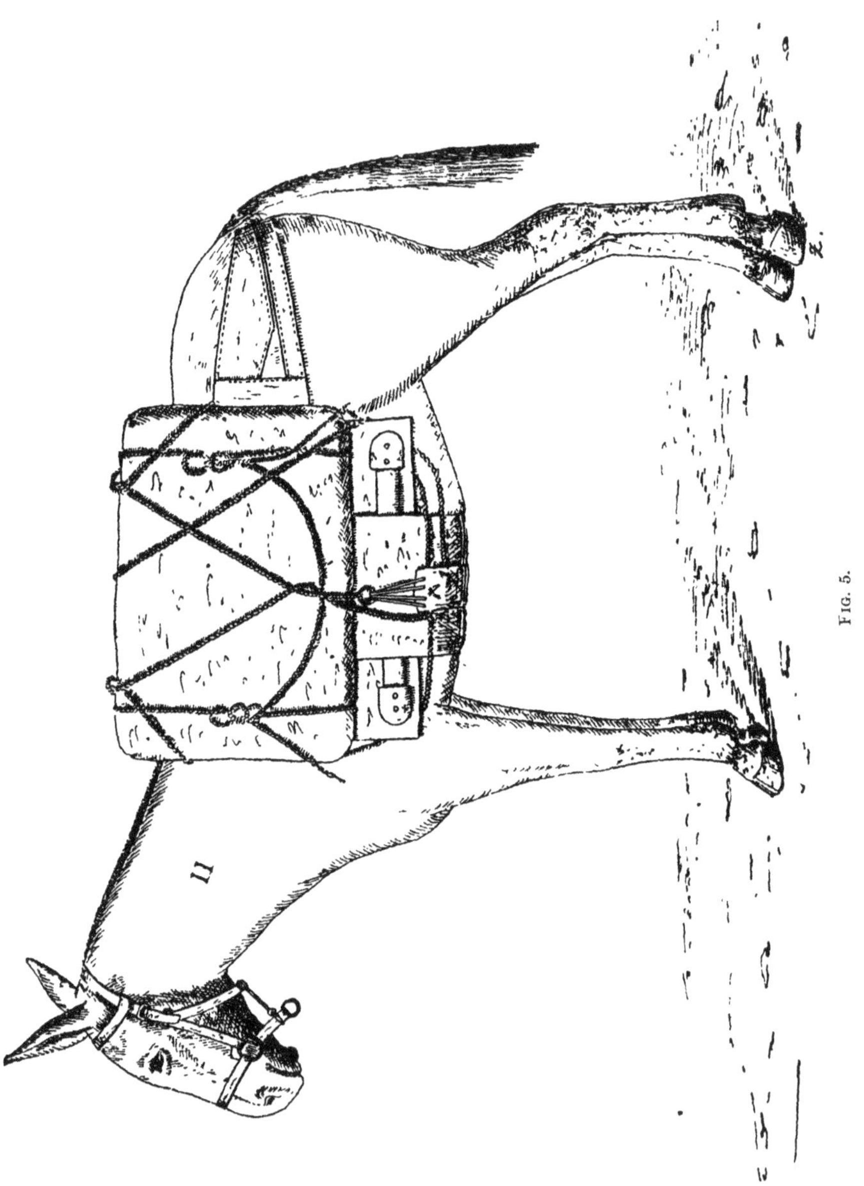

FIG. 5.

and Moore pack saddles. The conditions of this trial required a daily march of 25 miles to be made, each pack mule carrying a load of 250 pounds. In this contest, conducted under the supervision of Capt. R. J. Duff, Eighth Cavalry, as referee, it was developed that the Moore pack saddle is entirely unsuited for severe field service.

It is recommended that all pack equipment hereafter furnished for use in this department consist of the aparejo.

CHAPTER II.

ASSEMBLING AND CARE OF THE APAREJO.

SELECTION OF STICKS SUITABLE FOR RIBBING APAREJOS.

SEC. 4. The selection of suitable sticks or withes to rib the aparejo is usually governed by locality, and as the willow is found in all the States and Territories, it has been generally employed. While there are five species of the willow family that may be considered suitable—the gray, the black, the red, the button, and desert willows—the first named is preferred, having less pith, being tougher and more springy, straight as an arrow, and with few blemishes. Arrowwood and dogwood are found in Texas and Arizona, but are of scrubby growth. When found suitable, however, they make a most excellent stick for ribbing aparejos; it has less pith than the willow and holds life or spring longer, resembling the guayaba found in Cuba and the Philippines—the best stick for ribbing aparejos that has been tested. Ash, hickory, and pecan "sprouts" are a superior stick to any of the former, due to longer life in spring; these three last woods in sprout form are not numerous, so that they may not be classed in the list of available sticks for ribbing aparejos.

The essential requisites in determining suitable sticks for ribbing aparejos are toughness, spring, and taper, together with straightness and freedom from knots and other blemishes.

SELECTION OF HAY SUITABLE AS PADDING FOR APAREJOS.

SEC. 5. For padding or filling aparejos, nothing can compare with suitable hay. For this purpose fine, soft, elastic hay that will admit of mixing similar to curled hair is best suited as padding for aparejos.

Such hay as furnished by breweries for packing bottles in barrels answers this description, and no doubt can be procured in bale form.

This class of hay has the elasticity of curled hair, and admits of separation, straw by straw, a condition impossible in curled hair, black moss or lichen, sea grass, and excelsior, an essential quality when fixing for a "bunch."

To sum up, any padding that has the life and spring of curled hair, that will admit of separation when fixing for a bunch, without disturbing the rest of the bed of hay in the aparejo can be classed as suitable padding for aparejos. This class of hay is termed by packers "aparejo hay."

SETTING UP THE APAREJO.

SEC. 6. First, soak the aparejo in tepid water, say from ten to fifteen minutes (double the time if cold); take out and drain, and place on bench or ground, and prepare two sticks, termed the "boot sticks," of suitable hard wood 21½ inches long, 2½ inches wide, and three-quarters of an inch thick; the ends must be rounded on one side. The rounded or tapered ends to face the inside of back piece of the aparejo; it is *positively* forbidden to insert a "boot stick" in the aparejo that requires *force* to adjust it across the bottom of the boot, by so doing, when the aparejo dries, the ends of the boot stick project over the sewing at ends of the aparejo, and soon wears itself through the leather, as well as bursting the sewing at ends of the aparejo. A good substitute is the straight portion of a disused wagon bow.

Introduce a "boot stick" through hand-hole on each panel, and adjust it across the bottom of the boot, the side of the boot stick to be parallel with the sides of the aparejo, the flat surface of stick to face the inside of belly piece of the aparejo.

As the aparejo will take from twenty-five to thirty sticks (willow) on each side—that is, when laid side by side—it is well, before commencing to "rib up" the aparejo, to make three divisions of the sticks to be employed, say twenty in each division, rejecting any that are not straight or have any malformation, the largest for No. 1, the medium for No. 2, and the smallest for No. 3; commencing with the first that fits under the collar of the aparejo, which may have a diameter of three-quarters of an inch, lessening the diameter progressively to the last at rear, the diameter of which must be three-eighths of an inch.

Now take two sticks of division No. 1, largest size, and mate them as to size and toughness, one for each side, to fit under collar at front of aparejo.

Before introducing the first four or five sticks it is well to provide a taper of about 2 inches long on butt end of sticks, as they can thus keep position all the better on the flat surface of the boot stick when placing them in position under the collar of the aparejo.[a]

In measuring the length of stick, place the stick on the aparejo, butt end resting on lower edge of boot stick and in alignment under the collar; mark the stick in line with the stitching of collar at its forward part and cut off with pocketknife; round and smooth off the top surface.

Introduce the stick through slit provided on each side at center stitch line, butt end first, and press to forward corner of boot, the end of stick resting against and over[b] the flattened surface of the boot stick, then bring the stick to place under the collar at the forward edge of the aparejo.

Under no circumstances permit a stick to take position that is too long or too short, throughout the operation.

Having placed the first two sticks in position, one on either side of the aparejo, under the collar, select two more in similar manner as the first two, but be careful that they are not of greater diameter or toughness; this rule must *positively* be adhered to in the taper and toughness of each corresponding pair of sticks throughout the operation from front to rear. Any departure from this rule will mark

---

[a] A flat surface provided on butt end of sticks will prevent their rolling from position at the front corner of the boot; these sticks, being of larger diameter, are apt to be pressed out of position during the process of ribbing.

[b] This occurs in the process of ribbing. The aparejo is spread out its full length, the belly or body piece upward. When the aparejo stands on its boots, the sticks show they are against and under the boot stick.

the mule by "bunching;" taking out the hay, as in fixing for a bunch will not remove the trouble

Having ribbed up as far as slit at center of stitch line, commence at rear, using the smallest stick, increasing the diameter of stick until the center is again reached, and the aparejo is properly ribbed.

The aparejo having thus been "ribbed up," in order to fill the sides or panels with hay, proceed as follows:

Stand the aparejo up on its boots, the hand-holes facing out, and procure a tamping stick; an old broom handle is good for the purpose.

Take a pocketknife or drawing knife and shave end of stick so as to leave two sides flattened, tapering toward end of stick; thickness at end, one-quarter inch. Concave or hollow the end on flat side, so that it may grip the hay in tamping. In tamping manipulate this stick with the hands; do not use a hammer.

Introduce the hay through the hand-hole, a little at a time, and press into the corners of boots. It is well to commence at front corners always. Tamp down with stick. In tamping do not hold the hands well out from the aparejo, but rather lean the stick against the top of aparejo; the point or end of stick is then not so apt to pass between the ribs in tamping.

Be careful in tamping corners that you do not use too much hay at one time, or in each course. You will thus be enabled all the better to get the corners solid. This tamping should extend back about 6 inches from the corners on either side, and should be thoroughly done. Be careful to get the four corners equal. Tamp lightly along center of boot. Three or four courses of hay will fill the lengths of boots 4 inches in depth and thickness or nearly so.

Now, spread out the aparejo to its full length on the ground, or place on bench, hand-hole upward, and introduce the hand to ascertain if the ribs have been misplaced at top or bottom.

Ribs being in place, proceed to fill along top or center. Use the stick in pressing the hay into the corners under collar, and at the rear of the aparejo, but only far enough back or toward you to enable the hand to be used in filling the rest. Lay two courses through the body of the aparejo, spreading each course evenly. Do not allow the hay to lay in lumps, as it will "bunch" or wound the animal.

After the aparejo has been used a while, and the hay has been well settled in its place and made compact, the thickness of the filling through the body should be about 2 inches. The aparejo should have a thin appearance through the body; it should not appear stuffed and swollen.

The thickness of the filling decreases gradually from the boots to the hand-hole of the aparejo, being about twice as great in the boots as in the center of panel or hand-hole.

At the top or center the normal thickness extends to within about 4 inches of the center stitch line, the thickness gradually decreasing from there to the middle seam, where it is practically nothing.

The packer now proceeds to put in additional filling, so as to adjust the aparejo more accurately to the mule's shape, i. e., he proceeds to "dress" or to face up the aparejo, as it is called.

First, dress or face each front boot, the dressing to extend inward each way from the front corner toward the hand-hole, say 7 inches, and must be of oval shape. In introducing the hay hold the palm of the hand upward, so as not to disturb the bed of hay underneath the hand, increasing the width and depth of dressing as you recede from the front corner, and the inward edge of dressing to be of semicircular form; for the next 4 inches decrease the thickness rapidly as the hand-hole is approached. This will leave the filling of the front boot obviously greater than the rear boot. The difference should be about 1 inch for mules of ordinary girth in barrel; mules of larger girth will necessarily require more hay in the front boot to make the aparejo sit on the animal with the boot sticks parallel.

Next, make a dressing under the collar of aparejo for the withers of the animal.

For this purpose keep the palm of the hand up and carry the hay well into the corners at front, using as little of the hay at each time as possible, so as not to disturb the bed formed beneath the hand; carry this dressing back from the corner, increasing the width and depth of dressing as you recede from the corners, the outer edge of dressing to be of semicircular form.

The upper point of the semicircle should not approach the center line within a space of 4 inches. The whole line of semicircle should gradually decrease in thickness as the hand-hole is approached to within 4 inches of hole. The depth of this dressing will be governed by the height of the animal's withers. The aparejo when cinched on the mule should be level from front to rear. In similar manner the boots must be parallel and horizontal.

The front edge, between boot and collar, may now have an additional dressing 3 inches wide and about 1 inch in thickness, tapering each way toward the center, so as to give opportunity for the aparejo to brake or conform to the body of the animal, in the act of cinching; and the aparejo is properly "set up."

Now stand the aparejo up; that is, cause it to stand on its boots. Next, procure a crupper (standard size), and two lace thongs each about 7 feet long and one-half of an inch wide; at heavy end of each lace thong, and three-fourths of an inch from each end cut a slit 1½ inches long, introduce the light end of each thong through the upper hole on each end of crupper and pass the end through the slit on opposite end of thong and draw down snug; next procure two lace thongs, length of thongs, say 12 inches, and attach the crupper to the "carrier" pieces, and tie down; this helps to hold the crupper in the operation of lacing.

Now pass the end of crupper lacing through the second hole on front facing (counting from the collar), from above down or, as may be said, from outside toward inside, and draw thong snug.

Next, in similar manner, pass the thong through the second hole on crupper, then through the fourth hole on front facing, again through the fourth hole on crupper, and, lastly, through the bottom or end hole on front facing and crupper, and tie down. Always finish the tie on the last hole of the crupper; never on the front facing, as action of the crupper, which should bind or steady the aparejo is lost by such action.

It must be remembered that the lacing must *positively* pass through holes on front facing and crupper from above down, in order that lacing may not render or slip when the aparejo is fitted to the mule.

Next, punch two holes, one-half inch apart, at each extremity of the center line of the aparejo, and between the two outside stitch lines. Procure thongs and fit aparejo cover. Punch two holes correspondingly in the cover and tie down.

Procure cincha; place the latigo along center of its length and double the cincha, causing the upper surface of cincha carrying finger piece to be inside. Place cincha on aparejo in center, leaving the ends on the "off" side with ends of finger loop on top.

Turn crupper and rest dock on center of aparejo.

Procure a corona; double it and place it on aparejo, its ends facing to the front, numbered side up.

The aparejo is now set up and ready for use.

SETTING UP THE "DALY" APAREJO FOR USE.

SEC. 7. Owing to the heavy loads necessitated by the carrying of mountain guns (Vicker's, Maxim, etc.), the principal parts of which are carried as "top" loads, it has been found advantageous to supply boot and saddle bars of suitable wood, each bar being shaped so as to conform to that particular part of the aparejo coming least in contact with the body of the animal, i. e., that portion of the aparejo that should not rest on the animal's backbone, and be clear of the mule's belly. Slots are provided on bars to receive the ribs and hold them securely in position. Nine ribs are provided on each side, serially numbered with the corresponding number of the aparejo for which intended, the ribs being graduated in length of taper from front to rear, following the lines of the willow-stick method.

The boot bars conform to the shape of the boots, as formed by the padding of hay, with the provision of adding a sufficiency of hay over the upper portion of the bars where that portion of the boot comes into contact with the body of the mule.

The saddle bars, in similar manner, with the provision of adding a sufficiency of hay over the lower portion of the bars, where the weight of load is carried by the animal.

To rib up the aparejo with boot, saddle bars, and ribs a slit 12 inches long is provided on the back piece at rear, with holes punched on either side to receive lace thongs, and a "hand-hole" is provided, cut around to within a space of 2 inches at top, so as not to meet the "hand-hole" on opposite or belly side of aparejo. A hole is punched on lower edge of lid, with hole to correspond on back piece for lace thong, to secure lid of back piece. The "hand-hole" is provided as a help to guide the ribs to proper position in setting up the aparejo.

1. *To rib up.*—Unlace the slits and hand-holes; soak the aparejo in tepid water for about fifteen minutes; drain it and lay flat, back pieces up; insert the boot stick and the saddle bar through the slit in rear and press them to their places at the boot and the center stitch line, slotted sides up; insert the numbered set of nine ribs through the slit in rear in their numerical order, and seat them in that order from collar to rear in the slots of the boot stick and saddle bar, butts at the boot; secure the top of each rib as it is seated by inserting the key bar at the front edge below the collar and passing it over the rib in place; fasten the key bar to the collar by the thong.

NOTE.—Aparejos are issued to the service with ribs in place. Ribs are furnished in sets of nine. Each rib is numbered at its butt to correspond to its proper numerical position in the panel, counting from the collar to the rear. Each rib is also stamped with the size of the aparejo for which it is made. The aparejos are furnished in 58, 60, and 62 inch sizes. The ribs for a 60-inch aparejo are therefore marked 1–60, 2–60, 3–60, etc. Should repairs or alterations make it necessary to rib up, the butt of the fifth rib is seated in its slot, the overlap at its slot in the saddle bar is marked and cut away, and the other ribs are cut to the exact resulting length.

2. *To fill or pad.*—Turn the aparejo over, belly pieces up; procure about 6 pounds of fine, soft, elastic hay; taking a little at a time, tease or "mix" it carefully; insert it through the hand-hole, and thus gradually fill the body of the aparejo with a smooth and even layer not more than 2 inches thick.

NOTE.—Other filling may be used in necessity, such as moss, excelsior, curled hair, sea grass, but these substitutes are difficult of manipulation in alteration necessary to accommodate the rigging to injuries of the mule. By teasing or "mixing" is meant the arrangement of the straws so that they will cross one another. The body of the aparejo is that part which comes in contact with the body of the mule. As 3 inches of the lower portion of each boot stick and 3 inches of the upper portion of each saddle bar must not come into contact with the mule, no filling should be pressed within 3 inches of the end of the boot or within 3 inches of the center stitch line. The body course tapers, however, so as to overlap the boot stick and saddle bar, and also tapers toward front and rear.

3. *To face or dress.*—To adjust the aparejo more accurately to the shape of the mule introduce filling and press it well into the corner of the front boot; working toward the hand-hole, continue the facing along the boot stick and front edge, gradually increasing its thickness to about an inch at 7 inches from the corner and forming its inner edge into the arc of a circle concentric with the hand-hole, the thickness tapering to the ends of the arc; continue this for 3 inches more toward the hand-hole, rapidly decreasing the thickness to nothing; proceed in exactly the same way at the collar; under no circumstances should the collar facing reach within 7 inches of the center of the hand-hole. Connect the front boot and collar facings by a dressing along the front edge about 3 inches wide and an inch thick, decreasing in thickness toward the hand-hole and toward the middle of the edge.

NOTE.—In facing up introduce the filling with the hand, palm up, so as not to disturb the body course. In case the leather will not yield enough to permit the filling to be introduced well into the corners, the tamping stick may be used to raise it. This stick, used with the commercial aparejo, is 4 or 5 feet long, 1¼ inches in diameter, wedge shaped for 4 inches from one end, the edge of the wedge being about one-fourth inch thick and grooved. The object of the boot facing is to cause the boot stick to carry horizontally and parallel to the center of the mule and give free action to the mule's elbow. Mules of large barrel will require a thicker facing than described. The object of the collar facing is to cause the saddle bar to carry horizontally and parallel with the center of the mule and to protect the mule's withers. Mules with high withers will require a thicker facing than that described. In setting to the shape of the mule the aparejo bends at the middle of the front edge. It is important that the body course remain undisturbed during dressing, and that the instructions given be carefully followed to avoid sore withers and tails and body and belly bunches.

4. *To attach the crupper.*—Stand the aparejo on its boots in its normal position; secure a lace thong to the front hole on the upper facing of the crupper on each side and fasten the crupper with short thongs to the center holes of the carrier pieces on the rear of the aparejo; pass the crupper lace thong through the second hole from the top of the front facing of the aparejo, through the second hole of the crupper, through the fourth hole of the aparejo facing, through the fourth hole of the crupper, and so on, finishing through the bottom holes of the facing and crupper and tying to the crupper hole.

NOTE.—In lacing the crupper to the aparejo, the thong must be passed through the holes from the outside and must not be twisted, the lacing must not cross, and it is important that the tie be made on the last hole of the crupper instead of the aparejo.

NOTE.—Guayava, willow, dogwood, hickory or any other wood combining the qualities of permanent elasticity and strength may be used to replace broken ribs.

When the set up aparejo is to be filled, no soaking is necessary; instead make the belly pieces pliable by rubbing with a wet sponge.

Mules weighing 850 to 900 pounds require a 58-inch aparejo; 1,000 pounds, 60-inch; 1,100 pounds, 62-inch; for heavier mules requisition should be made for larger sizes.

When the mule is loaded the cincha, in travel, should free the elbow by about 1 inch; more than this will prevent a proper grip on the belly.

If the boots ride high on the body of the mule, or if they reach under the belly, even though they ride horizontally and parallel to the center of the mule, the aparejo will be likely to turn easily. This fault encourages injuriously tight cinching and sore tails.

If one or both boots flare out or turn in toward the mule, cinch sores and sore tails result, or belly bunches are caused.

The width of the collar arch clearance should be at least 6 inches. If it is too narrow or too wide, or if the saddle bars slope downward toward the front, there will be sores on the withers; if they slope to the rear there will be injuries over the loins, called kidney sores.

If the lacing of the crupper is drawn too tight at the bottom the lower edge of the crupper will rub the buttocks and cause abrasions.

The object to be attained is the uniform distribution of the weight of a load over the portion of the mule's body anatomically suited to carrying a burden; so that the saddle will ride with little motion and without friction of the bearing surface on the body. The contact of the bearing surface of the saddle must be close at all points. As the mule's body swells from front to rear, the more or less cylindrically shaped aparejo after the body course is laid must be modified by facing up so as to provide a concave surface to fit over a convex surface. But, as the barrel of the properly conformed mule is nearly cylindrical through the rear half or more of the contact surface, no facing is necessary, as a rule, in the rear part of the aparejo, although conformation may require it exceptionally.

CARE OF THE APAREJO.

SEC. 8. *Care of the aparejo.*—Packmasters should attend to the cleanliness of the rigging (aparejo proper) at least once a week.

The following directions for cleaning and preserving the leather equipment should be carefully followed:

To preserve the life of leather equipments they should be cleaned whenever dirt, grit, or dust has collected on them or when they have become saturated with the sweat of the animal. In cleaning each part do not separate the crupper from the body of the aparejo, except where attached to the carrier pieces, using a lather of castile soap and warm water. If the equipment is cared for frequently this method is sufficient, but if the leather has become hard and dry a little neat's-foot oil should be applied after washing with castile soap. When the oil is dry the equipment should be sponged lightly with soap and water, which will remove the surplus remaining on the surface. If a polish is desired a thin coat of russet leather polish issued by the Ordnance Department should be applied and rubbed briskly with a dry cloth.

Particular care should be taken not to use too much oil on the body piece, as the result will cause the belly piece to become baggy, as the more firm the leather of the belly or body piece is, the better it will hold the padding of hay to its place. In no case should leather be dipped in water or be placed in the sun to dry.

All accessories of the aparejo and other equipment of the train will likewise be kept clean.

CAUSES OF BODY AND BELLY BUNCHES, SORE TAILS, SORE WITHERS AND LOINS, OR KIDNEY SORES, ON PACK MULES, AND DIRECTIONS FOR THEIR PREVENTION AND CURE.

SEC. 9. The term "bunch" is applied to a swelling or "puffing up" of the skin, caused by the stopping of the circulation of the blood at that part of the body; it shows unevenness in the ribbing, or placing of the padding (hay), causing undue bearing or pressure on that part of the body.

Use as little hay through the body of the aparejo as possible. When the hay has become packed the thickness should not be greater than 2 inches.

If through unevenness of the filling a "bunch" is caused on the body of the animal, mark this "bunch" by wetting it with water; wet the face of the "bunch" only, as its shape on the animal's body is what must be indicated on the aparejo. Now place the aparejo on the animal, without corona or blanket, where it rests when cinched on; do not turn crupper. Place a hand on each side and rock the aparejo so that the wet surface on the body of the animal will leave its imprints on the aparejo. Raise the aparejo clear of the animal and extend it on the ground, inside facing up, and it will show the location where the "bunch" has been caused.

Remove the hay under the wet surface, and nowhere else, and take it out down to the ribs. The better this can be done without disturbing the bed, but only where it has been marked, the more confident one can be that the "bunch" will disappear on the next travel. If not traveling, a "bunched" animal should be loaded with pack and exercised sufficiently to reduce the "bunch;" otherwise the "bunch" will develop into a "steadfast."

Do not overlook any "bunches," no matter how small; reduce them at once and animals can always be kept sound, and sound animals will always carry their load and do so with comfort.

Should the animal be "bunched" under the belly, take out the hay on both sides for a space of about 4 inches above the boot, clear to ribs, and across width of aparejo, leaving a little at both edges. The aparejo, when cinched on the animal, will now shape itself to the animal's body and relieve the pressure on the belly.

The "bunch" will disappear when the animal is loaded; one or two hour's travel is sufficient to bring it down. Where hay has been removed, replace a little from day to day, until its proper filling is regained.

The evidence of a "belly bunch," plainly indicates there has been too much padding (hay) used in the boots of the aparejo, as also from the boots to the "hand hole;" this undue filling of hay causes the boots of the aparejo to stand or flare out from the body of the mule, and prevents the shaping or bending of the aparejo to the conformation of the mule's body, the result is too much pressure brought on the belly in cinching the aparejo to the conformation of the body of the animal, the circulation being stopped by the cinch, and on its removal the skin "puffs up," and we have what is termed a "belly bunch." Therefore to prevent a "belly bunch" the cause must not be provided, and if provided, must be removed; what is wanted is an even pressure bearing surface covered by the cinch and aparejo. As the cinch binds the aparejo to the body of the animal, the body of the aparejo and its boots or ends must bend and shape itself without undue compression of the ribs and belly of the animal; otherwise "body" and "belly bunches" will be sure to occur.

Sore docks or tails.—This trouble is not clearly understood by the average packmaster and cargador; therefore, to clearly understand the description here given, it will be necessary to remember the meaning of the following terms in reference to the aparejo:

First. It is said the aparejo is too long or too short. The obvious meaning is, that in fitting the aparejo we attach the crupper and determine by the lacing (crupper) how far forward or rearward the aparejo shall work. When the aparejo is too far forward, or long, the cinch of the aparejo causes an abrasion of the elbow, and interferes with the travel of the animal; if too far rearward, or short, the aparejo will not hold its place; it works itself off to the rear in mountainous country, and will do so even on level ground.

Second. It is said the aparejo is too deep or too shallow. The obvious meaning is, that in selecting an aparejo to fit the mule, an aparejo is provided that is either too deep or too shallow to properly fit the pack animal; right here is where packmasters and cargadors are apt to provide conditions or the fundamental cause for sore tails. An aparejo that is too deep laps around the belly and has not sufficient grip on the body of the mule to hold the aparejo in its proper place; that is, the aparejo not having sufficient grip on the body of the mule, it slips forward and the dock of the crupper cuts the tail by the impact given, due to the weight of the load in the travel of the animal.

For similar reason, the aparejo when too shallow, the boots stand too high on the body of the animal, and consequently the aparejo, having no grip on the body of the mule, slips forward and the dock of the crupper cuts the tail. Therefore the object to be attained is to provide an aparejo that will properly fit the animal, and take sufficient grip on the body of the animal so that the aparejo will hold its place when "set up" and cinched on the pack mule.

Third. Next in importance is to "set up" the aparejo by a gradual tapering in diameter of the sticks from *front to rear*, and a gradual tapering in the filling of hay from *front to rear*, in such manner so that when the aparejo is cinched on the animal the ends or boots of the aparejo will carry horizontally and parallel to the center of the mule and give free action to the mule's elbows. In similar manner in forming the saddle on each side of the center stitch line, the center or top of the aparejo will carry horizontally and parallel with the center of the mule.

As a further aid to avoid sore tails, all aparejos should be not less than 24 inches wide, as the greater the width of surface of the animal's body that is covered by the aparejo, the better retaining grip it has on the barrel of the mule.

Mules supplied with newly "set up rigging" should be loaded (250 pounds) and exercised each day until the aparejos show they have assumed the shape, or as may be termed, a plaster cast of the animal's body, and for this reason changing of aparejos is *positively forbidden.* When in such condition the aparejos are fit for satisfactory service.

Should the aparejo cause the dock of the crupper to cut the animal's tail, it is evident there is too much filling of hay at the rear corners of the aparejo, as well as too much filling above the boots at rear, thus preventing a suitable grip of the aparejo over the swell of the animal's ribs (to hold the aparejo to its place), always bearing in mind that the aparejo is sufficiently deep to grip the body of the mule properly. This latter feature is the fundamental cause of sore tails, that is, the first and necessary requisite to avoid sore tails is to provide an aparejo that is deep enough to grip the body of the pack mule. A shallow rigging will always cause sore tails, from the fact that it has no grip on the animal's body and consequently works itself ahead by travel action of the animal, the weight of the load giving the dock of the crupper impact against the animal's dock or tail; continued action, or a day's travel, develops a sore tail.

First. Sore withers: There are two causes for this trouble; the first is in setting up the aparejo too weak; that is, in providing sticks that are too small in diameter to hold up a 250-pound load; the second is in not having sufficient hay or padding under or below the collar to hold the aparejo away from the withers of the pack mule.

Second. Sore loins or kidney sores: The same causes operate for this trouble as for sore withers.

Third. It should be remembered that aparejos "set up" with sticks of too large diameter are injurious to the pack animal; they are too hard to "break in," that is, they will not compress or shape to the body of the pack mule. They are apt to cause chafes along the shoulder blades, body bunches, and belly bunches; however, such rigging, to properly break them in, should be loaded with not less than 300 or 350 pounds on the pack mule, and exercised each day for at least ten days, average distance 10 miles per day.

Steadfasts.—There is but one cause for steadfasts, that is in neglecting to fix for "bunches," a neglect of twenty-four hours after the bunch has been caused and the bunch will become difficult to reduce; a neglect of thirty-six hours and the bunch will result in the flesh becoming hard and callous, and assume the condition and appearance of dried beef; this condition is termed a "steadfast." To remove the steadfast the knife has to be used and all appearance of the steadfast must be cut out; the animal experiences no pain until the sound flesh is touched. Apply a slice of fat bacon after the steadfast has been removed and the sore will heal in a few days; this will not interfere with the working of the pack animal.

If packmasters will exercise care as above outlined when setting up and fitting the aparejo, they can follow a troop of cavalry at any gait desired, or climb any mountain where an animal can find footing, without the least danger of losing load or aparejo.

In the case of aparejos ribbed with willow or other sticks, the main secret is "ribbing" properly, that is, the gradual lessening in the diameter of each stick from front to rear.

To keep animals sound requires the time and experience of experts at the business.

CHAPTER III.

INSTRUCTION OF THE INDIVIDUAL PACKER IN PREPARATION FOR HIS DUTIES IN THE PACK TRAIN.

SECURING AND COILING ROPES.

SEC. 10. *How to prepare lash, sling, and lair ropes for use.*—Take a rope, standard size and length (see table of sizes of rope and canvas, sec. 88), and form an eye or loop on one end and wrap or seize the opposite end in this manner:

To form the eye unravel about 6 or 7 inches of end selected and double this portion back so as to form a loop about 4 inches long; divide the strands in the order of their twist, placing the second or middle strand against the strand on rope selected. For this purpose do not keep the rope at a twist as held by the left hand, as the loop or eye when formed will be at a twist, i. e., not in proper alignment. Now untwist the strand selected sufficiently to pass the end of second or middle strand through opening thus made and draw snug. (See fig. 100.) Next untwist the strand at the left and pass the first strand through opening thus made and draw snug. (Fig. 101.) Now turn the rope over and untwist the remaining strand of rope and pass this third or last strand through opening thus made from *right* to *left* and draw snug. (Fig. 102.) By this operation each raveled strand passes between its mates on the twist of rope.

Now draw the strands more snugly against the free end or twist of rope, and commencing with either one of the three strands pass each one from right to left between its mates, following the twist of rope until the operation is performed twice; cut off the remaining portion of each strand, allowing about one-half inch extending. Now place the rope on something solid; place the foot over the splice thus made and roll rope under foot to smooth splice and the eye or loop is properly formed. (Fig. 103.)

On the opposite end a wrapping of canvas twine may be formed about three-fourths of an inch long; use a needle to pass the end of cord between each strand of rope, embracing the wrapping in doing so and draw snug each time. The cord may be waxed—beeswax is good for the purpose—or when a cord is not available untwist the strands for about 7 inches and hold the rope in the left hand close to strands. Now take a single cord of each strand and untwist close to the fingers of the left hand, bringing each cord to the front in the order of the strands.

Now hold the strands between the first and second fingers of the left hand, and with the right hand take the first cord and loop it over toward the second or middle cord, and place this second cord over the first, holding the end of this cord between the points of the second and third fingers; next take the third or last cord and bring it under the first, if not already there, then over the second and around the strands from right to left, its end passing into the eye or loop of first cord, and draw each cord down separately until the strands are firmly engaged by the cords.

This operation leaves the strands standing upward and the cords downward, the strands thus being held in the center; now pass each cord from right to left as before, as in the operation of finishing the splice for eye of lash rope.

This latter method is preferred by packers as more durable, as it will not become undone, and in similar manner is employed for the free ends of the sling rope.

The operation of preparing the lair rope is entirely similar to that of the lash rope.

SEC. 11. *How to do up a lash rope.*—Take hold of rope in the left hand near the cincha or by the lacings; coil with right, receiving coils in left hand; length of coils 24 inches. This operation is best performed by keeping the left hand extended downward (this permits of the cincha resting partly on the ground); now allow the right hand to slip down the running rope at arm's length from left to right. This operation will gauge the size or length of each coil (length of coil 24 inches) and permit of rapid formation in coiling the rope as well as a guide in giving an exact resulting length to each coil. The action of the right hand in this operation is similar to that of a pendulum of a clock, the left hand receiving the coils and the ground partly supporting the cinch and coils as rendered.

Take cincha in right hand, make one turn with it around the coils, and pass the hook through the loop formed by the coils. Draw the hook well up, causing the cincha to tighten snugly on the coils (*t*, fig. 1).

SEC. 12. *How to do up a sling rope.*—Take a sling rope and bring the ends together, grasp both parts in left hand about 20 inches from ends; coil as in the case of lash rope.

Take three turns of the loop around coils and pass the loop through the coils, as in case of cincha hook; draw coils up snugly against end. This should leave the loop out, not exceeding 4 inches; length of coils 24 inches (*vii*, fig. 1).

SEC. 13. *How to do up a lair rope.*—Take a lair rope by its eye, in left hand; pass the end through the eye and draw through until a coil of 24 inches is formed; hold and coil as in case of lash rope, taking three turns of the end around coils. Pass the end through, as in the case of cincha hook; draw coils snugly up, leaving not more than 6 inches of end out (*viii*, fig. 1).

LAIRING UP THE PACKS.

SEC. 14. *How to square ends of packs and tie before lairing up.*—By "lairing up" a pack, we mean wrapping it up in a manta, or pack cover, to prevent damage to the pack during transportation. (See fig. 6, etc.)

When cargo is composed of sacks of flour, coffee, beans, rice, corn, or oats, etc., it is necessary that the ends of packs be squared and tied before "lairing up."

The more compact the packs and the better the ends are kept square, the better the load will ride and the less danger there will be of the sacks bursting when dropped on the ground, through accident or negligence.

For this purpose old or unserviceable sling, lair, or lash ropes may be used. Cut a length, say, 20 inches and untwist; take one of the strands and form a bowline knot at one of its ends. (Sec. 46, fig. 79.) Always commence at bottom or seamless end of sack.

Procure a marline spike; cause pack to rest on its end; face one of the narrower sides; squeeze the sack about 4 inches below the farther corner with both hands, so as to bring the hands toward one another. Through the portion of the sack thus included pass the spike, and form hole large enough for strand to pass through.

Pass the end of strand through hole formed, and draw it through until bowline knot meets hole; hold strand taut; tap lightly on knot with heel of right foot, drawing slack as rendered by tapping. Should not sufficient slack be gained, tap lower down, 4 or 5 inches from knot, gradually raising until knot is reached.

Hold the rope taut; move around so as to face the other end of the sack; make a hole with the marline spike as before, and pass the free end of the strand through; tap with the heel, as described in the former case, and draw taut.

Now introduce end of strand through loop or eye of bowline knot, (see fig. 80), draw down snug, and secure. Turn up the other end and do likewise, and pack is in condition to "lair up." Sacks needing it should be doubly sacked.

HOW TO LAIR UP SIDE PACKS.

SEC. 15. Secure a lair rope and spread out manta; place pack diagonally in center of manta; i. e., with ends facing opposite corners.

Face a side of the pack; pick up the near corner of manta and bring it tightly over pack, lapping corner under sufficiently to make it just cover the pack. Place knees on this part; grasp the opposite corner and, turning it under also, bring it tightly over pack, its edge flush with near edge of pack. Place right knee to hold this part in place and face one end; smooth canvas squarely down, and turn in corners; reach out and grasp the end, and bring it tightly over pack, spreading canvas out, if necessary, to cover corners.

Place left knee thereon, face opposite end, and do likewise. In bringing this last corner across length of pack turn corner under when necessary to square with end of pack.

Place left knee on pack and reach for lair rope; bring the rope lengthwise under pack, leaving the eye near the upper edge. Place end of rope through eye, if not already there, and draw it through; grasp the running rope in both hands; place both knees on end of pack, and draw well taut. This should bring the eye about 6 inches over end.

Hold slack with left hand; grasp the rope with right about 2 feet in advance of the left; form a loop outward and inward, so that the right hand will come under the left, and the running part of the rope will ride under the standing part. Pass this loop under the pack about 6 inches from the end and draw taut. Face the other end, placing the knee on the intersection of the ropes; form a similar loop, and place it around this end; holding taut with left hand, turn the pack over, passing rope over middle of end. Place foot on pack and draw taut.

Now pass the end of rope over and under the middle of cross rope at nearer end of pack; then over and under cross rope at farther end and draw taut.

Pass rope over middle of end of pack, turning the pack over, and securing the rope to the cross part at the intersection of the ropes.

If length of rope permits, take a turn around the center also.

The parts of the lair rope are designated as *l*, figs. 13 and 14.

In making up side packs keep the sides and ends square. Never make up a side pack in ball shape, or get it any longer than the width of the aparejo, when possible to avoid doing so.

HOW TO LAIR UP A SIDE PACK OF ROPES WITHOUT THE AID OF PACK COVER OR MANTA.

SEC. 16. Take a lair or sling rope, hold an end in each hand, and spread out the loop. Place the end held in left hand on the ground; draw sufficiently on the end in right hand, so that when this end is folded to the front the rope will lie in three equal lengths. This leaves an end of the rope and a loop at either extremity. Make the three ropes equally distant from one another at the center. Place lengthwise across the center as many coiled ropes as it is determined to form into a side pack.

When ready, another packer will assist to "lair." The two packers face one another on opposite sides of the pack, each draws on his end of the rope until opposite loop is close to side of pack; then passes his end of rope through opposite loop and draws slack. Each then places both knees on side of pack and draws taut, causing the loops to come near center of pack.

Each packer holding rope taut with left hand, with right hand passes rope over middle of end of pack to his left; assisting one another, they turn the pack over. Each now passes his rope to the other; then causing the ropes to cross at the center of the pack, each brings his rope to the middle of his side of the pack.

Resting their knees on the pack, the packers now draw the rope taut; then holding the slack, they turn the pack over and fasten the ropes together by a square knot on top of the pack.

HOW TO LAIR UP AN APAREJO AND RIDING SADDLE FOR STORAGE OR SHIPMENT.

SEC. 17. Without turning the crupper, extend the aparejo on the ground, inside facing up. Place the corona on it, full length, sweat-cloth facing up. Now procure a lair rope; bring the loop over one end of aparejo and place so as to lie along center of corona and aparejo. Cause the aparejo to stand on its boots; draw slack on rope so as to leave eye or bight of rope on top and in center of aparejo.

Proceed and finish as in lairing side pack and secure dock of crupper at top.

Ropes, canvas, and blankets should be made into packs of convenient size and laired; each pack to have a tag indicating its contents.

Each riding saddle should have its blanket folded; the bridle and blind are placed therein and rolled up and the roll tied to cantle of saddle.

The stirrups should be wrapped around saddle in convenient manner and the whole placed in a "gunny" sack, secured at top, and tagged to show its contents.

PUTTING THE APAREJO ON THE MULE—HOW TO FOLD AN APAREJO BLANKET.

SEC. 18. Hold the blanket by the corners, the short way up and down; fold across the longer edges, right hand holding corners, left holding folded edge at corner. Shake the blanket and spread it out on the ground, the hands still holding up the corners. Carry the upper edge to the front, so as to leave a portion of the blanket, 22 inches wide, on the ground. Then fold back, so as to leave the blanket in three equal folds, 22 inches wide and 42 inches long. Fold once more, bringing the ends together. It is now in condition to be placed on the aparejo before putting the aparejo on the mule.

HOW TO PLACE BLANKET ON APAREJO PREPARATORY TO PUTTING ON THE APAREJO.

SEC. 19. Place so that the ends will rest on front of aparejo. Its proper place, before putting the aparejo on the mule, is under the corona.

HOW TO BLIND A PACK MULE.

SEC. 20. Take hold of one of the sides of blind near end; hold animal by halter or halter shank; bring blind fully over animal's neck to "off side," allowing half of blind with tail to hang down; bring the crown of blind well to front and pass it over animal's ears with right hand, from right to left. Do not raise the hand in passing over, as the animal may duck from it.

HOW TO PLACE CORONA, BLANKET, AND APAREJO ON THE MULE.

SEC. 21. It is assumed that two packers, called, respectively, the "near" and "off" packers, work together in placing the aparejo on the animal and see that the aparejo is properly equipped—i. e., that the cincha is folded and placed on top of it; that the crupper is turned so as to rest on top of the cincha, and that the blanket and corona are on top of the aparejo.

A corona is placed in position on aparejo, as explained for the blanket (sec. 18), numeral or design on top.

With right hand take hold of the upper half of corona at the middle of the nearest side, fingers resting on top, thumb under; raise, and with the left hand grasp lower half in similar manner; raise, extend corona, and pass it over animal's body with right hand, the left guiding, to come in line over cross or birthmark on animal's withers, center of corona along center of back.

A blanket is handled and placed on corona in similar manner.

The "off" packer, in both cases, receives the "off" end of the corona and blanket as each comes over, and assists in adjusting them in place.

75927°—17——4

To place the aparejo on the animal, stand in front of aparejo and take hold near its center, in rear, with right hand; place the palm of the left hand against the front of the belly piece of the "off" side of aparejo, fingers downward and near to the boot of aparejo.

Now lean the aparejo well toward the body, thus raising the "off" side of the aparejo well off the ground, then, both hands assisting, raise and swing the aparejo over animal. Allow it to rest on animal's back slightly in rear of its proper position.

In the operation do not slap the aparejo on the animal's back, as the animal may jump from under.

HOW TO TURN THE CRUPPER.

SEC. 22. The "near" packer takes hold with left hand on lower edge of crupper, fingers under, the right palm down, near the dock; the "off" packer takes hold similarly, hands reversed; both raise crupper well up, press forward with palms, bringing edge of crupper toward them with the hand, and crupper is turned.

The quicker the action the easier turned.

HOW TO CINCH AN APAREJO.

SEC. 23. When crupper is turned, the "off" packer, with right hand, holds the upper edge of crupper well up and out from the animal's buttocks, and with left hand passes the tail up between the crupper and the mule's hips, and receives it with right hand; holds tail well up on animal's hips; presses crupper down under dock with left hand, and lets go of tail; raises tail partly with left hand and places dock of crupper well under animal's tail.

He then places his left breast against crupper to hold it in place; frees the animal's tail, observing that no hair rests on dock; places the palm of left hand on center of aparejo, the right hand on corner of boot, and pushes the aparejo forward to its place; steps to animal's shoulder, faces to rear, and places right hand on collar of aparejo.

While the "off" packer is thus engaged, the "near" packer draws the upper fold of cincha quickly toward him; allows the other end to pass over to "off" packer, guiding it to center of aparejo at top with left hand; retaining the leather facing of cincha on the near side of the aparejo; grasps latigo well down with right hand and calls out "Cinch!"

At the word "cinch" the "off" packer passes the end of cincha well under with palm of left hand, holding it in position until he feels it has been received by the near packer; he observes that cincha is over the center of boot of aparejo, places left hand on rear corner of boot and holds the aparejo forward to its place. Do not raise the aparejo in front.

The "near" packer takes hold of cincha with left hand on corner (never at its center or eye, as the hand will thus interfere), passes the double of latigo through eye of cincha from above, brings it up in front and passes it through rendering ring from above, grasps the double of latigo with left hand well under, and with the right hand passes the end through eye of cincha in *rear* of the other part, places the palm of left hand against the front corner of boot as a

brace and pulls taut with right hand. (This is termed a "primary cinch.")

Holding latigo in right hand, he takes hold of rear corner of boot, the left holding front, brings aparejo well forward to place, and calls out "Cinch!"

At this signal the "off" packer passing in rear observes that the aparejo is straight on the animal, takes hold of latigo in between the near packer and the mule, the palm of right hand up and of the left down, and places right knee on boot of aparejo.

The near packer holds latigo far enough back to permit him to raise his left foot to boot of aparejo, his left hand in front of his right, both palms up. The two packers then pull together, reach forward, taking a second and similar pull, and, if necessary, an additional pull to bring the eye or hole of cincha to edge of boot.

The cincha must be in center both at top and at boots of aparejo.

The "off" packer, holding slack of latigo with right hand, takes hold with the left below the right, palm down, the thumb grasping latigo underneath. He brings the latigo up, resting the butt of palm of left hand near top of aparejo, the fingers gripping the top thereof; with the right hand passes the end of latigo from above through finger loop and receives it with the two first fingers of the left hand; holds slack below left with right hand and pulls the end with left, taking slack well in. The latigo being drawn taut by this action, the end is engaged between the standing part of the latigo and the top of the aparejo and is thus caught in place. (See figs. 10, 11.)

FORMING THE LOAD PREPARATORY TO LOADING THE MULE.

SEC. 24. Take a coiled lash rope and unwrap cincha (sec. 11); hold coils and cincha at point of lacing in left hand; release as many coils of rope as will leave, say, from 10 to 15 feet extended. Swing the coils held in left hand toward the right and place on the ground, cincha underneath.

Now take the side packs, which make up a load, and place them lengthwise on lash rope, the heavier pack underneath. Take a coiled sling rope, unwrap and place crosswise on load. Then pick up the end of lash rope, extended on ground, coil and place on load.

In preparation for loading the mules the cargo is thus formed in separate loads according to the number of mules available. (See fig. 109.)

SLINGING THE LOAD—HOW TO PLACE THE SLING ROPE ON THE APAREJO.

SEC. 25. Take hold of the sling rope, about 5 feet from one end, with the left hand, the two last fingers gripping the rope; with the right form as many coils as may be necessary, according to the size of the load, and receive the coils between the thumb and two first fingers of the left hand, at the same time retaining the grip on the rope beyond the coils with the two last fingers of the right hand. Now receive the coils from the left hand, between the thumb and two first fingers of the right hand, and, retaining the grip on the free ends of the rope by the two last fingers of each hand, throw the coils over the aparejo to the off side, separating the ropes at the same time, as the length of the packs may determine. A loop of the rope is thus made to hang down on the "off" side of the aparejo, while the two ends called, respectively, the "front" and "rear" ropes, hang down on the near side. (See fig. 11.)

If, due to the size of the load, it is necessary to lengthen or shorten the loop on the "off" side, do so by taking or giving slack on the rear rope, never on the front rope; the latter should be allowed to hang nearly to the ground.

HOW TO LIFT SIDE PACKS AND PLACE THEM ON THE APAREJO.

SEC. 26. The "off" packer stands facing the sides of the packs; takes hold of the uppermost pack at each end, hands well under, and raises it to his knees; raises it from knees quickly to breast and carries it to "off" side. If heavy, incline the body forward and raise quickly, throwing the head and shoulders back. Rest lower edge of pack on aparejo and allow flat side of pack to come down on aparejo.

The upper edge should ride flush with the center or top of aparejo.

The "near" packer lifts in similar manner and places his pack so as to lap about four inches on top of "off" pack. Weight of packs being equal, this will permit the "near" pack, after "braking," to ride level with the "off" pack.

HOW TO SLING THE LOAD AND TIE THE SQUARE KNOT.

SEC. 27. The "off" packer, standing somewhat away from the mule, as a brace, supports his pack in place with left hand, palm against the center of the pack and slightly underneath it, so as to balance the weight of the pack.

With the right he picks up the front and then the rear parts of the loop of the sling rope and brings them up to center, the left hand receiving them between thumb and forefinger and holding them taut against the pack.

He then passes the loop of the rope over his right shoulder, and when "near" packer calls out "Rope," he throws the loop lightly over with his right hand. If thrown hard it will bound back. Should there not be sufficient rope to pass to "near" packer, he pulls on the rear rope sufficiently to do so.

The "near" packer takes a similar position to that above described for the "off" packer and supports his pack with the left hand in the same manner. With the right hand he picks up the front rope and brings it to the center of the pack, the left receiving it between the thumb and forefinger and holds it taut against the pack.

Now take the end of this rope in the right hand, call out "Rope," to "off" packer, and quickly place the rope on top of the loop as it comes over. Pass the end through the loop from above and draw down taut, letting the right hand slip down on rope to near the edge of pack.

The load is now held in place by the rope as though caught in a bight. The loop of the sling rope should never be placed above or below the swell of the pack, as the rope then loses its retaining hold on load. This does not apply to box loads.

Now place the left-hand edge of palm resting on top of rope below its engagement on the swell of pack, raise the rope with the right hand so as to give opportunity for the last two fingers of the left

hand to grip it, and keep the rope compressed against the palm, the free end hanging down.

Now reach down with right hand and pick up the rear rope, bringing it up snug against pack in rear of the front rope. Receive it between the points of thumb and first two fingers of the left hand, allowing the free end, or portion, to hang to rear—*never* allow this portion to cross over the front rope, to avoid confusing them. You will learn this.

The fingers of the left hand now hold the front and rear ropes, the free ends of each rope hanging down.

Now take the front rope in the right hand, pass it over and under the rear rope from right to left, and pull taut, allowing the last two fingers of the left hand to escape from under the rope as it comes down taut, and allow them to fall in front of the rear rope (not in rear or behind it).

Now, again, bring the "front" rope over the outer or free end of "rear" rope from right to left and up toward the thumb of the left hand, receive the rope by allowing the thumb of the left hand to fall down on the crown or loop of the front rope formed by this operation, and bring the thumb-holding rope toward the palm of the hand, and hold it there.

Now take or grip the "rear" rope, and pull down taut, and the square knot is tied. (K, fig. 14; see also fig. 63.)

Coil up the extra rope, pass the coils from rear to front between the rope and the top of the pack, and draw snug.

(The parts of the sling rope are designated as "s" in figs. 13 and 14).

NOTE.—In forming a granny knot in distinction from the square knot the loop at top and bottom divides the running ropes. In the thief knot in distinction from the square knot one end of the rope is on the left and the opposite end on the right, whereas in the square knot both ends are on the right. (See figs. 63, 64, 65.)

HOW TO "BRAKE" A SIDE PACK.

SEC. 28. The "off" packer does not "brake" his pack; if put up properly it is already in position. The "near" packer "brakes" the load.

The "near" packer, the square knot being tied, calls "Hold," indicating that the "off" packer must hold his pack in position. To do so, he will place a hand on each corner of pack, stand well out, and brace against load.

The "near" packer places a hand on each lower corner of pack, raises the lower edge well out and up, causing the front edge to work down and in, even with the off pack. If found difficult, when the pack is well up alternate the hands down and up until the pack is flush with off pack; then allow or cause it to settle on aparejo.

"Near" pack having been lapped four inches, packs of equal weight should "brake" flush. When the weight of the two packs varies, lap accordingly, and brake until rope becomes taut, and settle. Do not try to brake a box load, as it will stand out from aparejo; "hold" and settle.

Always remember the more equal the weights of the two packs the less trouble they are when traveling, and the closer they are slung together the better they will ride.

HOW TO DOUBLE SLING SIDE PACKS WHEN LENGTH OF PACKS REQUIRES IT.

SEC. 29. Place the sling rope on the aparejo, with the loop on the "off" side, leaving only enough of the ends on the "near" side to tie with. The packs being in place, the off packer proceeds and passes loop to near packer, as in single slinging, separating ropes as much as possible.

The "near" packer supports his pack with left arm, and grasps the rear part of the loop on top of pack with left hand, with right reaches down, picks up the rear rope on aparejo, and ties the two ropes together by a square knot, getting the packs well together in doing so; then throws the front of pack well up, to come even with rear end, picks up ropes in similar manner as at rear, and ties square knot. "Brake" and settle packs in usual manner.

HOW TO CROSS SLING SIDE PACKS WHEN TOP PACKS ARE NECESSARY.

SEC. 30. The "near" packer takes a sling rope by its middle and passes the ends over to "off" side, retaining sufficient of the loop so that when "off" pack is in place the loop can be passed up to its upper edge.

The "off" packer then puts his pack in position and supports the pack with his left hand, at center of pack. With the right hand he picks up the front and rear rope and brings them up to center of pack; receives them in left between thumb and forefinger, ropes pressed taut against side of pack.

With right hand he coils the ropes hanging down, coiling on left thumb, and throws coils over center of pack to "near" side. He then separates the front and rear ropes. The right hand now supports the pack, and the left receives the loop when passed up by "near" packer.

The "near" packer, after the off pack is in position and the ends of ropes have been thrown over, passes the loop to the "off" packer; he then separates the ropes on "near" side. Placing "near" pack on, he calls out "Rope," and proceeds to tie as in single slinging. (Sec. 27.)

The top pack is now put in place between the two side packs and above the sling rope.[a]

Just before tying the sling rope it is sometimes found necessary to get packs closer together. In such a case the "off" packer takes hold of the rear rope and pulls toward him from below, the "near" packer giving slack on front rope, as held in bight of sling, and pulling down on rear rope to take in the slack as rendered by the "off" packer. When enough has been taken the "near" packer calls out "Good."

If the "near" packer desires more rope to enable him to tie, the "off" packer will pull on the rear rope from above with the left hand until the "near" packer takes slack by drawing on the front rope, thus pulling the bight or loop of the sling farther over to his side.

If packs are high the "off" packer passes sling to rear with left hand, the "near" packer reaching from behind to receive it.

In passing loop to "near" packer over load, or from behind, it is well for the "off" packer to hold the loop with the thumb, the fingers extended, as he can thus more readily indicate position of rope to

[a] In the operation the side packs should be carried high enough to support the weight of the top pack to bind the load

"near" packer. Always place the packs lengthwise. Top packs should never be carried when possible to avoid them. They cause delay and are troublesome.

HOW TO DOUBLE CROSS SLING SIDE PACKS WHEN LENGTH OF PACKS REQUIRES IT.

SEC. 31. The *near* packer takes a sling rope by its middle and passes the ends over to the "off" side in similar manner as in single cross sling with the exception that the rope is evenly divided—that is, by retaining as much of the loop on the near side as the ends indicate on the "off" side; proceeds and ties as in double slinging, i. e., at rear and front.

LASHING THE LOAD—HOW TO FORM THE DIAMOND HITCH.

SEC. 32. In the formation of the diamond hitch and tightening of the load, two packers are employed. One, termed the "near" packer,

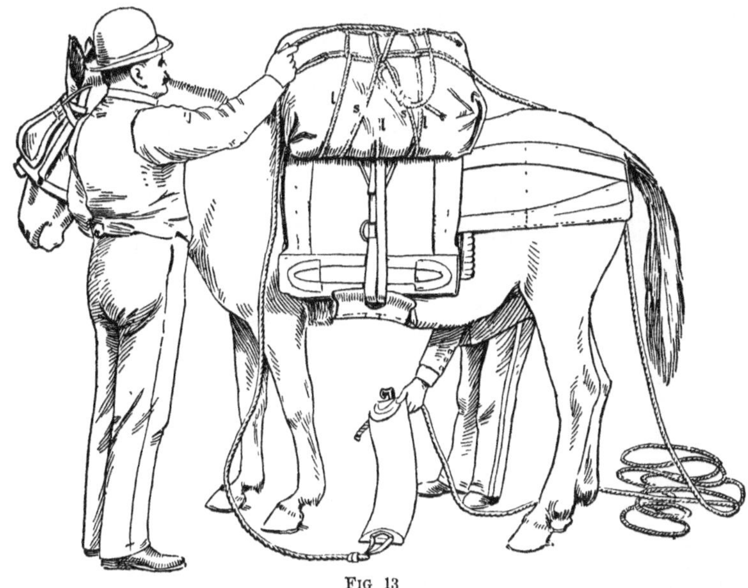

FIG 13

stands on the "near" side of the animal, looking toward rear; his mate, termed the "off" packer, stands on the "off" side, facing toward the front. The side packs being slung on the animal (secs. 26–27–28) the "near" packer throws the end of the lash rope in rear of animal, and the cincha portion under the animal's belly, convenient to the "off" packer, who picks them up and holds them in the left hand, as indicated in fig. 19, and stands erect.

(1) The *near* packer now picks up the rope, about 5 or 6 feet from cincha, and holding about 2 feet of rope between the hands, stands close to the animal's neck; now with both hands extended downward, he draws the right hand backward, to give impetus to the motion, and with one motion he swings the rope fore and aft between the side packs, clearing the animal's haunch in the action, allowing the rope held by the left hand to drop. (See fig. 13.)

Now, holding on to the rope held in the right hand, he draws on the running portion between the packs, bringing the right hand down by the side, arm's length, and reaches up with the left hand and grips the rope, so as to have the back of the hand upward. This brings the thumb under the rope (do not get the fingers under). He then draws on the running portion between the packs, in similar manner as done by the right hand, bringing the left hand down by the side, arm's length; do not let go of the rope held in each hand.

Now, with an outward and circular motion, bring the left hand holding the rope to the elbow of the right arm—this leaves the rope, or loop, on the outside of the right arm—and raise both hands to the position as seen in fig. 14.

Next bring the right hand to the center of the pack, and with one motion, both hands assisting, throw the "standing" rope, held in the

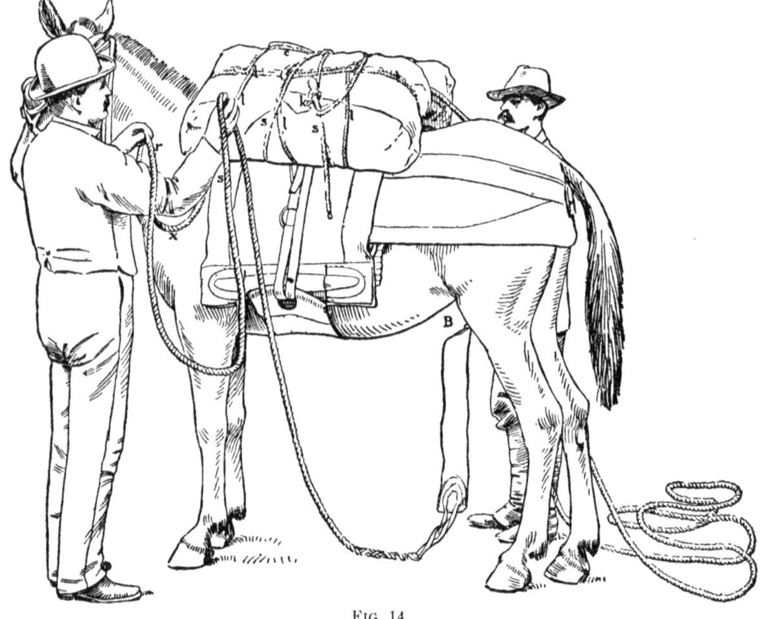

FIG. 14.

right hand, over the center of the load, to the "off" packer; the "running" rope, held in the left hand, over the mule's neck.[a] (In this action the back of the left hand rests on the mule's neck as seen in fig. 15.)

Now, draw sufficient slack on the "running" portion between the packs, about 6 or more feet, to form the rear half of the diamond, and throw this rope to the rear of the "*near*" pack, allowing the rope to go free from the hands. (This rope now becomes the "rear" rope.) Next take hold of the running rope on the mule's neck, the left hand forward of the right, and with the assistance of the "off" packer, bring this running rope to the center of the load (fig. 16), by

[a] The separating of the standing from the running rope is done purposely, to avoid confusing the "off" packer; both ropes should never be thrown together. Further, when throwing the standing rope over the load, *do not* give the rope a wild outward and circular swing, else the standing portion below the hand will become engaged around the rear corner of the aparejo and cause delay, with perhaps a strenuous expression from the "off" packer.

the side of the standing rope; both packers should perform this action together, never singly; it causes confusion and delay.

The right hand now slips down the rope to a point about midway between the pack and the "boot;" reach for this rope by passing the left hand *between* the standing rope and the aparejo, and grip the rope above the right hand; now, both hands assisting, slip down the rope and parting from each other, on each side of the standing rope, hold the rope in a horizontal position, with a space of about 10 inches between each hand; jam this portion down between the two cinchas under the aparejo, and the hitch is "*formed*" on the "near side," ready to tighten. (See figs. 17 and 18.)

FIG. 18

To avoid confusion, I have explained the formation of the hitch by "near" packer, in the first instance, as is customary in the practice of instruction. Now, we will take up that portion in the formation of the hitch devolving on the "off" packer.

(2) The *off* packer, having picked up the end of the rope and cincha, holds them in left hand, mouth of hook to the front, stands erect and waits for the standing rope to be thrown over the center of the load. (Fig. 19.) As the rope comes over he grips it as high as the arm will conveniently reach (fig. 20) and immediately places the cincha hook in position under the aparejo, about 6 or 8 inches, and draws down the slack on the standing rope, by one or two quick pulls, and lowering the hook for convenience, he engages the standing rope

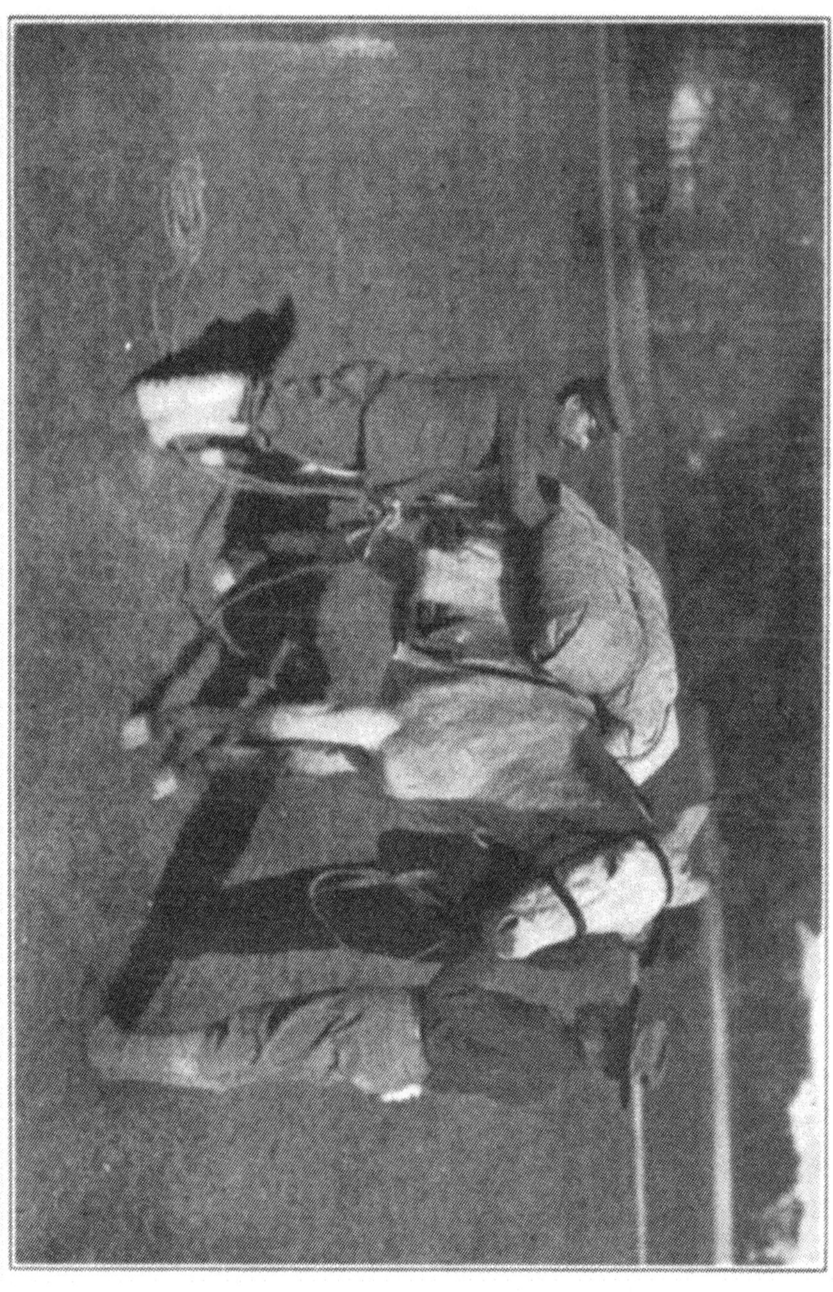

on the hook from in, out; or from above, down. This leaves the standing rope next to the aparejo and the running rope on the outside of the hook. (Fig. 21.)

(After engaging the rope, do not hold the rope taut on hook.)

Now, place the left hand, holding the end of the rope on top of the running rope, between the right hand and hook, and grip both ropes, the thumb under the running rope; now allow the right hand to slip upward on the running rope, and with the assistance of the "near" packer, bring this rope to the center of the load. (Fig. 22.) In this operation the left hand will immediately follow the right to the center of the load; this will bring both hands together. (Fig. 23.)

Now, with the right hand draw the end of the rope forward, held by the left hand, so that about 12 inches will fall on the "near" side of the animal's neck and the hitch is formed on the "off" side, ready to tighten the load. (Fig. 18 for the "near" side and fig. 24 for the "off" side.)

It will be seen that the hitch is now laid ready to tighten. This tightening is a progressive action, beginning on the near side and going by the rear all around the animal, assisted greatly by the taking of the ropes out of their line of direction.

(3) The *near* packer, to tighten the load, places the left hand, palm down, on the side and center of pack; with the right hand he grips the running rope in the rear of the standing rope on the side of the pack (fig. 25) and brings it between the thumb and index finger of the left hand; now bearing against the pack with the left hand as a brace, he holds the running rope taut and calls out "Go!" indicating he is ready to receive the slack from the "off" packer.

(4) The *off* packer, at the word "Go," takes hold of the running rope as near the hook as possible, and placing the left knee against the end of boot of the aparejo as a brace, he pulls all the slack possible by bending the body well over, as seen in fig. 26, and gives this slack to the "near" packer quickly, in such manner as if trying to hit the aparejo with both fists; do not let go of the rope. Now take a second and similar pull and call "Tie," indicating no more slack can be taken on the standing rope; then step quickly to the rear and throw the "end" rope forward of the pack (this rope now becomes the "front rope") and grasp the rear rope between the packs, ready to receive the slack from the near packer.

(5) The *near* packer, at the call "Tie," brings the right hand holding the slack down toward the aparejo in the rear of the standing rope; the left hand receives this rope and slack by bringing the hand under the standing rope, gripping the rope above the right hand, so as not to loosen the slack, and brings it forward. Now, with both hands, jam the rope upward, between the standing rope and pack; the running rope is thus held firmly, as if caught in a bight. In this operation pull the rope quickly toward the breast. (Fig. 27.)

Now bring the free portion of the running rope below the bight, around the front boot of aparejo with the left hand, and step to rear of aparejo and with the right hand grasp the rope in rear of the cincha and receive the slack from the left hand; now bring this rope up in the rear of the boot and place the left hand below the right, both hands bringing the rope up quickly to the upper corner of side pack, and hold the slack taut, the palm of the left hand compressed against the pack, the right hand indicating how much slack has to be

taken in by the "off" packer (fig. 28) who then receives it, hand over hand, quckly, and prepares to pull on the rope. To do so take hold of this rope, termed the "rear" rope, with both hands, and pull the rope taut (fig. 29); do not let go of this rope until you see the body of the "off" packer "setting" on the rope, then let go of the rope quickly; learn to turn the rope loose at the proper time; the difference will be noted. Now step forward of the load and face to the rear, and grasp the end of rope, and wait for slack from the "off" packer. (Fig. 30.)

(6) The *off* packer having taken in the slack from the "near" packer, hand over hand, takes a wrap of the rope around either hand, and leans the body forward, toward the animal's haunch, takes a forward step with the right foot and in line with the animal's body,

FIG 24

never outward, and sets back on the rope with all his weight. (Figs. 31–32.) He now holds the slack with the left hand, and with the right brings the free or running portion under and around the boot of the aparejo to the front; steps forward and faces toward rear; now grips the rope with the left hand below the right, and brings both hands quickly to the upper corner of pack, the left holding the rope compressed against the pack, the right indicating how much slack has to be taken by the "near" packer. (Figs. 33–34.) This is termed the "front" rope.

(7) The *near* packer having gripped the end of the rope (fig. 30) proceeds to take in slack, hand over hand, until he has about 6 or 8 feet; this portion, or end of rope is thrown over the center of the load to the "off" packer; he then continues to take in the remainder

of the slack. Now, likewise, he takes a wrap of the rope around either hand and leans the body forward toward the load (fig. 35) and "sets" back on the rope (fig. 36), giving the slack in similar manner as described for the "off" packer; the "near" packer now holding the slack with the left hand brings the free or running portion with the right hand under and around the boot of the aparejo and partly toward the center of the load, and calls out, "Rope." (Fig. 37.)

(8) The *off* packer, having given the slack to the "near" packer, steps to the center of the load and grasps the end of the rope, and at the call "Rope," takes in all slack, hand over hand, coiling the rope in the operation, and holds coils in the right hand.

At the call, "Take slack" (fig. 38) from the "near" packer, he places the left hand palm down against center of pack, as a brace,

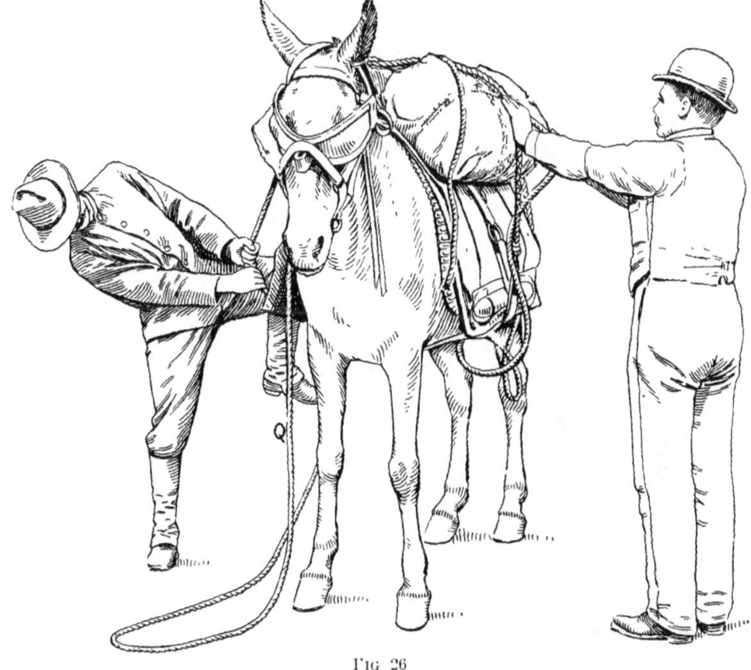

FIG 26

and receives the slack from the "near" packer. (Fig. 39.) He now grasps the standing portion of the rope above the coils and raises this portion high enough above the load to permit placing the coils on top of the load; in this action swing the coils from rear to front and bring the standing portion of the rope down on top of the coils, to hold them there, and secure the end of the rope; to do so take a wrap of the standing portion of the rope from right to left between the standing and running ropes and pack; holding the end of loop in both hands jam the double of the rope well up, so as to be caught in a bight, and take a similar turn between the standing and running ropes and jam this portion up likewise, and the load is tightened. (Figs. 40 and 41, showing completion of the hitch.)

NOTE.—The act of tightening, taking the standing and running ropes out of their line of direction, forms the "diamond" on top of

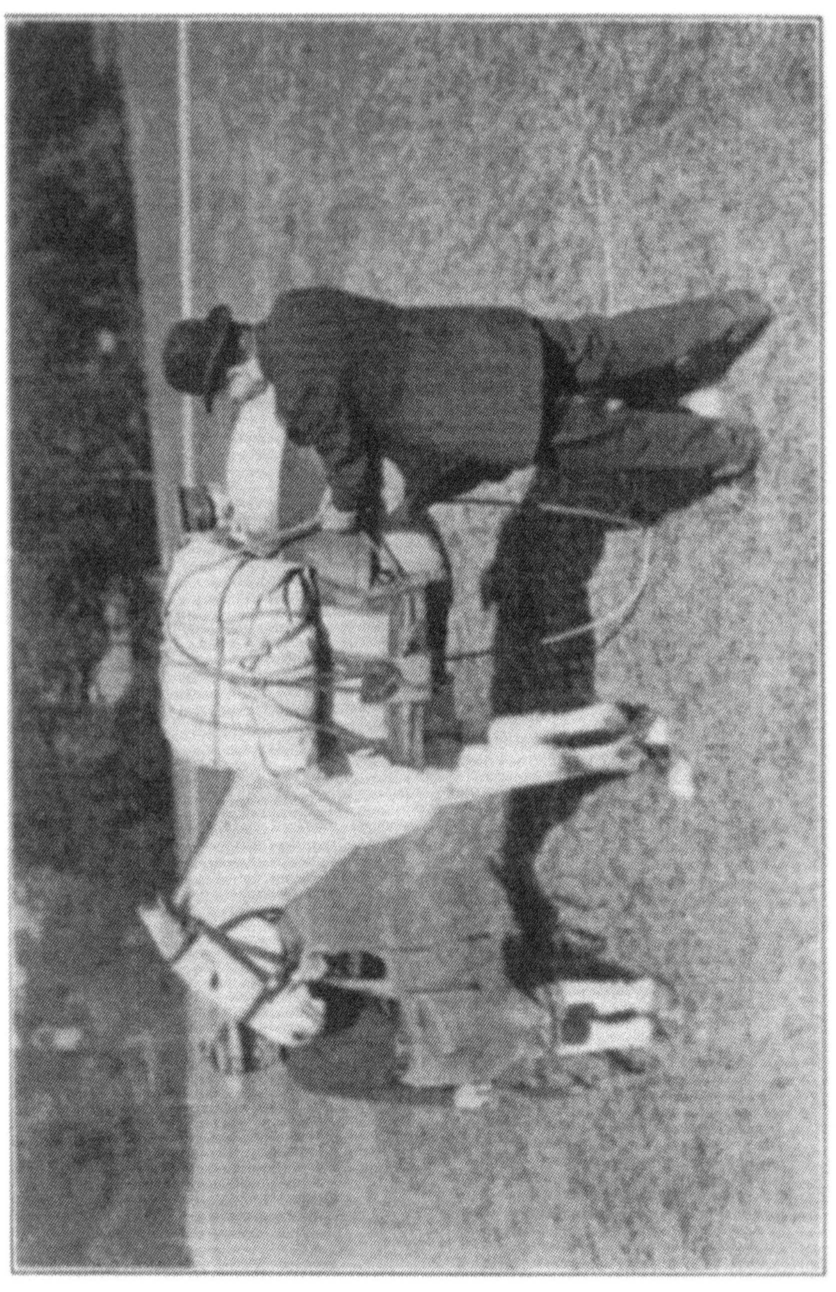

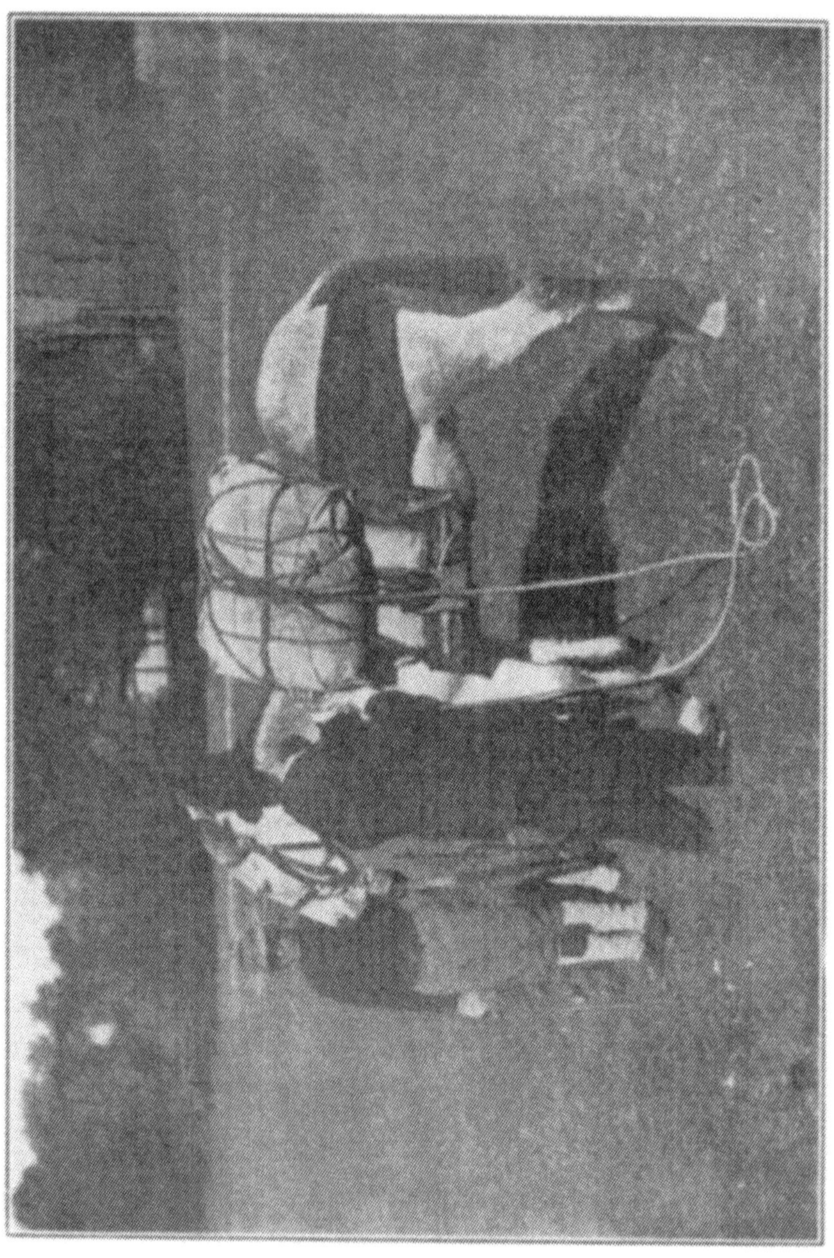

the load; hence the name given this form of hitch. In its formation a single knot is made, and when undoing the hitch the end, or top rope, when freed, is pulled or drawn from between the standing and running ropes; this leaves the lash rope free of knot.

In the formation of the "diamond" the rope has six designated names:

On the "near" side we have the standing, running, and marking ropes, and the front, rear, and top ropes.

On the "off" side we have the standing, running, front, rear, and top, or end ropes.

The standing rope is that portion encircling the mule and load to point of engagement on hook. (Figs. 40 and 41.)

The running rope, from hook going back over center of load to center of pack on the "near" side. (Fig. 40, to R, fig. 41.)

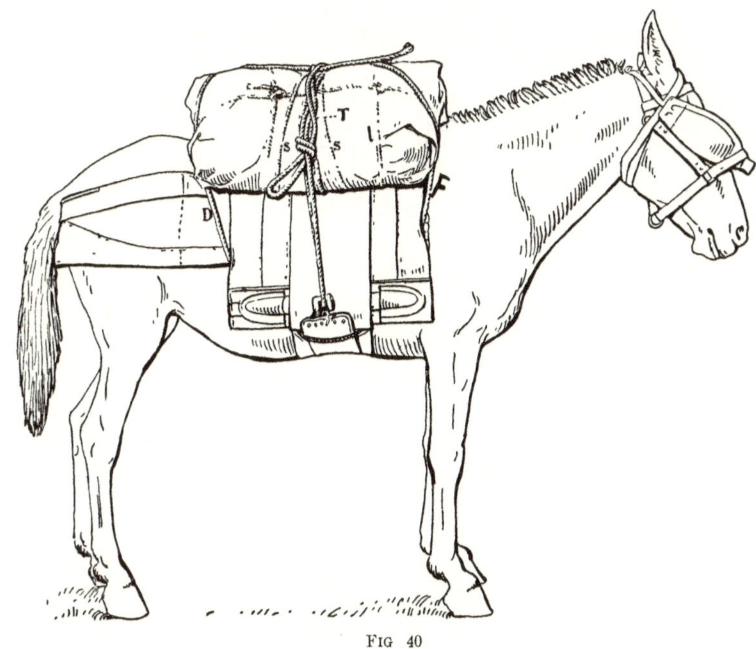

FIG 40

The marking rope, from the center of side pack on the "near" side, from point were jammed under the standing rope and front corner of boot of aparejo. (Fig. 41, R and M.)

The front rope passes over the front corners of the load; the rear rope, in similar manner, over the rear corners; in both cases, on each side, the rope passes under and around the boot. These ropes are sometimes referred to as the quarter ropes. (F and D, fig. 40, and D and F, fig. 41.)

The top rope, from the rear corner of the boot on the "near" side, running up toward and across the center of the load (fig. 41) to the center and side of the "off" pack, where the wrapping of rope indicates completion of the hitch. (Fig. 40.)

It may be added, there are various methods of finishing the hitch, as conditions of loading may suggest to the experienced packer.

The "top" rope may be used as a marking rope by bringing the rope to rear of the near pack instead of to the center, to indicate that the load has been tightened, in lieu of the marking rope, and by many packers is preferred as a better method of marking the load.

The formation of the "diamond" hitch and tightening of the load is performed in from twenty-five to thirty seconds.

The operation of loading a pack mule (this includes putting on the aparejo) is performed by experts in from forty-five to sixty seconds.[a]

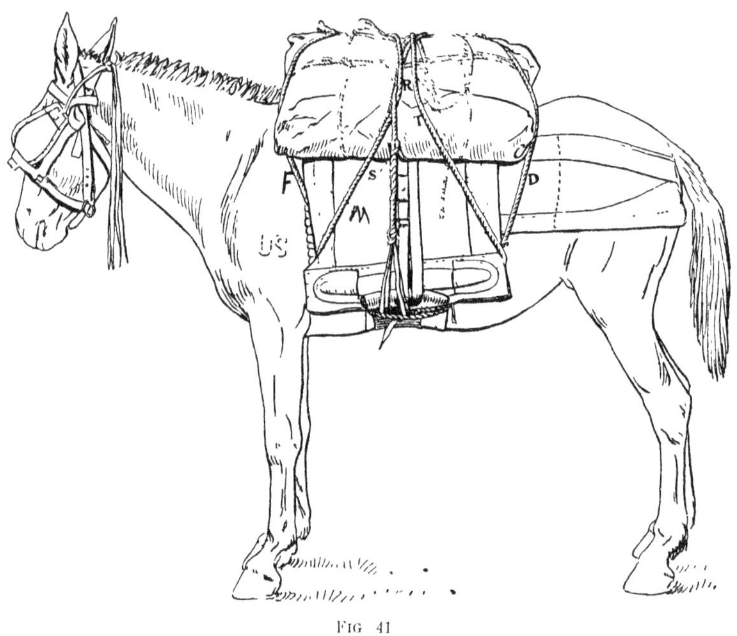

FIG 41

HOW TO FORM THE DOUBLE DIAMOND.

SEC. 33. This hitch is sometimes used when employing top packs or top loads, kegs and barrels excepted; for these latter the "double hitch" is employed.

The *near* packer takes a lash rope and uncoils about 15 feet of the free end, and passes it over the animal's haunch to the "off" packer, who in turn passes the rope between the top and side pack and allows the end to fall over the animal's neck to ground.

---

[a] As an aid to learn how to form the diamond and other hitches, a wooden horse, such as used by "carpenters" may be provided

It should stand 4 feet high, the center or ridge pole to be 6 feet long, the legs to be spaced 9 inches on each side, from center of ridgepole, so as to have 18 inches spread on each side. Bevel the upper ends of legs adjoining ridgepole so that their extremities will stand on the ground about 2 feet apart As a reenforce supply a small cleat of wood on the upper and outer ends of legs underneath the ridgepole.

Now place the corona, blanket, and aparejo on this wooden horse, turn the crupper and cinch the aparejo in the customary manner; place the sling rope on the aparejo and proceed to put on the side packs, forming the load as described in sections 25 to 38.

The *near* packer, in similar manner, brings the rope between the top and side pack; in both cases the top corners of each "side" pack retain the rope in position during the formation of the hitch.

The *near* packer will then hold the cincha with the right hand, and allow the coils held in left hand to drop to ground.

Now throw or pass the cincha to the "off" packer, under the animal's belly, and form a loop, and pass the standing rope over the load; the running rope over the animal's neck, as in forming the single "diamond," and, after the "off" packer engages the standing rope on the hook, the near packer throws, or passes, all rope on ground to rear; this forms the rear half of the "diamond."

Next, with the assistance of the "off" packer, bring the running rope up to center of load, and pass the running rope from rear to front, between the standing rope and cincha, as in forming the single "diamond."

Now bring the end of rope between the standing and running ropes from in, out, and draw 3 or 4 feet of the end forward and a "diamond" is formed on the near side. (Fig. 42.)

The *off* packer, to form a "diamond" on the "off" side, takes the end rope, as resting between the "top and side" pack, doubles a portion, forming a loop, and brings this loop between the standing and running ropes from in, out, and allows the loop to fall down; the loop comes under the boot in the tightening of the hitch, separating the rear and front ropes, thus forming a "diamond" on the "off" side. (Fig. 43.)

The hitch is now formed, ready to tighten the load.

In tightening the hitch, proceed in similar manner as in the single "diamond," with the exception that the rear and front rope, in tightening, passes along the face of each end of top pack, to retain the top pack in position. This formation gives a "diamond" on each side of the load; hence the name, "double diamond." (Fig. 44 for near side and fig. 45 for off side.)

HOW TO FORM THE DOUBLE HITCH.

SEC. 34. This form of hitch should never be used, except when packs are so narrow that the "diamond" will slip over them, as in the case of kegs, a single barrel, coils of rope, etc.

The double hitch is made as described for the single diamond hitch, with the two following exceptions:

(1) The "near" packer, before passing the running rope to rear of pack, brings the running rope up, from the animal's neck, and lays it on the center of the load, in front of the standing rope. He then takes sufficient slack on the running rope between the packs, and lays or throws it to rear of load, thus causing it to ride over *both* the running and the standing ropes; he then takes the rope in front of the standing rope and brings it down from right to left between the standing rope and pack and under the boot of the aparejo in the customary manner.

(2) The "off" packer, instead of placing the end of rope *between* the standing and running ropes, places it under *both*, then raises to center of load, and drops about 12 inches of end on "near" side of animal's neck, and hitch is formed ready to tighten.

The hitch is tightened in the usual manner as in the operation of the "diamond."

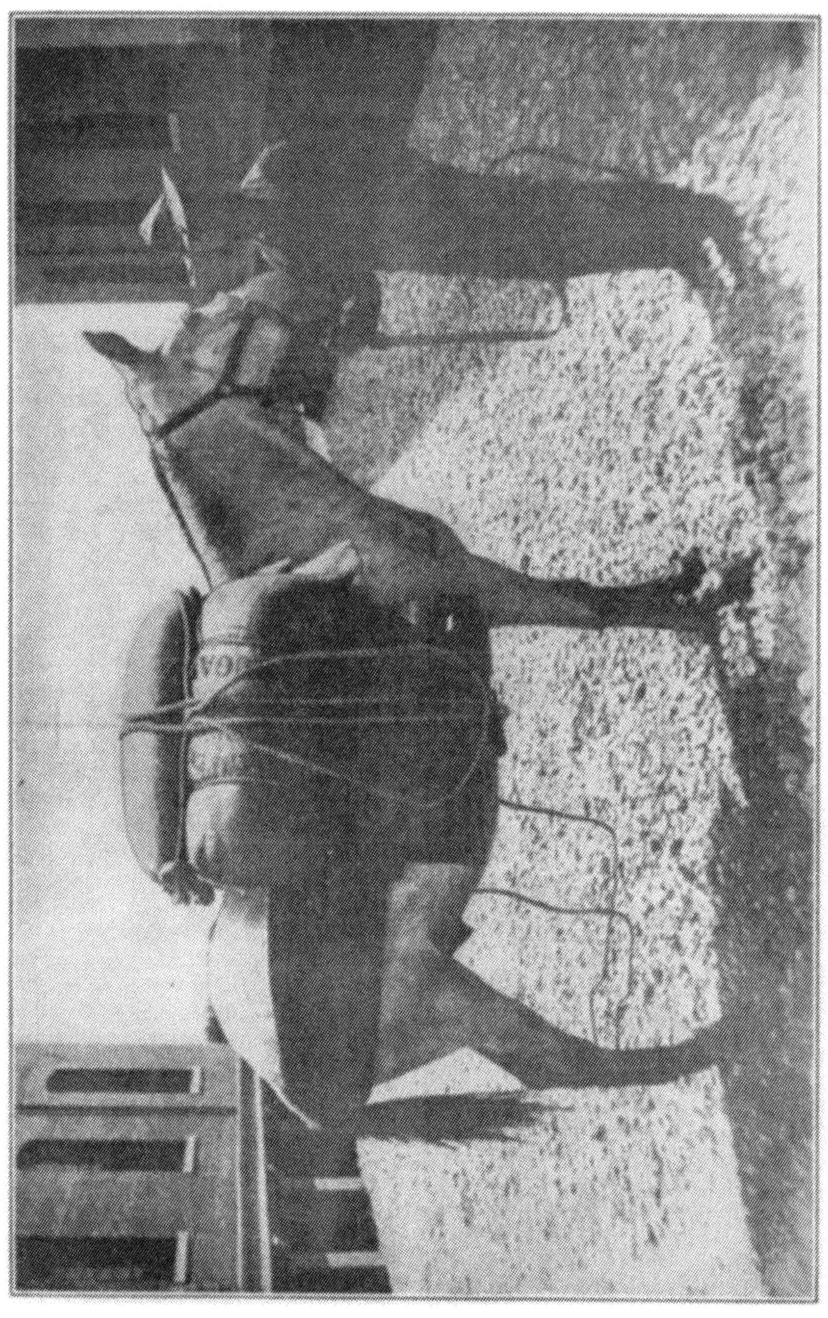

HOW TO FORM THE DIAMOND HITCH WHEN THE CINCH HOOK IS LOST OR BROKEN.

SEC. 35. First, the *near* packer will remove cincha from lash rope and place it on top of load; then throw the lash rope as usual.

The *off* packer picks up the end of lash rope, and, as the standing rope is passed to him by the "near" packer, he brings the end of the rope from rear to front around the standing rope; holding standing rope in loop he forms a bowline knot on end of rope; this leaves the standing rope in loop of bowline knot. (See fig. 80.) Then proceed with the diamond hitch in the usual manner.

To take the lash rope off undo the bowline knot.

HOW ONE PACKER CAN SLING THE LOAD AND FORM THE DIAMOND HITCH.

SEC. 36. Take the lash rope and grasp it with both hands, about 3 feet apart, anywhere near the middle of rope; bring the portion of rope between the hands under the boot of the aparejo, and bring the hands together above the boot of the aparejo and grasp both ropes with left hand.

Now, grasping the rear rope with right hand forward of the left, pass a loop of it over the aparejo, of size proportionate to the size of the pack. Lay the standing part as close to the rear edge of the aparejo as length of pack admits and rest the running part on the animal's hips. Drop the rear rope from left hand; then grasp the front rope with right hand below the left and with the left hand pass the rope over to "off" side in similar manner as described for the rear rope, resting the outer or running part on the animal's neck. Now place the sling rope in position in the usual way (sec. 25). It should lie between the front and rear parts of the lash rope.

Take up the "off" pack and, from the "near" side, place it well up toward center of aparejo. Place the left hand at center and lower edge of pack to hold it in place. Take the rope resting on the animal's hips and bring the loop over the rear end of pack, letting the right hand relieve the left at center of pack and with the left bring the front loop over the front end of pack.

Now place the left arm with elbow supporting the pack; grasp the rear rope of lash rope with left hand, as explained in double slinging side packs (sec. 29). Grasp the front rope with the right hand, bring it under the boot of the aparejo, from front to rear, and up to the left hand. Tie the two ropes by a square knot, as before described (sec. 27). Then work the pack so as to settle it to off side, giving slack at square knot, if necessary to get it settled to place.

Pass to off side and bring the sling rope over the center of pack, resting the loop on rear corner of pack. Return to near side and place the near pack in position.

Reach for the loop of the sling rope from behind, bring it over center of packs, and tie the square knot in the usual manner (sec. 27); then brake or settle pack to place.

Untie the lash rope from under the packs and proceed with the diamond hitch in the usual manner, passing from near to off side, as required, until the hitch is in position to take in slack.

Then take in all slack possible on the "off" side, and to hold it *bring a bight of the running rope between the standing rope and the pack*, so as to make it bind.

Proceed to take in slack in the usual manner. After pulling taut, as shown in fig. 26, bring the hands toward the aparejo quickly and grasp both ropes, i. e., the standing as well as the running rope, and, holding both ropes with left hand, receive the slack above the bight, as caught under the standing rope. Take a second and similar pull and receive the slack above the bight as before and pass to the near side. *Note.*—Bringing the running rope between the standing rope and the pack forms a holdfast and retains the slack as taken above the bight.

Take the running rope from under the standing rope on "near" side, should it be there, and draw in all slack. Then bring the running rope under the standing rope as before. (Fig. 27.)

The taking of slack should be repeated until all is rendered. In the completion of the hitch, pass from near to off side, as necessary, taking up all the slack until the hitch is completed.

HOW TO FORM THE POLE HITCH.

SEC. 37. For this purpose a lash rope without cincha, or two sling or lair ropes joined together, may be used for the purpose.

The *near* packer takes a lash rope and removes cincha and passes one-half of rope over the load to the "off" packer. Each packer takes hold of rope with the right hand, with the arm extended downward, raises the rope, causing it to rest on the left arm, and reaches for the standing rope at pack with left hand. Now bring the right hand, holding rope, to and above the left hand, allowing the free end to drop downward, and part the hands, bringing each rope over the upper corners of side packs and the loop portion under the boots of the aparejo.

Pass each end over the load to the opposite side, the "off" packer bringing his end under the standing rope at center of pack, waits for the word "Go," and the hitch is formed, ready to tighten. (Figs. 46–47.) Also figs. 72, 73, 74.

The *near* packer, to tighten the load, holds the end of rope passed by the "off" packer over the load, and placing the left hand as a brace against the pack, calls out "Go."

The *off* packer will pull the slack on the running rope in the usual manner and call out "Tie."

The *near* packer brings the rope under the bight of the standing rope, immediately takes hold of the running rope at center of boot, and waits for the call of "Go" from the "off" packer, who frees the end of rope from under the bight and proceeds to take in slack in similar manner, each packer securing the end of rope as in completion of the "diamond" hitch or as convenience may dictate. (Figs. 48–49.)

The pole hitch is the formation of a half hitch over each side pack; no portion of the rope passes under the belly of the animal, distinguishing it from all other forms of hitches. While it compresses the load to extreme tightness, it affords no tightening of the aparejo to the body of the animal, a necessary qualification when climbing a mountain, or, in other words, the load may be compressed, while the aparejo may be loose on the animal. It should never be used when a lash rope is available. It may be used for packing odds and ends after cargo is loaded and a loose animal is available, and when pressed

75927°—17——7

for time. It is also used to secure travois to aparejo and improvised "litters." (See figs. 71 and 74.)

HOW TO FORM THE OREGON DIAMOND HITCH.

SEC. 38. This form of hitch is performed by one packer, and is closely related to the crosstree or sawbuck hitch.

Standing on the near side of the animal, take a coiled lash rope and free the coils, hold the cincha and allow the coils to drop to ground; now take sufficient slack on rope and pass the cincha over the load in such manner that the cincha will come under the animal's belly within easy reach; pick up cincha and engage the standing portion on hook from in out, bringing a portion of the running rope upward, and engage it under the standing rope from right to left, to hold it there; now take the free or running portion of rope and form a half hitch, or single loop, keeping the free end under, and draw sufficient slack to engage over the off pack and boot of aparejo.

Pass to the "off" side and pass the running rope from right to left, between the pack and standing rope, and press to place under boot of aparejo, as performed on the near side in the regular "diamond."

Now pass to the "near" side and take the end of the rope and pass it over and under the standing rope at front, draw sufficient slack and drop the end of rope over the animal's haunch to ground, and the hitch is formed, ready to tighten the load.[a] (Figs. 50–51.)

To tighten the load, pull on the running rope close to cinch hook in the usual manner, but be careful that the rope is not drawn from under the bight of standing rope, as its purpose is to retain the slack as given.

In giving slack, bring the hands quickly to standing rope and grip both ropes with the left hand, so as to hold the slack, then receive this slack above the bight on standing rope, and repeat the operation until all slack has been taken; pass to the "off" side and receive this slack in the usual manner. Now pass from the "off" to the "near" side until hitch is tightened, finishing the hitch in the usual manner, or as conditions may indicate. (Figs. 52–53.)

HOW TO SLING THE LOAD AND FORM THE CROSSTREE HITCH ON CROSSTREE OR SAWBUCK—HOW TO SLING THE LOAD ON CROSSTREE.

SEC. 39. It is assumed that the animal is equipped with crosstree and ready to receive load.

The *near* packer takes the sling rope and forms two half hitches on the "forks" at the front of saddle, and allows each half to drop to ground, on each side of the animal. See Figs. 71, 72, 73, and 74.

Each packer will then form a half hitch on the free end over the forks at rear, allowing sufficient loop on rope to receive side packs. The "off" side is entirely similar; in this operation the free end of rope should come under the loop thus formed. (Fig. 54.)

The *off* packer places the side pack well up toward forks and, holding it there with the right hand, palm down, against center of pack, proceeds to pass the rope along the lower side of pack, taking slack

---

[a] The running rope may be kept to front of the standing rope in the formation; the end of the rope will then be over the animal's neck on the off side instead of over the haunch.

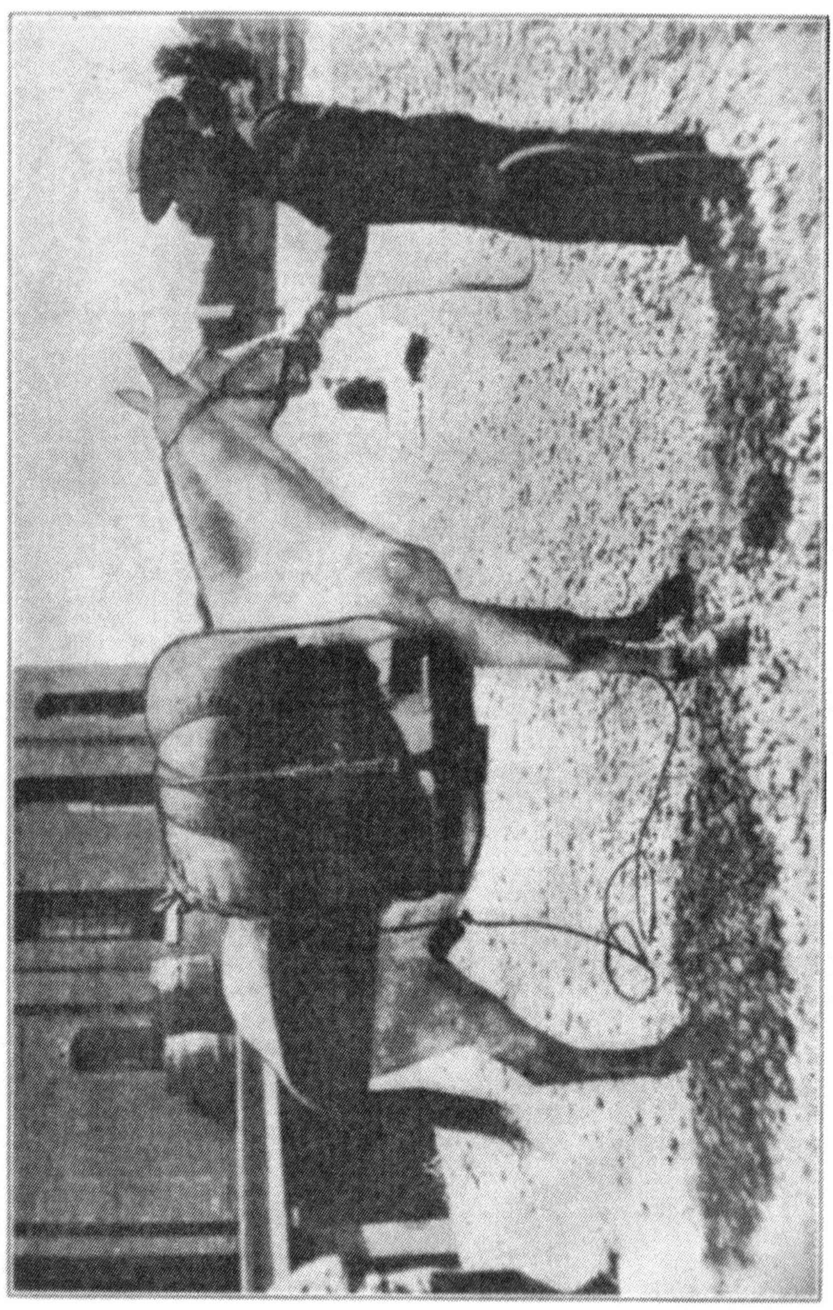

on free end of rope at rear and brings this portion under the pack to center, then with the end of the rope take a turn around the rope along the side of the pack at center and draw snug. This will hold the pack or support it, and forms a bowline knot on end of rope; he now brings the rope upward at center of pack and waits for the call, "Rope!" from the "near" packer.

The "near" packer proceeds in similar manner (without forming bowline knot), and when ready calls out "Rope!" He will then pass the end of rope over and under through the eye of bowline knot and draw the packs well together, each packer holding packs well up, to assist in doing so, and secure the end of rope at bowline knot, or at center of side pack at turn of sling rope, as it is always within easy reach. (Fig. 55; same on "off" side.)

This operation may be performed by one packer.

Another method in common use is, the *near* packer forms two half hitches on the "forks" at front of saddle and allows each half to drop to ground on each side of the animal.

The *near* packer places the side pack well up toward forks and, holding it there with the right hand, with the left he brings the rope upward and over the side pack, and then forming a loop or half hitch, he brings this loop over the forks of the saddle; in forming the loop keep the free end under and draw the pack well up, or as may be determined, if carrying one or more top packs, change position of hands and with the right hand bring the fore or running rope to rear and form a similar loop or half hitch on the forks at rear and draw all slack taut; now bring the fore or running portion under and over the pack at rear and form a similar half hitch over the forks and tie at intersection of ropes below the forks; the operation for the *off* side is entirely similar. This operation may be performed by one packer.

HOW TO FORM THE CROSSTREE HITCH.

SEC. 40. For this purpose take a lash rope with cincha, about 35 feet long, and stand on the near side of the animal, facing the load; take the cincha and throw or pass it over the load in such manner that the cincha will pass under the animal's belly, convenient to packer; pick up the cincha and, taking in all slack, engage rope on hook; now bring a portion of the running rope up to side of pack, double this portion, and pass it under the standing rope from rear to front, so as to be caught in a bight between standing rope and pack; this will hold the rope.

Now bring the running rope upward, double the rope and bring it under and *forward* of the standing rope, and take slack on double of rope, then form a loop or half hitch on this portion, keeping the free end under and turn loop over, drawing sufficient slack on rope to pass over the "off" side pack, from front to rear; step to "off" side to place rope over upper corners and along the lower side of pack; now come to "near" side, and bring the running rope around the lower side of pack, and pass the end over and under the standing, running, and rear ropes at center or top of load, from above down, and take in all slack, in similar manner as performed on the "off" side, and the hitch is formed, ready to tighten the load.

Or, in forming the hitch, after engaging the rope onto hook, bring the running rope upward and then pass the rope to rear without

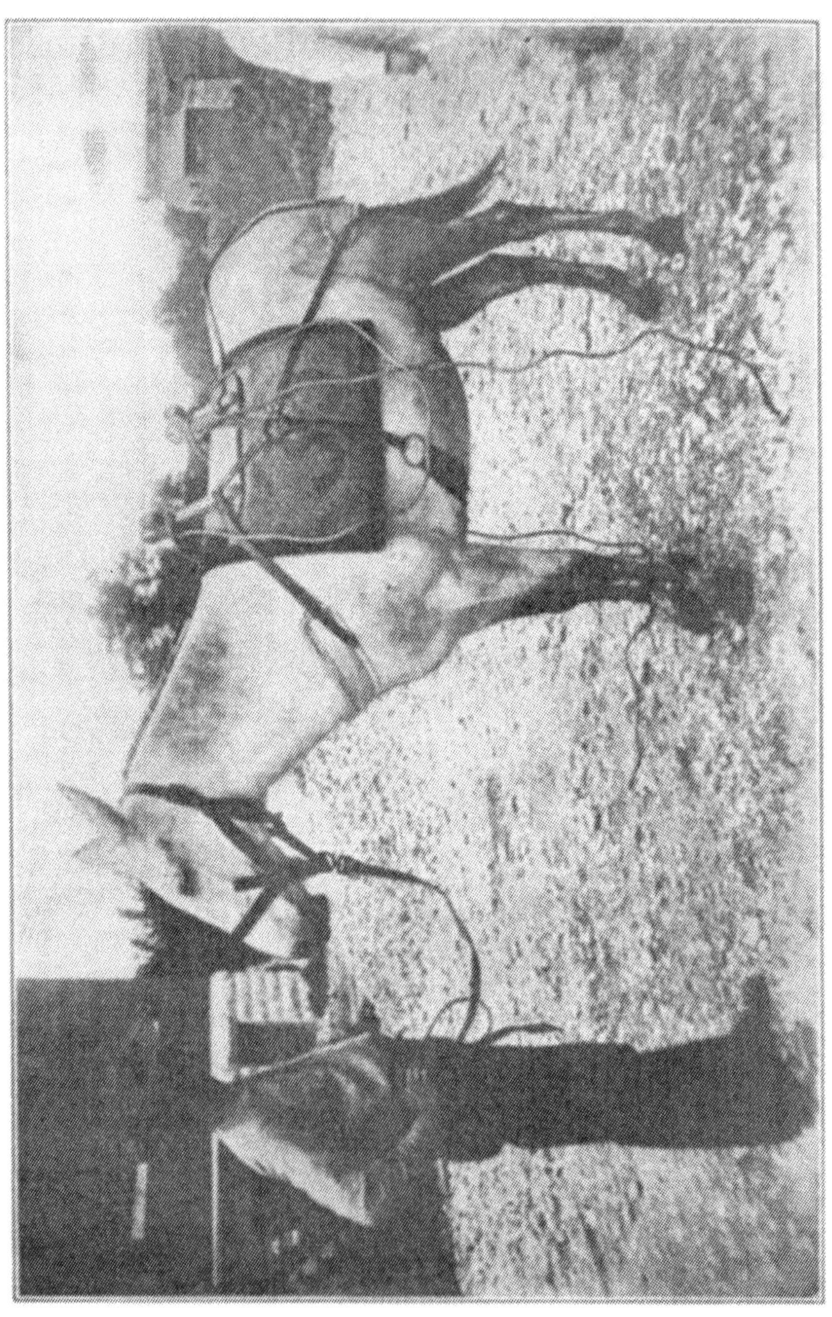

forming a loop, and then under and around the pack to front; now bring the end of the rope over and under the standing and running rope and draw sufficient slack on rope to pass under and around the pack on the rear side to the rear; now bring the end of the rope over and under the intersection of the standing, running and front rope, and drop the end of the rope over the animal's haunch on the off side of the animal, and the hitch is formed ready to tighten the load.

To tighten the load, bring the running rope under the standing rope so as to be caught in a bight, now, take hold of the running rope, close the cinch hook and take all slack possible, allowing the hands to come quickly to standing rope, and grasp both ropes with the left hand; receive this slack from above the bight, pass to the "off" side and take in all slack from front to rear, keeping the rope against the lower edge of pack; pass to "near" side, and take in all slack by pulling the end of rope and place the rope in similar manner as for the "off" side and secure the end of rope on the near or off side or on top of load. (Figs. 56, 57.)

The forks of the saddle act as a holdfast in keeping the packs from moving fore and aft, the lash rope tightening the load at the center of side packs.

NOTE.—This form of hitch is the parent of all other hitches used in pack-train service. The change in not bringing the loop under the standing rope forms the "Oregon diamond," the latter leading to the "diamond," "double diamond," etc. This hitch is used by prospectors, miners, hunting parties, the Bureau of Forestry, and is known and practiced in many countries.

HOW TO FORM THE STIRRUP HITCH.

SEC. 41. This form of hitch is used principally by cattlemen ("cow punchers") on the "round-up" or trail, the ordinary riding saddle being sometimes employed for the purpose.

Assuming that the load is properly slung on the crosstree, take a rope about 30 feet long, without cincha, and pass the rope over the load, so as to have an equal division on each side; now form a loop on top and center of load. Each packer will now take the end of rope and pass it from above, down into the loop at top, taking sufficient slack so as to leave a loop long enough to place the foot therein.

Each packer will then pass the loop held by the foot to each other under the belly of the animal, and receive it by passing the end of the rope into the opposite loop and release the foot. (Fig. 58)

Before taking slack it is well to spread the rope at top of side packs, so as to grip them more securely. At the call "Ready," each packer will place his foot against the animal's body and draw rope taut, and secure end of rope to loop on center of load; or a bowline knot may be formed on end of rope on the "off" side, sec. 46, fig. 79, the "near" packer passing his end through loop; the "off" packer giving slack in the usual manner, and secure rope at bowline knot. (Figs. 58, 59, and 60.)

TAKING OFF THE LOAD AND APAREJO—HOW TO TAKE OFF THE LASH ROPE AND THE LOAD.

SEC 42. (1) *Off packer.*—The "off" packer releases the end of the lash rope, as secured on the "off" side (fig. 40) and passes it quickly over the animal's neck to near side. This should be done quickly,

75927°—17——8

so as to cause any coils of the end that have been placed under the top rope to fall to the ground.

Grasp the front rope, draw on the slack sufficiently to bring it over and to rear of packs, stepping to rear as you do so. Then draw in the slack, hand over hand, coiling the rope in the operation, and receive the coils in the left hand, until the end of the rope has been freed from between the standing and running ropes. (This is the reverse of the process illustrated in figs. 22 and 24.)

Now step to center of aparejo, and when slack is rendered on running rope at bight of standing rope (R, fig. 41) by "near" packer, free the cincha hook from the rope.

(2) *Near packer.*—The "near" packer grasps the rear rope (D, fig. 41) with right hand, and when slack is rendered by "off" packer, he draws enough slack on the "marking" rope (M, fig. 41) to free the running rope from under the standing rope at center of pack (R, fig. 41). He allows sufficient slack to the "off" packer to enable him to free the rope from the hook.

The hook being freed he grasps with the left hand the running and rear ropes and the standing rope near the lacings of the cincha, and calls to "off" packer, "To rear."

(3) *Off packer.*—The "off" packer, at the call "To rear," grasps the running, standing, and rear ropes in right hand, passes them back over the animal's haunches, and swings or throws the coils held in left hand to the rear, in line with the "near" packer.

(4) *Near packer.*—The "near" packer, holding ropes in left hand, coils them with right, receiving coils with left hand, leaving from 10 to 15 feet of the end extended.

He then steps forward and partly in front of the animal swings the coils toward the rear and places the lash rope on the ground, cinch underneath. (See footnote.)

(5) *Off packer.*—The "off" packer, having passed the ropes to the rear, steps to center of load and with left hand frees whatever portion of the sling rope that may have been placed between the packs and allows it to drop to ground on near side of the animal. He now places a hand on each end of pack as a support and waits for the knot to be untied by the "near" packer.

(6) *Near packer.*—The "near" packer, having placed the lash rope on the ground, steps to center of load, places left hand, palm down, on center of pack, and calls out "Ready!"

He then frees the knot with the right hand and, changing the position of the hands, he frees the front rope from the bight of the sling and allows it to drop to the ground.

Grasping the pack at ends he allows the pack to come down against his breast, carries and places it lengthwise on the coiled lash rope.

(7) *Off packer.*—The pack being freed, the "off" packer receives it against the breast, allowing the sling rope to be caught between the pack and breast; carries pack and places it on top of the "near" pack, coils the sling rope, and places it crosswise on the packs; then takes the end of the lash rope where extended on the ground, coils and places it on top of pack. The load is now formed as described in section 24.

NOTE.—When occasion requires in forming cargo, the lash ropes may be passed to the front instead of to the rear, i. e., over the animal's head instead of the haunches. This is effected in a manner entirely similar to that described above.

HOW TO UNCINCH AN APAREJO AND TURN THE CRUPPER.

Sec. 43. With the left hand loosen the end of the latigo or cincha strap and with the right hand draw the latigo down. Loosen and release the latigo from the rendering ring; then pass the latigo over to the "off" side, causing it to lie along the middle of cincha.

Grasp the lacings of the cincha with the right hand, the left arm resting on top of the aparejo as a support, the thumb engaged under the latigo as a guide to keep the latigo in the middle of the cincha and draw the cincha downward so as to have about four feet. Now, place the left hand, fingers extended, on cincha, and fold the end over with the right hand. This should leave the cincha doubled on top of the aparejo, equally divided.

Step to the front, place left hand on collar, right on corner of boot, and push the aparejo slightly to the rear; if necessary, alternate each hand. Step squarely behind animal, with the right hand grasp the end of the animal's tail, raise it to the right and upward, resting it on the animal's haunch, and hold it there with the left hand. With the right raise the crupper so as to free the tail and allow the tail to drop.

Take hold of the upper edges of the crupper with both hands, about 10 inches from the dock on either side. Raise and bring the hands together. Take both edges in the left hand; place the right palm under the lower edge of crupper, and while the left hand is pressing downward, press upward with the palm of the right, thus turning the crupper upside down. Allow the dock of crupper to rest on the center of aparejo.

The animal should be held throughout the operation by retaining the end of the halter shank in the left hand.

HOW TO TAKE OFF AN APAREJO.

Sec. 44. Take hold with right hand, near the center of the aparejo on the near side and at rear, the left at front corner of boot; press in quickly with left, and pull toward body with right. This gets the aparejo quartering on the animal's back. Pass left hand over to off side, palm against inside of belly piece of aparejo; raise the aparejo with left hand, to clear animal's back, and place it on the ground. It will be observed that the position of hands is the same as when putting on the aparejo.

Note.—In taking off the aparejo packers *must not place* the aparejo on the ground with force.

MISCELLANEOUS

HOW TO FORM TWO HALF HITCHES—THE POLE (CLOVE) HITCH.

Sec. 45. Take a rope at point determined to form hitch, and hold in left hand, the last two fingers pressing rope against palm, the thumb and first two fingers ready to receive the hitches as formed.

Grasp the rope in the right hand in front of the left and at a distance from the left determined by the size of the loops or hitches it is desired to form.

By an outward and inward motion of the right hand make a loop in the rope, the part held in the right hand passing under that held in left. Allow the first finger of left hand to receive this loop.

Make a second and similar loop and place it on top of the loop first formed, receiving it between the thumb and loop already formed.

Render slack either way, to permit of hitches being of similar size. Place hitches over object and draw taut. (See Figs. 71, 72, 73, 74.)

HOW TO FORM A BOWLINE KNOT.

SEC. 46. With the left hand, palm up, grasp the rope, say, about 12 inches from the end, the standing part of the rope extended out from you.

With the right lay the end or running portion over the standing part, in front of the left hand, and grip both ropes with the thumb and first two fingers.

Now bring the left hand, holding rope forward, passing over the end of the rope as held by the right hand, and lay this loop or eye on top of the standing rope and grip both ropes between the thumb and first two fingers of the left hand. This operation leaves the end of the rope standing upward in the eye of rope as thus formed.

Now take the end of the rope in the right hand and bring it forward, then under and over the standing rope and back again into the eye of bowline, grip the end between the two first fingers of the left hand and pull taut on the standing rope. See Fig. 79. The rope d forms the loop or eye; the rope c is that portion first engaged in the loop, as seen in the eye adjoining; d, the rope; a, in first position, adjoins d, as seen in the eye; now follow this rope around, as seen at c and a, and the bowline knot is formed.

HOW TO FORM THE BOWLINE AND BIGHT.

SEC. 47. Take a rope and double it at any point determined to form the bight; now grasp the double or loop at end with the right hand, and with left reach forward and grasp both ropes as far as the size of the loop may be determined; bring the loop end of the rope over and under both ropes and into the "eye" thus formed.

Now with the right hand grasp the loop or double and draw sufficient slack to pass the right hand, palm up, from above down through the loop end only. Now grasp the double of the rope in the center of the eye and hold it there. Next bring the loop end forward against the standing part, and turn the rope over, as seen at a, Fig. 81, and pull taut on the double of the rope held by the right hand until the loop end compresses on the standing part, and the bowline and bight are formed.

NOTE.—In the first instance, the end of rope held in the right hand and brought into the eye is, in the second instance, brought under and back to the standing part extending forward, the double of the rope enclosed in the eye is drawn toward the body, this forms the loop as seen on the right of d; the loop at d forms the eye or bight.

This form of knot is used in stretching a picket line, etc.

HOW TO FORM A SHORT SPLICE ON ROPE.

SEC. 48. Take two sections of rope of same size diameter and unravel the strands of each section about 6 or 8 inches long; now place the *back* of one section on the *front* of the other section so that the strands of one section will pass between the strands of its mate, bring each section snug up and tie down with cord across the intersection or middle, to hold the strands to place during the operation.

NOTE.—There is a back and a front in the formation (or twist) of all ropes, and also in the formation (or plaiting) of all ropes, whips, etc. The back is that portion facing toward the body; the front is that portion facing from the body and is the under or bottom side of the twist in the formation of the rope; therefore, in short splicing place the back of one section on the front of the other section so as to follow the twist in splicing the rope; now pass each strand from right to left over and under its mate on the twist or section of rope; then take two more turns, drawing each strand down snugly during the operation; turn end for end and proceed in similar manner; cut off all remaining portions of the strands extending from the splice or rope; roll the splice under foot or something smooth and solid and the splice is formed. Neatness or handiness in the packer is everything in forming all splices, knots, and hitches. See Figs. 95 to 98.

HOW TO FORM A LONG SPLICE ON ROPE.

SEC. 49. Take two sections of rope of same size diameter and unravel one strand of each section about 12 inches long, or as long as may be determined; now place the rope held in the right hand on top of the rope held in the left hand, so as to have the unraveled strand of top section adjoining the unraveled strand of bottom section (in the operation of the splice it may be well to tie the sections of rope with a cord at point of intersection of the unraveled portions); now, holding each section in the left hand, unravel the forward or bottom section of rope, same strand, one or two more turns and follow this unraveling by the unraveled strand of top section; continue the operation until about 4 inches of the top strand is reached; now take the strand of the top section and pass it over and under the strand of the forward or bottom section and draw down snug, so that the tie or slip knot will lay smooth; now turn the rope end for end, and hold the rope in the left hand as before, and unravel the remaining strands of each section until the last one or two turns are reached. In unraveling the last one or two turns be careful to have the strand of the top section meet the strand of the bottom section, so that the strand of the top section will follow up the vacant turn of the bottom strand until about 4 inches of the top strand is reached, and form a slip knot as before; if carefulness is used this will leave the remaining strand of top and bottom section in alignment, one with the other, showing there is no interference in the lay of the twist of the rope; now take the strand of the top section, which will be the strand adjoining the left hand, and pass this strand over and under the strand of the forward section and draw down snug; this operation leaves all the strands engaged, each strand having occupied the place made vacant by its mate. To finish the splice, unravel each strand until the slip knot is reached, divide the cords of one strand, and pass one division, or half the cords, from right to left over and under the adjoining strand of rope and draw down snug; proceed in similar manner with the remaining five strands, using one-half of the cords of each strand as before; now cut off all remaining portions extending on rope and roll the rope under foot on board or something smooth and the splice is formed; the operation when neatly done will show the rope of same diameter all through the splice. See Fig. 99.

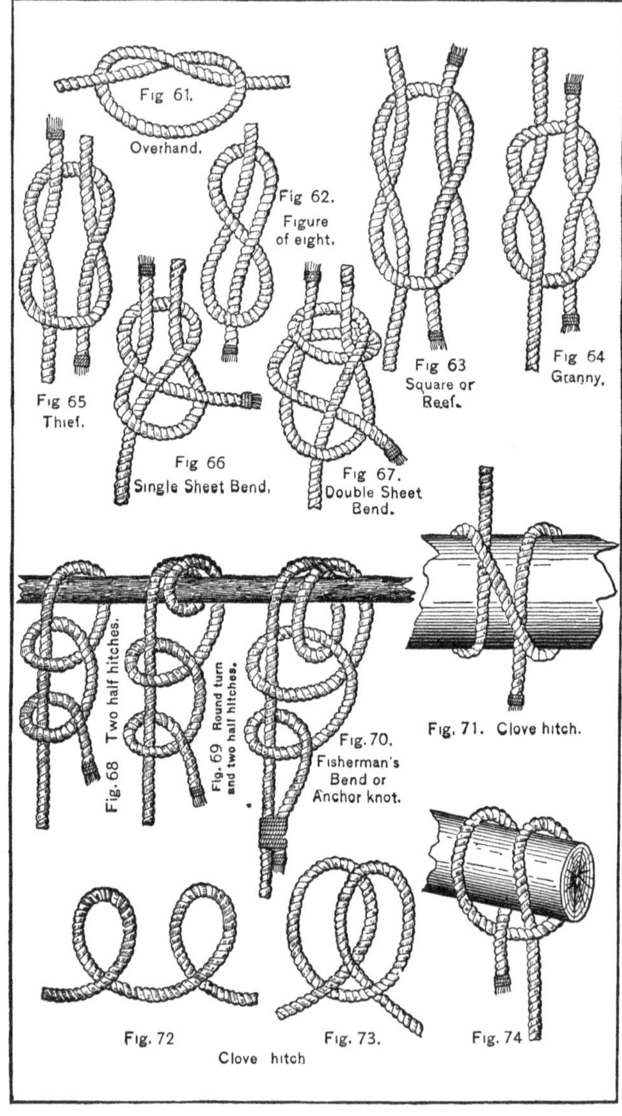
Fig 61.
Overhand.
Fig 62.
Figure of eight.
Fig 63
Square or Reef.
Fig 64
Granny.
Fig 65
Thief.
Fig 66
Single Sheet Bend.
Fig 67.
Double Sheet Bend.
Fig. 68 Two half hitches.
Fig. 69 Round turn and two half hitches.
Fig. 70.
Fisherman's Bend or Anchor knot.
Fig. 71. Clove hitch.
Fig. 72
Fig. 73.
Fig. 74
Clove hitch

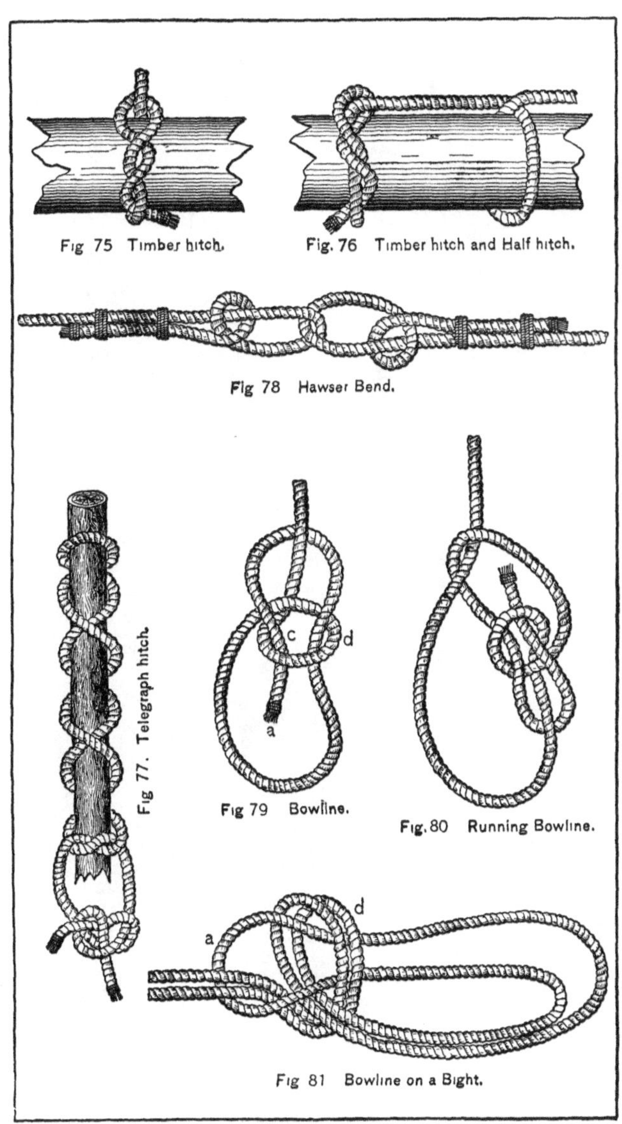

Fig 75 Timber hitch.

Fig. 76 Timber hitch and Half hitch.

Fig 78 Hawser Bend.

Fig 77. Telegraph hitch.

Fig 79 Bowline.

Fig. 80 Running Bowline.

Fig 81 Bowline on a Bight.

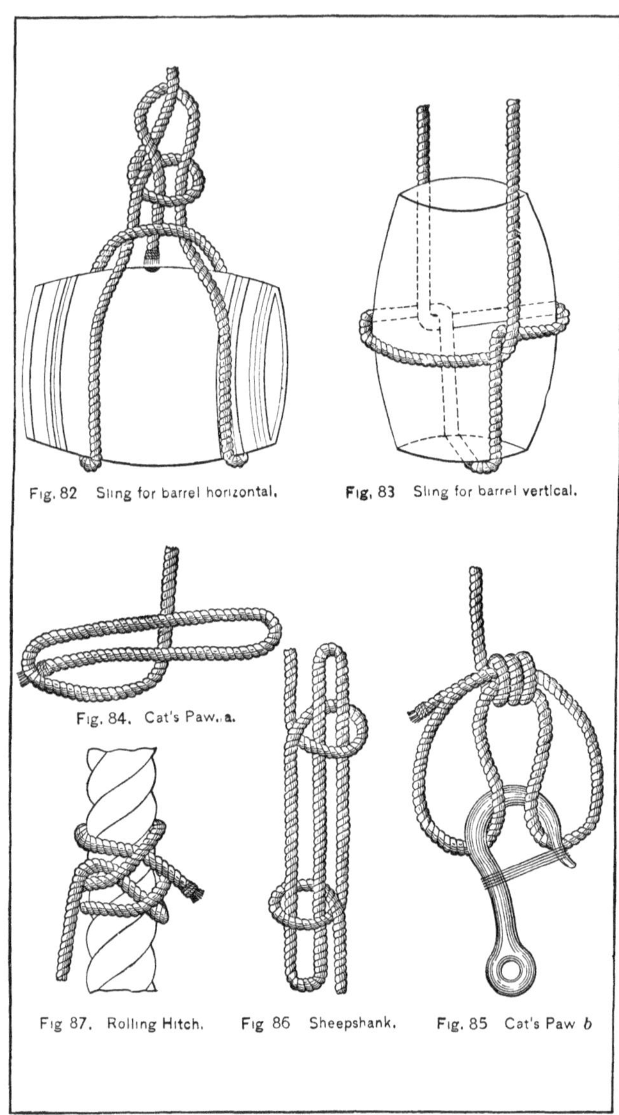

Fig. 82 Sling for barrel horizontal.

Fig. 83 Sling for barrel vertical.

Fig. 84. Cat's Paw, a.

Fig 87. Rolling Hitch.

Fig 86 Sheepshank.

Fig. 85 Cat's Paw b

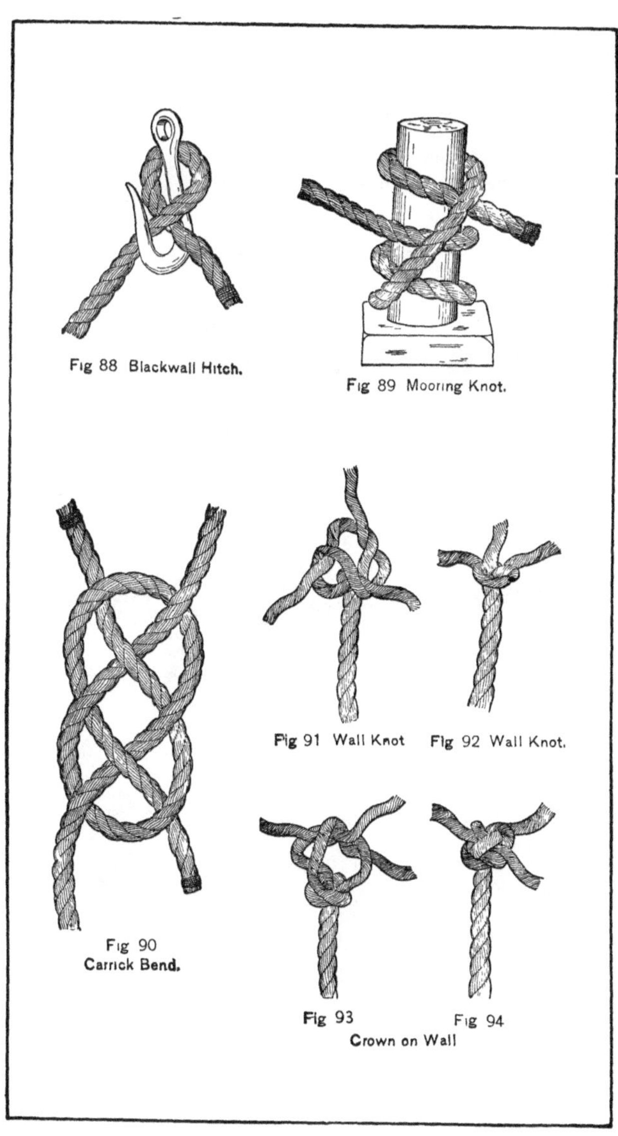

Fig 88 Blackwall Hitch.

Fig 89 Mooring Knot.

Fig 90 Carrick Bend.

Fig 91 Wall Knot

Fig 92 Wall Knot.

Fig 93 Fig 94 Crown on Wall

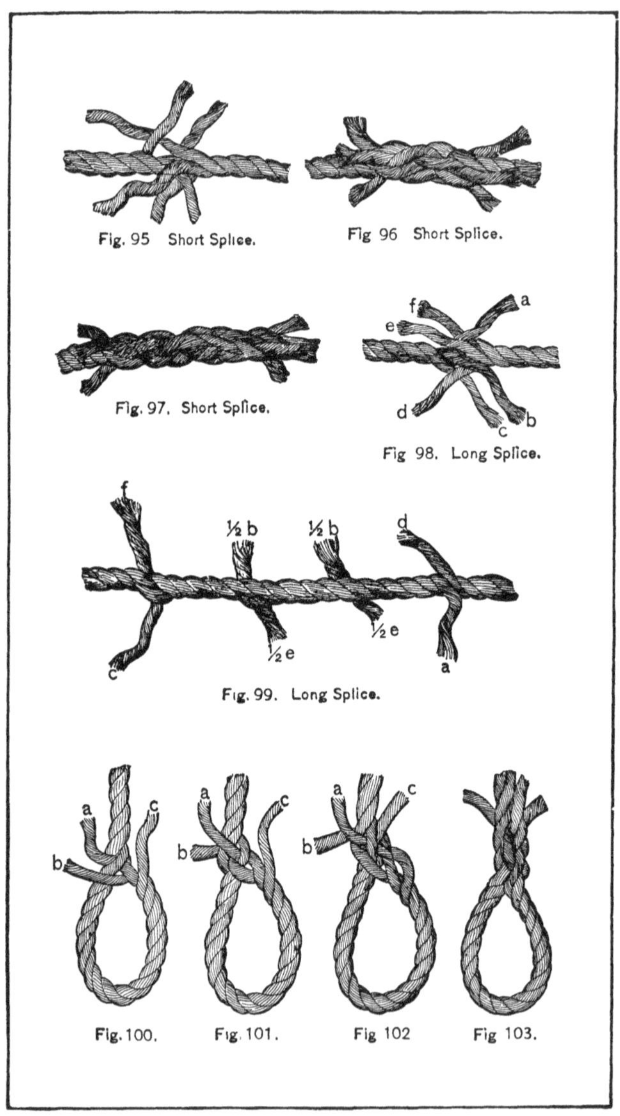

Fig. 95 Short Splice. Fig 96 Short Splice.

Fig. 97. Short Splice. Fig 98. Long Splice.

Fig. 99. Long Splice.

Fig. 100. Fig. 101. Fig 102 Fig 103.

HOW TO CONSTRUCT A TRAVOIS.

Sec. 50. Secure two poles from 14 to 16 feet long, as light as can be had, the diameter at the smaller ends being not greater than 2 inches.

Six inches from the butt end of each pole cut a notch deep enough to receive a sling or lair rope.

Take a manta and place poles thereon at opposite edges, leaving about 6 feet of the butt end of the poles extended beyond the manta. Roll the poles toward one another, leaving a space of 2 or 3 feet between the poles. Lace the poles to the manta by means of lace strings or small rope, or secure with horseshoe nails, always available.

Take a sling or lair rope and near middle of rope secure the butt end of each pole where the notches were cut. Use half hitches (see figs. 72, 73, 74) and allow about 18 inches of rope between the two poles.

Raise the poles and so place them that the center of the rope between the poles will rest on the center of the aparejo on the mule. Secure the poles to the aparejo with pole hitch. (Sec. 37.)

The construction should be strengthened by a distance pole lashed to poles below the manta.

One packer should lead the animal, and two should be in rear to hold up ends of travois in bad places or in crossing streams.

To enable them to hold the ends up, a rope should be attached to end of each pole.

HOW TO IMPROVISE A STRETCHER.

Sec. 51. Cut two poles 3 feet long; double sling them (sec. 29), and tie down to boot of aparejo. Cut two poles 2 feet long; place one in front and one in rear of aparejo, crosswise; mark and notch and secure to side poles. This should bring the cross poles 2 inches clear of the aparejo.

Cut two poles 6 feet long to form frame for stretcher. Take a manta and place the poles on the opposite edges of manta. Roll toward center, leaving a width of 20 inches between the outer edges of the poles. Lace manta to poles, or secure with horseshoe nails, which are always convenient. Place a distance pole at each end, notch, and secure. The plane of the canvas should ride on top. Secure body to stretcher by a lacing over body, clearing the stomach. Secure poles of stretcher at front and rear to each crosspiece and lash stretcher to aparejo. (Figs. 104, 105, 106, 107.)

Fig. 104 shows adjustment of bamboo frame to the aparejo prior to lashing litter thereto.

Fig. 105 shows method of attaching litter to bamboo frame, the crosspieces passing through legs of litter at front and rear as a holdfast and lashed to aparejo—near-side view.

Fig. 106 shows position of wounded on litter, fig. 107 showing off-side view. Jolo pack train carrying wounded soldiers to the sea from the interior.

Note.—The writer is indebted to Maj. Gen. H. L. Scott, Chief of Staff, United States Army, for the above views.

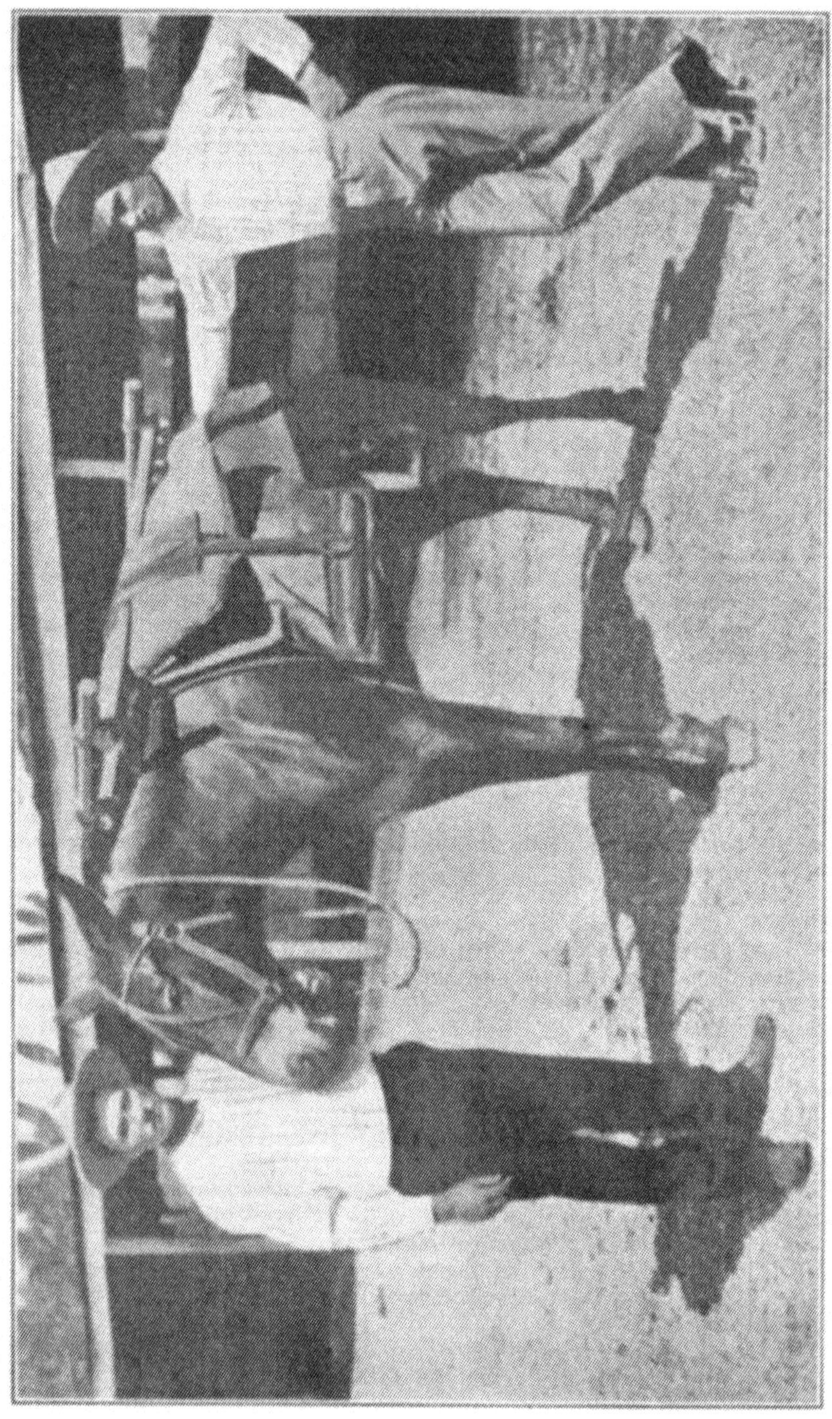

CHAPTER IV.

INSTRUCTION IN THE SERVICE OF A PACK TRAIN.

1. SUMMARY OF DUTIES IN LOADING AND UNLOADING A TRAIN.

SEC. 52. The operation of loading a train, or of unparking, in preparing for a march, may be summarized as follows:

(1) The mules follow the bell horse and take their places at the rigging. They are tied together by means of their halter shanks as they stand facing the rigging.

(2) The packers then put on the aparejos. Each animal, after receiving his aparejo, is tied to the lash rope under the load he is to carry. (Sec. 58.)

(3) The aparejos being on, the packers begin at once to load the animals. As each animal receives its load it is turned loose, and certain men are detailed to keep the animals in the neighborhood of the "bell."

In the operation of unloading a pack train, or of parking, after a march, the elements of a pack train are arranged as follows:

(4) The cargo is formed by the cargador. (Sec. 53.)

(5) The rigging is placed in an orderly manner, convenient to the cargo. (Sec. 54.)

(6) The animals, if not on herd, are tied to a picket line, placed conveniently in rear of rigging. (Sec. 75.)

(7) The kitchen is placed convenient to water and nearest to cargo.

In this order a pack train is parked in camp or bivouac.

These various operations are described in detail in the succeeding sections.

2. LOADING A PACK TRAIN.

HOW TO FORM CARGO PREPARATORY TO LOADING THE MULES.

SEC. 53. In selecting ground for the cargo always choose the highest available, so that water will drain from it.

In first forming a cargo at the place where the stores to be transported are received, the coiled lash ropes are all placed on the ground in order before the loads are laid on them.

Take the middle of the ground selected for the first rope. Undo a lash rope (sec. 11) and place it on the ground, the cincha underneath the coils, the end of the rope extended 10 feet. Get a sling rope and place it on top of end of lash rope about 2 feet from coil. Take another lash and sling rope and place them similarly near those already in position, the heads of the coils adjoining and about 6 inches apart, the ends of the lash ropes extended out in opposite directions.

The remaining ropes are then placed in a similar manner in position on either side of these two, thus leaving them in two lines, with a space of 6 inches between the lines and an interval of about 2 feet from center to center of lash ropes in the same line.

Now place the loads on top of their respective lash ropes.

In selecting packs to form a load, cargadors should be careful to get both side packs of as nearly the same weight as possible, always, however, placing the heavier pack on the bottom. Form loads according to their kind as much as possible, as a mixed load is always troublesome.

Place the packs lengthwise on the ropes, but with the flatter side of the packs down.

When cargo is in place on lash ropes, commence at ends and place the sling ropes on top of loads crosswise; then coil the ends of the lash ropes and place them on top of the sling ropes.

In parking a pack train the cargo is formed as here described, except that the lash ropes are placed only as the loads are removed. See Fig. 109.

HOW TO PLACE THE RIGGING.

SEC. 54. Preparatory to loading, the rigging is placed together, either in line or in some other formation, as an L, a half circle, a horseshoe, etc., as convenience or the nature of the ground may dictate.

If to be arranged in a straight line, the aparejos are placed so that each will have its boots abutting squarely against those next adjoining. The line is parallel to the line of the cargo and about 10 paces from it.

If an L, place the first rigging in prolongation of the line of the cargo and 10 paces from the end of the cargo. Then run ten rigging in line perpendicular to the line of the cargo; turn at right angles and run the rest parallel to the line of the cargo. The cargo is thus included in the angle of the L.

If a double L, start as in the case of a single L, and run ten rigging in line perpendicular to the line of the cargo; turn and run thirty parallel to the line of the cargo; then turn again and run the last ten perpendicular to the line of cargo.

If half circle is desired, incline boot of each aparejo toward the boot of the next aparejo, already in place.

In each of these last two cases, the cargo is included between the extremities of the line of rigging.

In placing, always watch the front corners of the boots of the aparejo; for as they are inclined or squared, so will the line run.

As one stands in rear of the line of rigging, facing the front, the "head rigging" is on the right, the "end rigging" on the left. See Figs. 108, 109.

HOW TO TEACH ANIMALS TO COME PROPERLY TO RIGGING.

SEC. 55. Pack animals should be early taught to "come to the rigging." The first and necessary requisite is to teach them to come in from the herd ground properly. That is, they should string out behind the "bell" animal, and should not bunch together like a flock of sheep. A thoroughly organized train, if brought up in a bunch, may take their places at the rigging without trouble; but a "shave-tail," or unorganized train, never will.

The object of the instruction is to teach the animals to approach the rigging quietly and take their places in line in rear of it, facing toward the rigging.

As the animals approach the rigging from the rear, in single file, packers should take station on either side of the column.

One packer holds the bell animal, facing the third rigging from the head rigging. By the time all the animals are in place, the "bell" will have been crowded down, opposite the first or head rigging. The mules are then guided, so as to form in line, facing the rigging, on the flank of the "bell" animal. (Figs. 108, 109.)

To do this, one packer, in rear of the "bell" animal, guides the first mule to the proper flank of the "bell" animal; while one packer, immediately in rear of the rigging, crowds the mule up toward the "bell" animal. As the mules come in these two men gradually work down the line, guiding each successive mule to his position. Three packers are stationed on each side of the column of approaching animals to assist in guiding them in place. Should any animals break away, the herders must be prompt to round them up and get them back in place.

The pack master and the cargador should stand in front of the rigging to prevent the animals from jumping over.

To more readily teach them to come to rigging, the animals may be fed there, the feed covers being spread on rigging for that purpose. This, however, should be discontinued as early as possible.

HOW TO TIE ANIMALS AT RIGGING.

SEC. 56. The animals having taken their places as described in section 52, they are next tied together by means of their halter shanks. (Figs. 108, 109.)

The packers station themselves in rear of the animals and keep them well up to the rigging. The pack master and cargador are in front. The cargador places a blind on the last animal.

The mules, as they come in from herd, have the halters on, the halter shanks detached. These shanks are piled conveniently, one-half at the head, one-half at the the end of the rigging.

The pack master beginning at one end and the cargador at the other now work toward the center, attaching the halter shanks to the halters.

This is done by means of the "snap" at one end of the shank.

Then working from the center to the ends they tie the animals together. Additional packers will be detailed to assist when necessary.

This is done as follows: Take the case of the man who is working from the center toward his right or toward the "end rigging;" he takes the halter shank of the first mule, i. e., the one nearest the center, about 9 inches from the snap, and forms a bight or loop in it 6 inches long. Holding this in the left hand he grasps the halter shank of the second mule about 2 feet from snap and brings it from front to rear over the loop held in left hand, retaining it in place on the loop by the pressure of the forefinger of the left hand. Then, with the right hand, he grasps the free or running part, passes a bight of it under the loop and under and over the standing part; then down through the loop held in left hand. Holding the original loop in the

left hand he grasps this bight of the running part in the right hand and pulls taut.

This knot is immediately unfastened by pulling on the running or free end of the shank.

In tying the third animal form the loop in the halter shank of the second animal between the snap and the knot just tied. Then take the halter shank of the third animal and proceed as before. So continue to the flank until all are tied.

In the case of working from center to left (or toward head rigging) along the line of mules the knot is formed similarly. Note, however, that in this case the first loop is formed each time in a *free* halter shank, and that the running or free part of the halter shank on the right is used in making the knot.

HOW TO "DO UP" THE HALTER SHANK BEFORE TYING ANIMAL TO HIS LOAD.

SEC. 57. To keep the halter shank out of the way and prevent it from dragging it is secured in the following manner:

With the left hand hold the animal by the cheek piece of halter on near side, and with the right pass the shank over the animal's neck to the off side.

Grasp the shank over the animal's neck and pass it between the ears so that it will lie between the crown and ear on near side and along in front between the ear and eye on off side, keeping the arm well over the animal's neck in doing so.

Now bring right hand to near side, reach for the shank under animal's neck and, bringing it up snug, pass it up from rear to front under the buckle piece of the halter at point below brow band. Draw sufficient of this loop through to permit its being passed from rear to front under crown piece above brow band. Then pass the loop down between the halter and the shank; draw snug; take the end of the shank and pass it through the loop. (Figs. 40–41.)

HOW TO TIE AN ANIMAL TO HIS LOAD.

SEC. 58. Lead animal to load selected and take the end of the lash rope. Pass this end (or bight of it) into chin piece of halter from above, with left hand, and receive it in the right hand. Then with this end form a single slipknot on the standing part and draw up snug.

HOW TO LOAD A PACK TRAIN FOR THE DAY'S MARCH IN THE MOST EXPEDITIOUS MANNER.

SEC. 59. The following is the routine in the service of a pack train in preparation for the day's march:

It is assumed that the train has been properly parked, the animals being on herd or at the picket line.

First, the cook must be awakened one-half hour before the trainmen. He folds his blankets, places them in front of the head rigging, and immediately proceeds to get breakfast.

The moment the trainmen are awakened they must promptly arise and dress; then fold their blankets and canvas and place them in front of the rigging; the one first ready placing his blankets next in order after the cook's blankets; then so on with the other blankets until all are placed.

(It may be noted that the pack blankets are used for sleeping purposes by the men of the pack train while in camp or bivouac.)

The first two packers ready will remove the rigging covers (sec. 74) and fold them, placing them lengthwise, in front of such aparejos as the cargador may direct. Other packers will assist as soon as ready.

Commencing at head of rigging and working toward end, packers not engaged will place blankets on aparejos. (Sec. 19). Then two or three packers will step in rear of rigging and place the blankets under coronas.

Those packers not thus engaged remove the cargo covers (see sec. 73), fold and place them in front of rigging as directed. In the meantime the herd guard has brought in the animals, if on herd, and the animals are tied up at the rigging. (Sec. 56.) Packers then saddle their riding animals.

Breakfast should now be ready. Each packer should endeavor to be first at breakfast and first to put on an aparejo after breakfast.

PUTTING ON THE APAREJOS.

Sec. 60. The animals are either at the rigging or at the picket line. If at rigging, remove the blind from the last animal and place it on the next to the last. Untie the last animal and lead him around in front of rigging until his number or design is reached.

For convenience the packers should work in pairs. The mate assists in getting the animals up to the aparejo.

While one packer is blinding the animal the other puts on the corona. After blinding the animal, the first packer steps to off side to receive blanket and assist in adjusting it in place; or, if before the mate can get into position, he is quick enough to himself put the corona on, then his mate steps to "off" side to receive the blanket. One packer must not wait for the other to do what he can do first.

The aparejo having been properly cinched on the animal, the halter shank is tied up (sec. 57), and the animal is led to the cargo and tied to the load assigned him (sec. 58).

If animals are tied to picket line, to put the aparejos on, commence at end, untying the animals and leading them to their aparejos as before, and work toward the "bell."

When "bell" animal is removed and tied, the blacksmith takes up picket line and places it on load indicated by cargador.

Packers should not count how many aparejos they are getting on in excess of another set. The pack master is taking notice and will give due credit.

When an animal is tied to his load, do not stand waiting for the mate to bring the next animal around to his rigging. Time is not to be wasted in such a manner. Move and assist him.

PUTTING ON THE CARGO.[a]

Sec. 61. The mules, having received their aparejos, and having been tied to their respective loads, the packers begin at once to put on the loads.

Two sets of packers work at each end of cargo, working toward center. First ready, first choice of sides. Packers will soon learn

[a] For cargo, see Glossary.

which is the choice side. Do not unnecessarily move an animal around, causing loss of time.

Blind the animal, the mate in the meantime putting on the sling rope. Pick up pack and place it in position on "off" side, mate putting up the "near" pack and tying the sling. The "off" packer steps quickly around and grasps the end of lash rope. Swing it away back, as in so doing time is saved and labor with it. Get in position and wait for near packer to pass the loop of the rope over. Work quick and true, and above all things keep the mouth shut, for no packer has time to listen.

As each mule is loaded he is turned loose.

When cargo is nearly loaded, or before, if opportunity offers, the pack master will detail a packer to assist the cook to load, the kitchen mules being tied conveniently for the purpose.

Before loading, but after the rigging is on, the pack master causes the "bell" animal to be tied in some convenient place in as open ground as possible, so that the mules, as they are loaded and turned loose, will remain in the vicinity.

The blacksmith will keep loaded animals from straying away, and the cook, when ready, will assist. Each keeps count of the animals as they are turned loose, prevents them from lying down or straying away, and reports any accident to the pack master.

LEAVING THE PARK OR CAMP GROUND.

SEC. 62. Loads being on, the pack master calls out "Bell!" The cook, riding quickly, unties the "bell" animal and leads out in direction indicated by pack master.

Cargador and blacksmith count the animals as they string out, cargador reporting quickly if any are missing.

Time allowed.—Twenty minutes for getting blankets and canvas and riding animals saddled, fifteen minutes for breakfast, twenty minutes for rigging, and twenty minutes for cargo. Total, one hour and fifteen minutes. It can be done in less time with a well-organized crew.

3. DUTIES OF PACKERS ON THE MARCH.

SEC. 63. *In open country.*—On leaving camp packers must string out so as to take in five packs, one packer riding opposite every fifth animal, and about 30 yards from near side of train, dust or conditions of country permitting. Each packer should not only watch the five packs in front, but also those in rear, as far back as his eyes can detect whether a pack is riding straight or not. Circumstances permitting, packers should ride in the order of mate following mate.

SEC. 64. *On bad and narrow trails.*—Packers must ride on trail one behind each fifth animal. If a pack needs attention, the packer in rear calls out to packer ahead, who will assist him in catching animal and straightening its load.

While the two packers are thus engaged, those in rear ride forward and take their places in the train.

When the two packers have straightened load and turned animal loose, they will immediately fall in, in places made vacant by those who have gone ahead.

SEC. 65. *Up and down a mountain.*—In traveling up or down a mountain a pack master should have one or two packers with him at the head of train. He will ride far enough in advance, when nature of country indicates danger, to enable him to station either one or both packers, as emergency requires, to keep animals in trail and guard against accidents.

The same rules apply as in the case of bad or narrow trails, though when possible packers will work on side of train.

Be especially vigilant in watching the condition of packs, giving prompt attention thereto when needed.

SEC. 66. *In crossing streams, either fording or swimming.*—Packers must always be stationed on the downstream side and at the most dangerous points of crossing, keeping the animals well up and clear of obstacles that may endanger their footing.

If ford is such that animals have to swim, packers should remain on lower side, likewise keeping animals well up and riding close up to the weakest swimmers.

HOW TO CATCH A PACK ANIMAL WHEN HIS LOAD NEEDS ATTENTION.

SEC. 67. A packer, noticing a pack that needs attention, will call out to his mate the name of the animal. Both packers will then ride far enough in advance of the pack animal to gain time to tie their riding animals before the pack animal comes up.

Let one packer cross the trail and the other remain on the near side. They should keep far enough away from trail to keep therein any that show a disposition to break out. When the pack animal approaches they will close in; one will stand squarely in front of the animal—never on the side—reach out and take him by the halter, and lead him out on near side of train.

Blind the animal, loosen the lash rope, and straighten the load as quickly as possible. Do not detain him a moment longer than is necessary. The animal knows how far he has to travel to catch up and work back to place in the train. Packers should bear this in mind.

Eager to get back into place in the train, the animal will become unmanageable and be apt to throw his load. Should the animal break away before his load is straightened he is certain to throw it, and then, running through the train, dragging the lash rope after him, he will scare others in the train and perhaps cause other packs to fall off.

The animal will stand a reasonable length of time, but no longer. The animal having once broken away, the "bell" animal has to be stopped, the animal caught, led back, and its load put on; three packers are needed, one to hold him, while the others put on the load.

Certainly no good packer will cause such trouble and delay.

Packers can not be termed first class if loads fall off while traveling; attention must constantly be given to animals and their packs.

HOW TO TIGHTEN A LOAD AND INDICATE IT HAS BEEN TIGHTENED.

SEC. 68. The "off" packer releases the "top" rope (fig. 40) and passes it over the animal's neck to near side; loosens the "front" rope, drawing the slack toward him, and steps to center of aparejo.

The "near" packer steps to rear and pulls on "rear" rope so as to loosen it, then steps to center of aparejo and loosens the "marking" rope (M, fig. 41)—that is, pulls from rear to front on rope at front corner of boot and draws it from under the standing rope (R, fig. 41).

The "off" packer pulls on the running rope so as to slacken the tension at the cincha hook.

The hitch is now loosened throughout.

The "near" packer adjusts the load in its proper place, and the two packers then begin and tighten the hitch, taking up slack as prescribed in paragraphs 4 to 8, section 32.

To indicate that the load has been tightened, however, the following variation is made in the hitch:

The "near" packer passes the bight of the running or marking rope under the standing rope, as usual (R, fig. 41), but does not bring it around front corner of boot. He allows the marking rope to drop down to center of boot; then with the right hand he receives the slack as usual, in rear of cincha. The hitch is then finished as usual; or the top rope may be passed to rear of near pack in finishing the hitch; this latter method is preferred by some pack masters.

HOW TO TEACH SADDLE MULES TO STAND.

SEC. 69. For this purpose, when in bivouac and using a picket line, the riding mules should aways be tied at the opposite end of the line from the bell horse; this rule should be followed when stables are provided. In preparation for the day's march after "saddling up," tie the animals as far away from the bell horse as opportunity offers. On the trail do not endeavor to be always rear the "bell;" and when necessary to catch a pack mule, when his load needs balancing, tie the riding mule with the shank of the bridle rein, when other opportunities are not convenient, to either hind leg above the hock; in doing so bring the mule's head well around so that should he endeavor to travel he will "mill," or travel in a circle. Should the animal get loose and endeavor to overtake the "bell," do not maltreat him when caught as he will become more difficult to catch on the next occasion; instead, pet the animal—that is, treat him kindly. A crust of bread or a little sugar is a great aid to teach the mule to become attached to its rider. In time the animal will show a disposition to wait for its master, who, in turn, should show appreciation by patting the animal's neck or other kind attention. Kindness will teach the riding mule to wait for its master or approach him when called for.

SIGNAL CODE.

SEC. 70. When desiring to slacken gait of pack train the pack master raises either hand above the shoulder, fingers extended.

To increase the gait he raises the hat vertically.

Requiring the assistance of two packers at head of train he waves the hat in front of him from side to side in such manner as to be distinctly seen.

Requiring the assistance of all packers but one, driving in rear, at head of train he waves the hat in circular motion over his head.

When a halt is necessary he will extend both arms sideways; or, "bell" animal will be led to one side of trail and brought to a halt; packers then ride quickly to head of train and give attention to packs, the packer in rear riding quickly forward keeping the animals well rounded up.

4. HOW TO PARK (UNLOAD) A PACK TRAIN

OUTLINE OF DUTIES.

SEC. 71. A pack master in parking his train will give the highest ground to cargo; next to the cargo comes the rigging, and then the picket line.

The camp is arranged so that the kitchen is near the cargo and convenient to water. The cargo is formed in a double line as described in section 53.

The ground being selected for cargo, the cargador should place the first lash rope. Placing it in the middle of the ground selected its position indicates how the cargo should run.

As the loads are removed by the packers the animals are turned loose, being kept in the vicinity by the herders.

If the animals are to be at once tied to picket line, the latter is now stretched. The loads being removed, the animals are caught in succession and the aparejos taken off, as described in section 72. The aparejos are placed by the cargador, as described in section 54.

If the animals are to be herded at once for grazing, they are then sent out under charge of the herd guard. Ordinarily two packers are detailed daily on this duty. The cargador then has certain packers detailed to assist in cleaning the coronas. (Sec. 76.) The cargo is covered as described in section 73; the rigging as in section 74. The picket line is stretched as in section 75.

HOW PACK ANIMALS SHOULD BE LED TO CARGADOR, FOR CONVENIENCE IN TAKING OFF THE RIGGING.

SEC. 72. Packers catch the animals, undo the halter shanks (see sec. 57), and lead the animals in single file to the cargador, who removes all the aparejos and places them in the order desired.

Just before reaching the cargador with an animal, the packer uncinches the aparejo, and, removing any canvas which may be under the cincha, places it on the ground lengthwise, in front of an aparejo already in place.

The aparejo being uncinched (sec. 43), the mule's halter shank is passed to the cargador, and the packer passes to rear of the animal.

Each mule in turn is then brought to the cargador, those in rear closing up as the line of rigging advances. No packer should be permitted to lead in ahead of the animals in his front; he should close up and await his turn.

If the animals are to be sent out on herd at once, the cargador, after removing an aparejo, unsnaps the mule's halter shank and turns him loose. Halter shank should never be thrown on ground in front of rigging, but on top or in rear of rigging. If not herded, the mules are tied at once to the picket line.

HOW TO COVER CARGO AND TIE DOWN.

SEC. 73. Before placing covers on cargo, coil up ends of lash ropes, and place the coils on top of their respective loads. (Sec. 53.) The ropes of the two packs at each end, however, should be left entirely uncoiled, the load resting merely on the lash rope cincha. These ropes are used for securing the covers on top of the cargo.

Unfold the covers (see sec. 79) and bring them lengthwise over cargo, lapping them over one another, and allowing ends of covers to come over ends of cargo, down to the ground. In doing this, notice the direction of wind, and lap covers so that end may not be raised by the wind.

In covering cargo four packers are needed, in order to work to the best advantage. Two work at each end, facing one another on opposite sides of the cargo. Each coils one of the corner lash ropes, and passes or throws the same down along the center of the cargo, lengthwise; working from ends toward center; each pair of packers will then exchange ropes, pass them into cincha hooks at the sides and bottom of the cargo, and repeat until center is reached. Then secure the ropes at the top, or at the last hook, as the length of the rope determines. The ropes thus form a lacing over the cargo.

HOW TO COVER RIGGING AND TIE DOWN.

SEC. 74. Two packers at each end of rigging, working toward center, unfold covers (sec. 78) and place them lengthwise along the line of rigging. In doing so overlap the cover adjoining, so that its end may be engaged in tying down on top of aparejo selected.

For securing covers in place sling or lair ropes are used when the animals are tied to picket line, halter shanks when the animals are on herd.

In the first case, take a sling or lair rope and pass an end of it from rear to front under the last aparejo on the line. This may readily be done by "whipping" the rope over and under the aparejo.

Then on top of the aparejo fasten the end by a slipknot to the running part of the rope and draw snug, so that the knot will be at the collar of the aparejo.

Proceeding to the third aparejo, pass the other end of the rope under it from rear to front as before; then bring the end up and, passing it under and over the standing part, draw taut, so that the intersection of the ropes will be at the collar of the aparejo. Take a similar turn of the rope around the sixth aparejo, and so on.

Lengthen the rope as needed by additional lair or sling ropes.

One rigging cover extends over ten aparejos. At every tenth aparejo the rope must consequently be made fast, so as to catch the covers where they lap. Thus the rope is made fast at the third, sixth, tenth, thirteenth, etc., aparejo. (Fig. 108.)

In the second case, when the animals are on herd the covers are secured by means of halter shanks. Pass the snap end under the aparejo from rear to front and tie the ends together by a square knot at the collar. As in the first instance "whip" the shank to more readily get it over and under the aparejo.

HOW TO STRETCH A PICKET LINE.

SEC. 75. For securing the ends of picket line, if other conveniences are not available, sink what is termed a "dead man" for each end and, if necessary, one also at the middle.

To do this cut two or three pieces of wood about 18 inches long. At the ends and middle of the picket line dig holes about 18 inches long, 12 inches wide, and 18 inches deep, or as deep as the nature of the ground may require, the length of the holes being perpendicular to the direction of the picket line.

For each "dead man" take a sling rope, tie its ends together, and give a single twist on rope and bring the loop ends together; this causes the folds to lie evenly. Twist again and bring the loop ends together as before.

Now hold the folds of rope in the left hand at opposite point, or part where ends of rope had been tied; at opposite part grasp the folds with the right hand and bring the folds to the middle finger of the left hand and receive them.

Now introduce the "dead man" through the folds of rope made by this formation, and allow the folds of rope held in the palm of the left hand to fall over the folds of rope held by the middle finger, and draw taut on "dead man," and the "dead man" is thus caught in a slipknot. As in the case, as seen in fig. 82.

Place the "dead man" in the hole dug for it, and keeping the end of the sling rope out, fill the hole and tamp.

The picket line is then stretched by being attached to these sling ropes.

As facilitating the tightening of the rope, the following is a convenient method of stretching the picket line:

If the picket line consists of a single rope, fasten one end to the sling rope of one of the "dead men;" bring the other end through the loop at the center "dead man." About 10 or 15 feet from this end form a bowline knot on the rope; then pass the end through the loop of the sling rope at the last "dead man;" bring it back and pass it through the loop of the bowline.

By drawing on the end all slack is now readily taken in, and the end is then secured.

If the picket line consists of two ropes, fasten each to one of the extreme "dead men;" take an end of one, pass it through the loop at center "dead man," and form a bowline knot in the end. Then pass the free end of the other rope through the loop of this bowline, draw taut, and secure as before.

Obviously the same method may be employed when the ends of the picket line are attached to other forms of holdfasts than the one here considered.

HOW TO CLEAN CORONAS.

SEC. 76. For this purpose a table knife is ordinarily employed, and for convenience a provision is supplied on selected aparejo. This is done by cutting a slit between the two inside lines of stitching on the "near" side of "front" facing, just wide enough to permit the blade of knife to pass downwardly; the handle of knife will hold it in position. Two or more knives may thus be provided for cleaning purposes.

Immediately after the aparejos have been taken off the packmaster or cargador details certain packers to assist in cleaning coronas.

Commencing at each end, spread corona, canvas side up, and allow it to fall on either side of aparejo, and with knife clean the canvas thoroughly. Before cleaning corona place corona on top of aparejo adjoining, and clean the canvas and dock of crupper thoroughly; then replace corona and proceed and clean, as explained.

Should the corona be wet, leave the canvas side exposed to dry; in due time fold coronas, cover, and tie down. (See sec. 74.)

HOW TO FOLD PACK COVERS.

Sec. 77. The operation of folding a pack cover is similar to that provided for the folding of a pack blanket, with this exception, that the pack cover is square. (Sec. 18.)

HOW TO FOLD RIGGING COVERS.

Sec. 78. For this purpose two packers are ordinarily employed; each packer takes hold of one end at corners, folds and brings the corners together, and holds corners with one hand; the packer at one end holds the corners with the right hand, while packer at opposite end holds corners with the left hand.

Now, with the free hand, each packer takes hold of the folded corner, and bracing from each other they draw taut on cover, to cause the folds to lay evenly. Then one packer lays his end on the ground, while his mate gives a quick swing backward, so as to cause the opposite end to come quickly toward him, and places end on top of opposite end.

Now fold one end, and fold opposite end on top of fold thus formed so as to have folds of equal length; or each end may be brought together and folded as may be determined.

HOW TO FOLD CARGO COVERS.

Sec. 79. For this purpose two packers are employed; each packer takes hold of one corner on the same side of cover and folds within the last section or strip; now fold this odd section or strip on top of fold already formed, then fold once more and draw taut. Now fold one end to near center of its length, and fold opposite end on top of fold thus formed, or as conditions may require.

HOW TO FOLD FEED COVERS.

Sec. 80. The operation of folding feed covers is entirely similar to that prescribed for rigging covers.

In preparation for the day's march, pack, rigging, cargo, and feed covers so folded are placed lengthwise in front of rigging selected.

In the operation all canvas should be well shaken in order that dust and other matter may fall therefrom. In no case must folded covers, when placed on the aparejo, reach within six inches of the boots or ends of the aparejo, or must the folds be wider than the width of the aparejo.

CHAPTER V.

MARCHES AND LOADS.

1. WHAT MAY BE REQUIRED OF THE PACK MULE.

SEC. 81. Under ordinary conditions, the pack mule carrying a load of 250 pounds will travel from 20 to 25 miles per day, and maintain a rate of speed of 4½ to 5 miles per hour.

With occasional days of rest he may be expected to perform this amount of work steadily; and this, too, without the aid of grain or hay.

It must be remembered, however, that except on extraordinary occasions pack mules should never be tied to a picket line, but should be herded as much as possible. In bivouac they should be taken to graze at night as well as day, packers being detailed as herd guard.

The "bell" horse being hobbled or picketed in the vicinity, there is no danger of the mules stampeding, as they will not leave the "bell."

If allowed to graze, mules will always keep in average condition, and on nutritious grasses will stand a twelve months' campaign and keep fat.

SEC. 82. *Mountainous country.*—In rough and mountainous country, the pack mule will carry the same load (250 pounds), and travel from 10 to 15 miles per day. He should not, however, be forced when traveling up or down a mountain, unless the occasion is very urgent. Uphill work is hard on man and beast.

SEC. 83. *Forced marches.*—In forced marches the pack animals should not be loaded in excess of 200 pounds.

If traveling with cavalry, the pack mule may not be able to spurt off at a 10-mile gait, but he will be pushing the horse before 30 miles are covered, and he has the horse at his mercy in a march of 75 to 100 miles in twenty-four hours.

The following instances, out of a great many, may be briefly mentioned:

In the campaign of 1881, under Colonel Buell, Fifteenth Infantry, against Chiefs Victoria and Nana, of the Warm Spring tribe of Apaches, a company of Indian scouts and one pack train made a march of 85 miles in twelve hours, loaded 200 pounds to the pack animal.

Later, in pursuing Indians of the same tribe, a company of Indian scouts and one pack train marched from old Fort Cummings to Fort Seldon, on the Rio Grande, about 60 miles, from sunrise to sunset; then went by rail to Fort Craig, N. Mex., loaded 250 pounds to the mule; marched across the valley, some 30 miles, to the San Mateo Range; struck the trail of Chief Nana and party; and, without making an all-night camp, followed the hostiles into old Mexico, south of the Hatchet Mountains.

This was a running fight the entire way. A distance of about 300 miles was covered in about four days.

During the "Loco" outbreak from San Carlos Agency, Ariz., in 1882, one company of scouts and one pack train, loaded 200 pounds to the mule, made a forced march of 280 miles in three days.

During the Garza campaign on the Rio Grande frontier, in Texas, in 1891 and 1892, a troop of the Third Cavalry and a part of one pack train marched 108 miles in sixteen hours; the mules were loaded 250 pounds to the mule.

In the same campaign another troop, with part of a pack train, marched 104 miles in a night and part of the following day.

In another instance, in the same campaign, a pack train made 90 miles in less than twenty-four hours, the animals carrying loads of 250 pounds. After such marches the mules were given twelve to twenty-four hours' rest to regain their normal condition.

It should be remembered that pack animals should be kept in condition by constant exercise, for if fat such marches will quickly kill them.

2. GAITS.

SEC. 84. When moving at a slow rate of speed the walk is the ordinary gait of the pack mule.

As the rate of travel is increased, however, a trained pack mule, instead of quickening the walk, falls into an amble or "fox" trot. This is for the reason that an extended walk or a "jogging" trot would transmit motion to the load, which would greatly inconvenience the animal. He has, accordingly, learned to acquire the gait which enables him to move to the best advantage without rocking his load.[a] At this ambling gait he is able to cover from 5 to 6 miles an hour without undue fatigue.

SEC. 85.—

3. Table showing loads and rates of travel considered practicable for a well-organized and seasoned pack train.

Weight of load.	Maximum rate of travel per hour.	Number of miles per day.	Number of days continuous travel.
	Miles.		
Two hundred pounds	8	25	7
Do	7	40	10
Do	6	50	7
Do	6	100	3
Do	5	25	365
Two hundred and fifty pounds	8	25	3
Do	7	40	7
Do	6	100	1
Do	6	50	5
Do	6	25	30
Do	6	20	60
Do	5	100	2
Do	5	50	10
Do	5	25	60
Do	5	20	90
Three hundred pounds	5	75	1
Do	5	50	7
Do	5	25	30
Do	5	20	60
Three hundred and fifty pounds	4	20	30
Four hundred pounds	4	15	30

[a] To acquire this ambling gait a young pack train should be taught to travel 5 miles an hour and under no circumstances should mules be allowed to straggle out, i. e., keep them in close order, one mule following the trail or step of the other. After a few practice marches they readily acquire this ambling gait. Occasionally one or two mules in a train seem to have difficulty in acquiring this ambling gait. Do not overload such animal in the endeavor to teach him, instead place the cincha sufficiently forward on the aparejo so that the elbow will rub against the cincha during travel, as soon as the elbow becomes sore the mule, to escape the cincha, will take short and quick steps in order to keep his place in line and thus readily learns this ambling gait. Do not continue the forward use of the cincha longer than necessary.

75927°—17——10

4. THE ENDURANCE OF THE PACK MULE UNDER PROPER CONDITIONS.

SEC. 86. As a prerequisite he must not be less than 14.1 and not over 15.1 hands high, of blocky build, weighing from 950 to 1,100 pounds, sound in body and limbs, age from 4 to 6.

Head well formed and intelligent looking, broad between the eyes, eyes clear, large, and full; ears flexible; teeth and tongue free from blemishes; neck full and inclined to arch; withers low and broad; back short and straight; belly large and deep; dock low and stiff; legs straight, standing well apart at front and rear, the former indicating good lung power, the latter full in buttocks; the hoofs sound, broad, and full.

The mule should have a pack saddle that will protect the body from all manner of loading—that is, capable of being adjusted so as to support heavy loading when necessary without injury to the withers and with a proper bearing surface on either side of the animal's backbone. For such a purpose there is no form of pack saddle that has ever been devised comparable to the aparejo.

As an instance of the adaptability of the aparejo to carry heavy and unwieldly loading, reference to figure 110 will show what can be accomplished by the aid of the aparejo and expert packer. This cage mount of naval rapid-fire gun, weighing 540 pounds, was taken from the gunboat *Quiros* (Captain Walker, U. S. Navy) and carried 3 miles inland, island of Jolo, P. I., and back again on the same mule by order of Col. H. L. Scott.

To accomplish this feat Assistant Chief Packer Mora E. Smith made a wooden frame to fit over the aparejo as a base on which to rest the cage and lashed the frame to the aparejo. The cage was then lifted onto the mule and secured with lash rope. Such a feat could not be accomplished by the use of the crosstree or Moore pack saddle.

CHAPTER VI.

ORGANIZATION.

SEC. 87.—

1. Usual organization and equipment of a pack train.

PERSONNEL.

Pack master	1
Cargador	1
Blacksmith	1
Cook	1
Packers	10

ANIMALS

Bell horse	1
Pack mules	50
Riding mules	14

EQUIPMENT

Aparejos, proper	50
Head halters and shanks	65
Blankets, pack	50
Lash ropes with cincha and hook	50
Sling ropes	50
Lair ropes	100
Pack covers	100
Rigging covers	5
Cargo covers	5
Feed covers	5
Packers' blinds	14
Packers' saddles	14
Packers' bridles	14

EQUIPMENT—continued.

Blankets, saddle	14
Clothes or war bags	14
Hay pads	14
Bell (sheep) with strap	1
Pair hobbles	1
Mess or kitchen boxes	2
Field stove with kit	1
Package matches	1
Pack train mess kit	1
Wall tent with jointed poles	1
Tool sack	1
Cargador's box	1
Cargador's kit	1
Blacksmith's kit	1
Blacksmith's boxes	2
Mule shoes, Nos. 1 and 2 (fitted)	256
Horseshoes (fitted)	8
Box horseshoe nails, No. 6	1
Ax	1
Spade	1
Pick	1
Currycombs	10
Horse brushes	10
Feet of picket line, ¾ inch	150
Linen shipping tags	200

SEC. 88.—

2. Table showing size and quantity of rope and canvas required for one pack train.

ROPE

Article	Made of—	Length	Number required	Total feet
		Feet		
Lash rope	One-half inch	50	50	2,500
Sling rope	Three-eighths inch	30	50	1,500
Lair rope	do	30	100	3,000

NOTE.—The size of the above rope is measured by the diameter

A coil of half-inch best hand-laid manila contains 1,200 feet, weighs 85 pounds, and will furnish 24 lash ropes (Sec 10)

A coil of three-eighths inch best hand-laid manila contains 1,200 feet, weighs 55 pounds, and will furnish 40 sling or lair ropes. (Sec. 10.)

2. *Table showing size and quantity of rope and canvas required for one pack train*—Con.

CANVAS

Article	Made of—	Length.	Number required	Total yards.
		Feet.		
Pack covers	72-inch No 4 cotton duck	6	100	200
Rigging covers	22-inch No 2 cotton duck	24	5	80
Cargo covers	28-inch No. 10 cotton duck	12	5	100
Feed covers	44-inch No 10 cotton duck	24	5	40

NOTE.—A roll of 72-inch No 4 cotton duck, containing 100 yards, weighs 312½ pounds, or 3 125 pounds per linear yard, and will furnish 50 pack covers or mantas (Sec 98)

A roll of 22-inch No 2 cotton duck, containing 100 yards, weighs 106¼ pounds, or 1 0625 pounds per linear yard, and will furnish 5 rigging covers. (Sec 99)

A roll of 28-inch No 10 cotton duck, containing 100 yards, weighs 78⅛ pounds, or 0 78125 pound per linear yard, and will furnish 5 cargo covers. (Sec 100)

A roll of 44-inch No 10 cotton duck, containing 100 yards, weighs 112 5 pounds, or 1.125 pounds per linear yard, and will furnish 12 feed covers (Sec 101)

3. ARTICLES OF EQUIPMENT IN USE IN PACK TRAINS.

The following articles are ordinarily comprised in the equipment of a pack train for the field:

MESS OR KITCHEN BOXES.

SEC. 89. Made of seven-eighths inch white pine, 26 inches long, 18 inches wide, and 11 inches high, outside measurements; dovetailed; no lid or cover.

PACKER'S FIELD STOVE, WITH KIT.

SEC. 90. One No. 2 army field range will be supplied each organized pack train.

COOKING OUTFIT, WITHOUT STOVE.

SEC. 91. This comprises 3 camp kettles, telescoping; 1 Dutch oven, with lid; 2 frying pans, short handles; 1 bread pan; 1 coffee mill (box); 1 butcher knife; 1 steel; 2 mess pans.

NOTE.—A small buzzacot may be used to replace the Dutch oven.

PACK TRAIN MESS KIT.

SEC. 92. To each packer 1 coffee cup, without handle; 1 pie plate; 1 knife; 1 fork; and 1 tablespoon.

CLOTHES OR WAR BAGS.

SEC. 93. These bags are ordinarily made by the packers, as follows:

Take a piece of 22-inch No. 4 cotton duck 30 inches long, double it across the shorter edges; lap the long edges over one another 1 inch and sew them together with a flat seam.

Now, to the edges at one end attach a round piece 11 inches in diameter, as a bottom for the bag; the edges are lapped 1 inch and sewed with a flat seam.

Turn the bag inside out and sew down the edges along the side and at the bottom.

As a flap for the bag, take a piece of duck 12 inches long and 3 inches wider than the bag when flattened out. Cut one of the shorter edges in semicircular shape and hem this edge. Attach the straight edge to the upper edge of the bag, lapping 1 inch. Then for securing the flap over the bag, fasten a lace string at the center of the semicircular edge of the flap and attach a corresponding loop 6 inches from the bottom of the bag.

PACKER'S WARDROBE.

SEC. 94. Packers are ordinarily permitted to carry 3 changes of underclothing; 3 overshirts; 6 pairs of socks, wool preferred; 2 overalls; 1 canvas coat; 1 overcoat; 1 slicker, or rain coat; 1 extra pair of boots or shoes; 1 pair of overshoes.

PACKER'S WALL TENT.

SEC. 95. The tent is a wall tent, regulation size. For convenience the upright poles are cut diagonally in two at the center; length of cut, 4 inches. For use the two parts of an upright are united by a collar or sleeve. This is made of stiff tin or iron, shaped to the pole and riveted to the lower joint, so that it will fit well over the diagonal cut.

The ridgepole is hinged on the flat side at the center of its length. The hinge is screwed on and the pole is then sawed in two at the center.

TOOL SACKS.

SEC. 96. Same as clothes or war bags, but instead of a flap at open end, use a double lace string, and secure as in drawing or closing up a tobacco sack. The sack is used for extra lace strings and for currycombs and brushes.

GRASS OR HAY PADS.

SEC. 97. Take a piece of 28-inch No. 10 cotton duck, 7 feet long; double across the long edges and sew the edges together all around with a flat seam. Cut a slit 10 inches long in center of one side and bind the edges of the slit all around with sheepskin. Attach a string for lacing.

These pads are used for carrying extra grass or hay, for readjusting the filling of the aparejos.

PACK COVERS.

SEC. 98. Made of 72-inch No. 4 cotton duck; cut 6 feet long; allow 1 inch at each end for hemming, to be sewed with 3-cord flax thread, machine stitch, six stitches to the inch. Two (2) for each aparejo.

RIGGING COVERS.

SEC. 99. Made of 22-inch No. 2 cotton duck; cut two lengths 24 feet long, to be sewed with 6-cord yellow machine thread, machine stitch, six stitches to the inch; ends to be hemmed in customary manner. Five (5) for each organized pack train.

CARGO COVERS.

SEC. 100. Made of 28-inch No. 10 cotton duck; cut five widths 12 feet long; lapped on border line and hemmed at ends; to be sewed with 3-cord flax thread, machine stitch, six stitches to the inch; ends to be hemmed in customary manner. Five (5) for each organized pack train.

FEED COVERS.

SEC. 101. Made of 44-inch No. 10 cotton duck; to be 24 feet long, hemmed at ends; to be sewed with 3-cord flax thread, machine stitch, six stitches to the inch. Five (5) for each organized pack train.

CARGADOR'S BOX.

SEC. 102. This is made, preferably of leather, 18 inches long, 9 inches wide, and 6 inches high, with lid.

It is reenforced on the inside by iron bands, 1 inch wide and one-eighth inch thick, riveted around the edges at top and bottom. Half of the upper iron band is left exposed above the edges of the box, serving as a support for the lid, when in place.

Thimbles for tools are sewed to the sides of the box on the inside. A slide handle of leather may be attached to the lid.

For a hinge, take a piece of leather the length of the box and about 2 inches wide, and sew it to the back of the lid and the back of the box.

For fastening, a strap may be used across each end, provided with buckle and held in place by means of leather keepers, and an attachment provided for a small Yale or other lock.

CARGADOR'S KIT.

SEC. 103. To consist of—

Half-round knife		1
Gauge knife		1
Riveting hammer		1
Rivet cutter		1
Rivet set		1
Spring punch		1
Hand punches, size $\frac{3}{8}$, $\frac{1}{4}$, and $\frac{1}{8}$ inch		3
Edge tool		1
Awl handles		3
Awl blades or points, assorted sizes		12
Saddler's needles, Nos 2 and 4	papers	2
Sailmaker's needles, assorted sizes		6
Palm		1
Sailing twine, No. "0"	ball	1
Shoe thread, "Barbour's" No 10	balls	6
Beeswax	pound	$\frac{1}{4}$
Black wax	do	$\frac{1}{4}$
Halter rings, regulation size		12
Halter snaps, "trigger," size $1\frac{1}{8}$ inches		12
Common japanned buckles, size $1\frac{1}{8}$ inches		12
Side of latigo leather		1
Side of bridle leather, "fair"		1
Oilstone, "small"		1
Tailor's shears, 6-inch blade		1

The leather is carried on one of the aparejos, between the aparejo and the aparejo cover.

NOTE.—One stitching horse, when stationed at post.

BLACKSMITH'S BOXES.

SEC. 104. Made of seven-eighths inch white pine, 24 inches long, 12 inches wide, and 9 inches high, outside measurements; to be dovetailed; inside tin lined; no lid or cover.

BLACKSMITH'S KIT.

SEC. 105. To consist of—

Horseshoe knives, blades 3¼ inches	2
Rasps, length 16 inches	2
Shoeing hammer	1
Hand hammer	1
Pritchel	1
Pincers	1
Cutting nippers	1
Clinch iron	1
Packer's field anvil	1
Blacksmith's apron (sheepskin)	1

To make the field anvil, take a piece of flat iron about 18 inches long, 3 inches wide, and one-half inch thick; shape this into a triangle about 5 inches on the side and weld together.

4. HOW TO ORGANIZE A PACK TRAIN.

SEC. 106. As an aid to more readily teach the animals in their duties a corral should be provided in which to arrange the rigging and cargo and to keep them off the ground. Procure some two by fours; space them 18 inches apart and hold them by crosspieces, on which to place the aparejos; for the cargo procure some boards to rest on the two by fours and form a platform 8 by 65 feet (it is not expected to provide these conditions in the field). Now, to teach the animals to come to rigging and prevent crowding and pushing the aparejos out of position drive five stakes in rear of the rigging and connect them by two by fours or suitable poles placed on top of the stakes and nail down; the height of stakes should not exceed 6 inches above the rigging. Next cover the rigging, tie down and spread the "feed covers" thereon. Along the line of covers pour sufficient grain to encourage the animals to approach the rigging in rear of the line of stakes or guard rail; for this purpose the gateway to enter the corral should be placed facing the line and end of the rigging, the first aparejo placed being considered the head, the last in line the end of rigging.

Before the train is brought into corral to "line up" the pack master and cargador should take position in front of the rigging to prevent the animals jumping over the guard rail. Six packers take station in rear of the guard rail facing the line of approaching animals, while one packer leads the "bell" horse, and the other packers remain on the outside of corral to keep the animals together.

The bell horse is tied to guard rail with halter shank at end of rigging, the packer taking station in rear of the animal and causing the other animals as they approach to fall in on the flank of the bell horse, the packers in rear of the guard rail causing the animals to fall in line in the flank of each animal following. As the line fills up the packers in rear of guard rail take station behind the animals until all are lined up. The pack master and cargador with the assistance of the packers that were guarding the mules on the outside of corral assist in tying the animals to guard rail; this should be done as promptly as possible, and under no circumstances should the animals be permitted to leave their positions first taken. While the animals are tied up at rigging, care should be exercised to prevent their wasting the grain and kicking each other. A small switch or aparejo stick in the hands of each packer will cause the animals to give attention—this should be used for correction, not for abuse,[a] which must not be permitted under any circumstances, remembering the more abuse the animal is given the more unruly or ugly it becomes, until it is classed as an outlaw; the animal is dumb—the packer is presumed to be intelligent and human.

In due time "turn loose," that is, unsnap the halter shank from halter. For this purpose always commence with the bell horse and then successively each animal in turn until all are freed; lead the "bell" toward opposite end of corral and cause each animal to follow the "bell" as turned loose. Packers should now go among them and approach as many as will permit, stroke the animals on the neck and back and call them by given name; animals like to be petted. The results will be astonishing in the short time in which a train of gentle mules can be loaded for the day's march.

A young train should be accustomed to line up at rigging twice per day at regular intervals, on each occasion placing a little grain on the feed cover, as they soon become accustomed to look forward in patient expectation for the morning and evening meal.

In due time as they learn to line up properly, the feeding at the rigging should be discontinued.

During the process of teaching the animals to line up at rigging, they should be loaded and taken out of camp a distance of 2 or 3 miles and the pack master should then round up the train and note the condition and fit of each aparejo in memorandum book, correcting those needing immediate attention; continue this practice each day until each aparejo is properly fitted and adjusted, when longer marches should be taken, to get the animals in good muscular condition and harden their backs.

After a period of four weeks practice marches should be reduced to four times each week, one day to the practice of lairing-up side packs, the last day of the week, Saturday, to cleaning up the rigging and other duties.

From four to six weeks, as noted above, should get the train in service for active duty.

Chapter IV, "B. Instruction in the service of a pack train," should be thoroughly understood and complied with; also Chapter VI, "Duties of individuals."

To maintain an organization and efficiency both men and animals must be taught their duties, and regular practice marches be had, together with stated inspections of both men and animals and equipments.

As pack trains are organized on the basis of one pack master, one cargador, one blacksmith, one cook, and one packer to every five

[a]Care should be taken to have the animals come quietly to the rigging; they should never be hurried unless the occasion is urgent.

pack mules in the train, it sometimes becomes necessary to divide the train into "sections" when traveling with a command of cavalry.

For this purpose ten pack mules are usually assigned to a "troop" with their proper complement of equipment. The pack master will see to it that the necessary cargador tools, mule shoes, nails, etc., are supplied, and packers will mess with the troop to which assigned.

The pack master should therefore school the packers in the requirements exacted of the "skilled" packer (sec. 108).

In case of the distribution of the five sections of the train the pack master will retain the bell horse, blacksmith, and cook with the first section, and will be considered headquarters of the pack train. The cargador will be assigned with the fifth section, or the one farthest away from the first or headquarter section of the train. It must then be the duty of the pack master and cargador to visit the intermediate sections, at stated or suitable intervals, to overlook the condition of the animals and equipments so as to maintain efficiency.

It should be remembered by commanding officers that pack mules (sections) should be reassembled as early as possible to maintain organization.

5. THE ESSENTIAL CONDITIONS IN THE SELECTION OF THE PACKER.

SEC. 107. He must know how to read and write; be sound in body, of athletic build, and not addicted to the excessive use of intoxicants or display of bad or ugly temper, and thoroughly imbued with an "esprit de corps" for the pack service.

Age, from 21 to 35 years. Height, from 5 feet 7 inches to 6 feet 2 inches. Weight, from 165 to 210 pounds. Honorably discharged soldiers will be given the preference.

THE SKILLED PACKER.

SEC. 108. Ordinarily one versed in the usages and customs of pack-train service.

As instancing the requirements necessary for the proper discharge of his duties, the following may be enumerated:

He must understand—

(1) The principles of "ribbing up" the aparejo, to keep the animal's back sound.

(2) The relative toughness in different classes of wood suitable for the "ribbing" of aparejos.

(3) The gradual tapering to give "ribs" necessary for conformation to the body of the mule.

(4) How to select grasses (hay) suitable for filling or padding for aparejos.

(5) Where and how much filling is necessary in the aparejo to give perfect conformation to the body of the animal, and the relative thickness necessary for the holding up of different weighty loads bearing on the proper surface on either side of the backbone and withers.

(6) The *cause* of "bunches," or wounds, on any part of the animal's body covered by the aparejo and cincha, and the proper adjustment to correct the same. (See Evolution of the aparejo, and sec. 9.)

(7) The *cause* for the animal's "dock" becoming sore, and the proper remedy to correct the same. (See sec. 9.)

(8) How to lace, fit, and cinch the aparejo to the mule, with due regard to the proper size of aparejo necessary.

(9) How many sections, giving the proper name, in the make of the aparejo, what comprises the aparejo proper and the aparejo complete, and how to make repairs to rigging (aparejos) and sew on canvas.

(10) The conformation of the hoofs and how the animal should be properly shod for warm and cold seasons.

(11) How to select "pack" and riding animals, with due regard to endurance, strength, and docile qualities.

(12) What remedies to apply in case of cutting of blood vessels.

(13) What remedies to apply in case of snake bite and how to prepare the wound for same.

(14) How to prepare, "form," and cover cargo, and tie down properly.

(15) How to arrange aparejos in an orderly manner, cover and tie down when in bivouac, as the nature of the ground will permit.

(16) All hitches, knots, and splices customary in pack-train service.

(17) How to construct a travois to carry wounded, and how to improvise a stretcher for similar purpose.

(18) How to put on a load in the most expeditious and satisfactory manner, requiring not over one minute for ordinary loading.

(19) How to catch a pack mule when his load needs attention.

(20) How to quickly readjust a load in less than one minute. (Experience will teach by sight and sense of touch how load is riding.)

(21) When traveling up or down a mountain how to cut or take as many turns as necessary to conserve the strength of the animals.

(22) How to guard against accidents when crossing a stream, either fording or swimming.

(23) He must be attentive to animals and loads, that none of the latter may fall off, impeding the progress of the train.

(24) Be quick to note weakness in animals during travel and relieve the same.

(25) Be quick to note conditions of country that may endanger the life of the animal and guard against accidents.

(26) Be watchful, both day and night, during travel that none may go astray.

(27) Be kind in his treatment of animals.

(28) Have a knowledge of the component parts of a ration and the allowance for thirty days; also the allowance of grain, hay, and bedding for horse and mule.

(29) Have a fair knowledge of cookery, especially the art of making good bread.

(30) Be prompt to obey all proper orders emanating from the pack master or other proper authority.

(31) Always be ready for duty in all conditions of country and climate.

(32) Be honest and honorable in all his dealings with his fellow-men.

THE NOVICE, OR UNSKILLED PACKER.

SEC. 109. One not versed in the usages and customs of the pack-train service, but otherwise qualified as called for in section 107.

INSTRUCTIONS TO PACK MASTERS.

SEC. 110. It should be the ambition of pack masters to keep the animals sound, equipments in good order, and maintain efficiency and discipline in the train.

Attend personally to the proper watering of the animals when in bivouac and during travel when opportunity offers.

Obey all orders promptly coming from proper authority. In like manner exact prompt obedience from members of the train and maintain perfect organization by schooling of men and animals in their duties.

6 DUTIES OF INDIVIDUALS

SEC. 111. *The chief packer.*—He will—

(1) At post, whereat stationed, report every morning to the quartermaster for instructions, unless otherwise instructed.

(2) On expeditions, report every evening to the quartermaster or commanding officer for instructions, unless otherwise instructed.

(3) When practicable, equip all pack trains, giving receipt therefor to quartermaster, and in like manner obtain receipts from pack masters; supervise the distribution of cargo according to the number of pack animals in each train and the strength thereof.

(4) Keep a roster of names of packers of each pack train, and positions occupied, when employed, when discharged, with cause therefor; their height, age, color of hair and eyes, weight; how long they have served and in what capacity, giving names of pack masters they have served under, and how long and in what States, Territories, or foreign possessions.

(5) Keep a descriptive list of public animals of each train, giving age, sex, color, height, marks and blemishes, and weight, as near as can be judged when scales are not convenient.

(6) When practicable select pack masters that are eligible, having due regard to length of service, experience, and the proper requisites in the control of men; and cargadors upon the recommendation of pack masters.

(7) In the employment of men as packers, give preference to honorably discharged soldiers filling the necessary requisites. (Sec. 107.)

(8) When directed by quartermaster, receive reports from pack masters every evening or morning, as the exigencies of the service may require, of the number of public animals, condition of train, amount of cargo on hand, and of what composed; also of any accidents happening to men or to public animals, making note thereof and report same to quartermaster.

(9) On expeditions form a pioneer corps, instructing pack masters to detail as many packers as may be necessary, who will provide themselves with ax, spade, or pick, as directed, looking to the clearance of all obstacles that may impede travel or endanger trains.

(10) When practicable, park all pack trains as directed by the quartermaster.

(11) Detail, as directed by the quartermaster, as many pack trains, or parts thereof, to commands, as the exigencies of the service may require.

(12) Have all trains in readiness at time specified by quartermaster or commanding officer.

(13) Exact from pack masters a constant adherence to the rules of packing, schooling of themselves and their men, and teaching of animals, looking to the perfect organization of the trains.

(14) Exact a prompt obedience from all pack masters to orders concerning their duties.

(15) Exert a watchful care over trains, that efficient and effective service may be rendered.

(16) Keep a memorandum book, giving a general description of country and climate, how country is watered and grassed, and incidents of note that may be of service.

(17) Hold pack masters strictly responsible for the perfect working, management, and condition of trains in their charge.

(18) Make stated inspections of pack trains, as may be directed by the Quartermaster-General, United States Army, looking to the maintenance and perfect organization of pack trains.

(19) Perform all other duties as the exigencies of the service may require and as directed by the Quartermaster-General, United States Army.

SEC. 112. *The assistant chief packer.*—He will—

(1) Assist the chief packer in the performance of his duties.

(2) On detached service, in the absence of the chief packer, or when in foreign service, he will assume the duties prescribed for the chief packer, as directed by the chief quartermaster.

SEC. 113. *The pack master.*—He will—

(1) At post whereat stationed, in the absence of the chief packer or assistant chief packer, report every morning to the quartermaster unless otherwise instructed.

(2) In memorandum book provided for that purpose, keep a list of property and descriptive list of public animals in his charge, number, age, sex, color, height, marks and blemishes, and weight as near as can be judged when scales are not convenient.

(3) Keep a roster of names of packers, when employed, when discharged, and cause therefor; their rank, date of rank in pack train, when first employed, lenght of service as packmaster, as cargador, as blacksmith, as cook, as packer, as instructor, organization assigned to, place of birth, age, height, weight, color of eyes, color of hair, complexion, giving names of pack masters they have served under, and how long, and in what States, Territories, or foreign possessions, efficiency and conduct.

(4) Keep a memorandum of number of days' rations drawn, how many men drawn for, the amount and description of cargo, how disposed of, and when and to whom issued.

(5) Report any accident, sickness, or death happening to men or public animals, to chief packer or his assistant, and in their absence, to quartermaster.

(6) Station men at bad or dangerous places, for the safety of the animals; likewise before crossing streams find out bad or dangerous points.

(7) In mountainous country he must know how to cut or make as many turns as the strength of the animals may indicate, giving opportunity when space will permit to rest animals and secure loading.

(8) Be ever watchful and quick to detect weakness in any animal approaching bad or dangerous places, lightening or relieving its load accordingly.

(9) Be just and fair with the men and exact prompt obedience to all orders.

(10) When opportunity offers, school the men in the system of packing, exacting a strict compliance therewith.

(11) Assist the cargador in "setting up" rigging and attend to the animals' bodies, keeping them sound.

(12) Keep equipment in proper order and repair.

(13) Keep a diary of the distance traveled, condition of country, how wooded and watered and grassed, and other incidents of note that may be of service.

(14) Compute the carrying capacity of train at 250 pounds to the pack animal; aparejo and accessories not included.

SEC. 114. *The cargador or assistant pack master.*—He will—

(1) With the assistance of the pack master, set up the rigging.

(2) Fix aparejo for all bunches or wounds, as their position indicates, being careful not to overlook any, no matter how small, remembering that a small one is more easily fixed than a large one.

(3) Attend to all needed repairs to aparejos and equipments, supplying himself with cargador's kit for that purpose.

(4) Make up all cargoes, mating packages according to kind, and equalizing all packs to the best advantage, loading animals according to their strength and condition.

(5) Keep a watch on animals and packs while traveling, and on packers, that they attend to their duties, reporting any inattention or disobedience to orders promptly to pack master, as they are necessarily under his immediate charge.

(6) Place cargo, rigging, and picket line as indicated by pack master.

(7) Assume charge of the pack train in the temporary absence of the pack master.

(8) Keep a memorandum of all cargo received, and to whom issued, with date, marking or tagging when necessary, and attend to the cleanliness of the coronas and cruppers.

(9) Keep two or three table knives for the purpose of cleaning coronas; for convenience, select certain aparejos on which to secure them. (Sec. 76.)

(10) See that rigging and cargo are covered and securely tied down; all halter stems gathered and placed half and half on head and end rigging, all blinds likewise placed between the two last rigging.

(11) See that all saddles, bridles, and blankets are placed on cargo before covering up; pack master's and cargador's at each end.

(12) Have all canvas and blankets spread out to dry, if found wet, and all canvas gathered up and placed in front of rigging.

(13) Count all rigging when taken off, halter stems and blinds, to see that none are missing.

(14) Name all animals according to sex, that they may be known and remembered, marking each aparejo fitted to the animal with the name and number of corona of that animal.

(15) Never abuse or maltreat the animals or permit others to do so, impairing their gentleness and usefulness; it tends toward dis-

organization. With sound and gentle animals it is possible to go anywhere they can find footing.

(16) Keep all animals' manes properly "roached," i. e., trimmed up.

SEC. 115. *The blacksmith.*—He will—

(1) Provide himself with blacksmith's field kit and shoe boxes, the necessary number of shoes, of the size numbers wanted; amount of nails and size numbers wanted; fit them up, shoe and keep the train properly shod. Remember that sound feet are as necessary as sound backs to the efficiency of the train.

(2) In addition, obtain and fit up 200 shoes, with sufficient nails, ready for field service.

(3) While train is being loaded keep the animals close to "bell," keeping correct count as turned loose, reporting any accident to pack master or cargador promptly.

(4) On leaving bivouac, with assistance of cargador, take count of animals, see that none are missing, taking station on each side of train when possible, and see that tally is correct, reporting any that may be missing to pack master.

(5) Take station at rear of train while traveling, keeping a watch on the animal's feet, so that he may know how many shoes have slipped during the travel, and call attention of packers to any loads that may need readjusting.

(6) At any and all halts, opportunity offering, come quickly to the head of train and keep animals rounded up, so that animals may not stray off, and in order that packers can give attention quickly to packs.

(7) On arrival at camp, when opportunity offers, call on pack master for all animals that need shoeing and necessary assistance. If animal is unruly tie up his foot. Do not abuse him; remember the animal is dumb and you are intelligent and human.

(8) Assist in putting on rigging and loading when necessary, and perform all other duties required as the exigencies of the pack service demand.

SEC. 116. *The packer.*—He will—

(1) Properly fit himself for his duties, study and perfect himself in the system of packing. For this purpose the pack master will obtain from the quartermaster the necessary number of books on Pack Transportation.

(2) Obey all orders emanating from the pack master, and in his absence, the cargador.

(3) Be gentle in his treatment of animals; never throw rocks, blinds, or in any way abuse them. The gentleness of animals, especially the quickness with which a train can be gotten out of camp, indicates the understanding of packers of their duties and is the test of organization and discipline of a train.

(4) Be watchful of loads when traveling, that none may fall off.

(5) Do not wait for others to do what he himself sees should be done.

(6) Work for the interest and good name of the train and be jealous of its reputation.

SEC. 117. *The cook.*—He will—

(1) As a necessary requisite, be a good bread baker, careful and saving with rations.

(2) Distribute short rations (one or two days' supply) in mess boxes, evenly, so as not to make one end of box heavier than the other or top heavy.

(3) When called, be quick to get up, and fold blankets and canvas and place in front of head rigging.

(4) Be quick in serving breakfast and dinner, especially during field service.

(5) Give variety of food as often as rations and extras will permit.

(6) Be clean, and keep utensils and surroundings clean.

(7) On arrival at camp, dinner being over, prepare for breakfast and dinner next day, and keep ready bread sufficient for two meals.

(8) As beans are a main staple in packers' fare and easily gotten ready, cook them before retiring for the breakfast and dinner meals.

(9) Always carry a little wood and kindling, so that a fire may be started quickly on arrival at camp.

(10) Get as near ready as possible everything designed for breakfast and dinner after supper and before retiring.

(11) Pack boxes, or as much as can conveniently be done, and secure them, and secure all packs opened before retiring.

(12) Keep kitchen ropes in a dry place.

(13) Have sufficient water for cooking, and wood and kindling to start fire quickly in the morning.

(14) Be called one-half hour before the trainmen, and call packers to breakfast promptly when ready.

(15) Secure riding animal and have him tied conveniently near.

(16) Time permitting, saddle up before breakfast; if not, while packers are eating; the kitchen animals will be tied conveniently close to kitchen.

(17) With the assistance of a packer, have the kitchen loads ready and loaded on the kitchen animals, so as not to cause unnecessary delay when the train has been loaded.

(18) Assist in keeping the animals rounded up, and at the call "Bell" be quick to untie the "bell" animal and lead out in the direction indicated, gaiting the animal as directed by pack master.

(19) Look back occasionally, should the pack master not be in the lead, and notice how the animals are coming, and whether the gait is too fast or too slow; if any accident happens, halt and wait for orders.

(20) Watch for and obey the signals of pack master.

(21) Look to pack master for all orders pertaining to kitchen.

(22) Look to pack master or cargador for orders on trail while traveling.

NOTE.—There is nothing that will add more to the comfort and good will among a crew of packers than a good, clean, and fast cook.

WHAT PACKERS ARE NOT PERMITTED TO DO.

SEC. 118. Packers must not—

(1) Throw rocks, blinds, or in any manner abuse the animals of the train.

(2) Tie riding or pack mules in front of saloons.

(3) Indulge in the use of intoxicants to the prejudice of good order and discipline in the pack train.

(4) Be absent from the train without permission from the pack master, and in his absence the cargador.

(5) Be insubordinate to the proper orders of the pack master, and in his absence the cargador.

(6) Read papers, books, etc., while on herd duty, or neglect to keep proper supervision over the animals that none may stray off or be stolen.

(7) Neglect to keep watch on pack mules on the march, night as well as day, that none may stray off during travel.

(8) Be inattentive to pack animals when their load needs balancing.

(9) Use coronas for bedding.

(10) Use the aparejo as a seat when in bivouac or permit others to do so.

FEEDING.

SEC. 119. In case grain is to be fed to pack animals, let it be given to them after the day's work is done—not before. In the latter case the grain is liable to sour on the mule's stomach; thirst, and possibly colic, results.

When grain is available it is fed at the picket line or on the herd ground. In the latter case, put it in separate piles, one for each mule, about 20 feet apart, the various piles being placed on the circumference of a circle.

When the mules are on herd do not picket the "bell" horse unless the urgency of the occasion requires it; "hobble" it instead. More freedom is thus given him in the selection of grasses.

If the "bell" horse is picketed during night herding, one of the herders should remain in its immediate vicinity in order to be prompt to render aid in case of accident.

If grain is not available for the train, but enough may be obtained for the "bell" horse, feed it separately, since it has not the same opportunities for grazing as the other animals.

If animals are fed at the picket line, the grain is placed on feed covers (sec. 80). These covers should be promptly removed after feeding. Two or more packers are detailed to be present to prevent animals from kicking one another and wasting the grain.

WATERING.

SEC. 120. It is very essential that animals should be watered at least once a day. Deprive them of water and they immediately grow thin.

Pack masters should personally supervise the watering of animals on arrival at bivouac.

Some animals are fastidious as to the quality of water they drink. Do not overlook them; see that they are properly watered.

Before fording streams, when there is reason to believe that animals are thirsty, always give them an opportunity to drink. Accident and delay may thus be avoided; especially in case the ford is boggy and dangerous.

GROOMING.

SEC. 121. Pack animals should be groomed daily. It is done while they are at the rigging.

In grooming, stroke with the hair, not against it; under the belly, stroke to the rear.

75927°—17——11

In a country where grass burs occur, see that none are on the animal's back or belly before putting on the aparejo.

TRAVELING.

SEC. 122. In warm climates, avoid traveling during the heat of the day. On the other hand, avoid making two marches in one day. It is better to do the day's work, if possible, and then go into camp.

In ordinary flat or undulating country, hourly halts are not necessary for pack trains. It is better to complete the day's march quickly, and get the loads and aparejos off the animals.

In mountainous country, however, halts should be made as opportunity offers, to rest the animals and secure the loads.

If the animals show the inclination, allow them to drink when opportunity occurs. They travel better in consequence.

On dark nights, when following a command, trust to the sense of smell of the riding animals. They will rarely leave the trail, the sense of smell guiding them more truly than sight. The animals, too, are more solicitous of keeping the trail at night than in the day.

Never adjust an animal's load while his head is uphill; always face him downhill.

During night travel, keep the animals within hearing distance of the bell.

Desiring to surprise an enemy, muffle the bell with a handkerchief, allowing a faint sound, if necessary.

In fording streams, do not permit the animals either to bunch up or to straggle out. After the bell horse has crossed the ford, rattle the bell, to encourage timid animals.

If in fording a stream a laden mule falls, cut the "standing rope" of the lashing, so as to free the load in case this becomes necessary in order to save the life of the animal.

A similar course may be pursued when an animal loses his footing on a mountain side.

Pack masters should always be provided with a heavy hunting knife for the purpose.

In traveling through dry and desert countries, two 10-gallon casks of water should be carried in a pack train. It will be found, however, that if available, canned tomatoes are a good substitute and quench the thirst better than a small allowance of water.

When expecting a dry march, do not eat beans or salted meats for the morning meal.

The "bell" horse should not be ridden.

CAMPING.

SEC. 123. In camping avoid low and swampy ground.

Always camp on the farther side of a stream in the direction of travel.

Do not camp in a "box" canyon, i. e., one which has but one practical outlet.

On getting into camp it is not necessary, as sometimes held, to loosen the aparejos and allow them to remain for half an hour or so on the animals.[a] It will do them more good to be relieved of the aparejos and allowed to roll.

USE OF BLINDS.

SEC. 124. A pack mule is always blinded when putting on the aparejo and the load; also, when the load needs tightening on the road. He is not blinded when taking off the load and the aparejo.

Blinds should always be carried on the left arm when traveling.

When putting on the aparejos the packer whose blind is not being used lays it on the ground in front of the mule. After an aparejo is on, the near packer removes the blind, places it on the collar of the aparejo and proceeds to tie up the halter shank. (Sec. 57, figs. 40–41.)

The off packer, after securing latigo, takes this blind off the aparejo and hastens to get another mule. The packer tying up the halter shank picks up the blind on the ground.

Mules should be taught not to move when the blind is on. Consequently, if necessary to change the position of a mule always lift the blind before causing him to stir.

KINDNESS TO ANIMALS.

SEC. 125. A mule remembers kindness and will recognize by sight and sense of smell the individual who has shown it to him. Be brutal in treatment of him and he will shy from you and avoid you.

Kindness will conciliate the most vicious animal and cause him to become docile.

If vicious, provide means to prevent his injuring any person.

In doing so do not maltreat the animal. Treat him kindly, but firmly, and he will soon learn to recognize you as his master, and obey.

Maltreat him and he will never forget you.

PRECAUTIONS.

SEC. 126. In malarial districts or hot climates wear a woolen bandage 12 inches wide wrapped from two to three times around the stomach.

Avoid fruit and nuts; lemons, however, in form of lemonade, may be taken, but not to excess.

Avoid spirituous liquors of all descriptions.

While traveling, sleep under canvas of some description to avoid the dew.

Procure twigs or brush, never green grasses, on which to spread blankets.

If possible, procure a hammock and always use it, especially during the rainy season. Above all things, do not sleep on the bare ground.

Boiled fresh milk is good for a weak stomach; condensed milk is a good substitute.

Keep a supply of quinine, but use it sparingly and only when necessity requires.

Keep the head cool, the feet warm, and the bowels in order, and fear no danger from sickness in any climate.

---

[a] Twenty-five or thirty years ago it was the custom to loosen the aparejos and allow them to remain on the animals for half an hour with the belief that if any bunches occur during travel this method would reduce them. This, however, is an error and affords no relief.

Keep on hand a small supply of needles, silk thread, and bandages in case of wounds.

Keep a small supply of ammonia for animals, in case of snake bite. Puncture the flesh freely around the bitten part and rub ammonia well in with fingers. Be careful, however, that the fingers have no abrasion.

For screw worms, keep a supply of chloroform, or crysilic ointment.

GLOSSARY

SEC. 127.—

Aparejo (pronounced "ap-pa-ray-ho") A pack saddle

Bag, war: A clothes sack (Sec 93)

Bell: Ordinarily a sheep bell, attached by a strap to the neck of the horse.

Bell horse: A horse with a bell strapped about its neck and used to lead a pack train of mules, sometimes alluded to as the "bell" in such expressions as "get the bell," "lead the bell," "stop the bell," "call the bell "

Bell sharp· Applied to mules that become especially attached to the "bell" horse

Blind. A hood of leather, made to cover the eyes of a pack mule when loading the animal or tightening the load (Figs 40–41)

Boot: Term applied to the end pieces of aparejo

Boot bar· A section of wood representing the finished product, when the boot of the aparejo is properly filled with hay by the skilled packer, and provided with slots to receive ribs of wood (In connection with the saddle bar, the boot bar holds the ribs in place, thus stiffening the aparejo)

Brake: To brake a pack, to brake a load—signifying the act of working the packs close together and into their proper relative positions after they have been tied together by a sling rope (Sec 28.)

Bunch: A puffing up of the skin

Cargo: The loads carried by a pack train, when spoken of collectively To "form cargo," i e , to arrange in an orderly and convenient manner an aggregation of loads. (Sec. 53)

Cargador: An individual who, in the organization of a pack train, is next in importance after the pack master He has to do with making up and forming the cargo, equalizing the packs, caring for mules, repairing aparejos, etc (Sec 114)

Carrier piece· A fold of leather sewed in between the back and belly pieces of aparejo at rear, to which, by means of lacing, the crupper is attached, and which thus serves to support the crupper and prevent it from hanging too low on the mule's buttocks. (*g*, fig. 1.)

Center stitch line: The stitch line which divides the aparejo into two equal parts. (*j*, fig 1)

Cinch (cincha): A broad canvas band, by means of which the aparejo is secured on the mule's back. (III, fig 1)

Collar: That portion of the aparejo which lies over the mule's withers. It is so shaped as to relieve the mule of all pressure on the withers (1, i, fig 1)

Corona: A saddle pad, which is placed on the mule's back before the blanket and aparejo are put on. A numeral is placed on one of its sides to distinguish it. (V, fig 1)

Cover, aparejo (or sobre-jalma): A canvas covering attached to the aparejo to protect the leather from wear and tear. Called by packers a "sovereian hammer, soldier hammer " (II, fig 1)

Cover, pack: A section of heavy canvas employed to wrap therein, by means of rope, certain packages that may deteriorate by exposure to rain or dampness

Cover, rigging: Covers used to protect the aparejos in camp or bivouac. (Sec 78)

Cover, cargo: Canvas used to protect aggregation of loads, termed the "cargo," in camp or bivouac. (Sec. 79)

Cover, feed: Canvas laid on the ground at the picket line, on which grain is placed for feeding the animals. (Sec. 80.)

Crupper: A leather band attached to the front facing and carrier pieces of the aparejo, and fitting under the mule's tail, its purpose being to steady the aparejo, and to prevent it from slipping to the front. (IV, fig. 1)

Deadman: A holdfast, sunk in the ground, to which the picket line is attached.

Diamond hitch: Name applied to the lashing, by means of which the load is secured to the aparejo, the two ropes forming a diamond or lozenge on top of the load

Dock piece· That portion of the crupper that fits under the animal's tail; also applied to that portion of the animal's tail under which the dock of the crupper rests.

Drag tails: Term applied to mules that are farthest away from the "bell" when traveling; also applied to a lazy packer.
Facings: Additional pieces or strips of leather, applied to certain parts of the aparejo to strengthen them (*d, e, f*, etc , fig 1)
"*Go.*" Term used by the "near" to the "off" packer, when hitch is formed and ready to be tightened.
Hand-hole: Hole made in the belly piece of the aparejo in the center of each side, to enable the packer to insert the hay or grass that forms the padding
"*Hold:*" Signal by the "near" to the "off" packer to hold his pack in position, while the "near" packer brakes the load
Lair: Term applied to the rope used in securing pack covers around pack Hence, to "lair;" "to lair up," meaning to secure the pack cover to the pack by means of the lair rope. (Sec 15)
Line up: Meaning to cause the pack mules to take position at rear of the rigging on the proper flank of the "bell" horse
Load: A pack or packs forming the burden for one pack mule Hence, "to load up," meaning to place the loads, as formed in cargo, on the pack mules
Pack: In the ordinary case, that portion of the load carried on one side of the mule's back. A load, however, may consist of a single pack or of several packs, depending on the nature of the articles to be packed, or the exigencies of the service.
Pack up: Meaning to load up; to place the loads, as formed in cargo, on the pack mules.
Packer, first-class: One skilled in the art of preparing cargo; loading a pack mule, adjusting a load so that it will balance evenly on the mule's back, etc ; one familiar with the "diamond" and other hitches used in securing loads, and versed in the usages and customs of the pack service.
Packer, second-class: A novice in the art of packing
Pack master. A master in the art of packing; one who has charge of a pack train
Ribbing up: Placing in an aparejo the sticks, or whatever may be used to give stiffness to the sides of the aparejo.
Rigging: Term applied to the aparejos in a pack train, particularly when it is desired to refer to them in a collective sense.
Saddle bar: A section of wood representing the finished product when the saddle of the aparejo is properly filled with hay or similar material, by the skilled packer, and provided with slots to receive ribs of wood In connection with the boot bar, the saddle bar holds the ribs in place, by means of which the aparejo is stiffened.
Set up: To set up an aparejo, meaning to prepare it for use by inserting the ribs, and then padding it with hay, so as to adjust it properly to the shape of the mule's back (Secs 6 and 7)
Settle: To adjust packs to their places on the aparejo, as in the case of simple box loads. Here it is not necessary to brake the load, i e , to work the near pack up and down, until it is in place, as the two packs may readily be settled on the aparejo so as to ride evenly.
Shoe: Term applied to the protecting sticks of the aparejo cover (l II, fig 1)
Sling: Term applied to the rope used in tying the packs together on the mule's back prior to being lashed Hence, "to sling" the load, "to cross sling," "to double sling;" and "to double cross sling " (Secs 27 to 31)
Snap up: To tie animals together by their halter shanks, while standing at the rigging. (Sec 56)
Stem or snap: Names sometimes applied to halter shanks
Sticks, protecting: Used on the aparejo cover to stiffen the ends Sometimes called shoes (l II, fig 1)
Sticks, tamping: Used in tamping hay, etc , in the corners of the aparejo
Tie Signal from the "off" to the "near" packer that all slack has been rendered on the running rope. Also signal from the "near" to the "off" packer for the latter to secure the end of the rope, on completion of the hitch
"*Tied.*" Signal from the "near" to the "off" packer, in slinging the load, that the "square" knot has been tied
Trail A path, usually narrow, hence incumbent upon animals of a train to move in single file "To trail" means to follow in single file after the "bell" horse
Train, pack: A pack train is an organization comprising fifty pack animals, a proper complement of men, and a complete equipment. (Sec 87)

7. SPECIFICATIONS FOR PACK AND RIDING MULES

SEC. 128. The mule must be sound in body and limbs, of blocky build, of kind and gentle disposition, with free and springy action at the walk or trot, and to conform to the following description:

The pack mule must be in fair condition, from 4 to 6 years old; weight, depending upon height, to be as follows:

Pack mules should weigh from 950 to 1,025 pounds, and be from 14.1 hands to 15 hands high.

Head of medium size, well formed, intelligent looking, broad between the eyes; eyes clear, large, and full; ears long and flexible; teeth and tongue free of blemishes; muzzle well rounded and firm.

Neck, stocky, broad and full at crest, and inclined to arch.

Withers, low and broad, indicating strength in shoulders.

Chest, low and broad, with division well defined, holding the fore legs well apart, showing good lung power.

Knees, wide in front and free of blemishes.

Back, short and straight, indicating strength in back over region of the kidneys.

Barrel, deep and large, indicating a good feeder—not hard to please in either food or water—a most essential requisite in the selection of pack mules.

Hips, broad and well rounded.

Dock, low and stiff, offering resistance, showing endurance.

Hocks, standing well apart and strongly made, showing well developed buttocks.

Pasterns, muscled, short, and strongly shaped.

Hoofs, sound, broad, and full, with frog well developed, elastic, and healthy.

Riding mules will conform to the above conditions, with the exception, they may be deeper from point of withers to brisket.

WHAT TO AVOID IN THE SELECTION OF PACK MULES.

SEC. 129. Head: Avoid a long and large head, dish face and Roman nose, narrow between the eyes, eyes small, round, and sunk well under eyebrow, the eye inclined to snap and show the white; ears erect and stiff, indicating advanced age; teeth long, pointed and flat on upper surface, with bean well worn; tongue cut or other blemish; mouth cut at inner corners, and under lip hanging down.

Neck, long and thin, inclined to be ewe-necked.

Withers, high and narrow.

Chest, high at center or chicken-breasted, lacking vitality.

Knees, small and out of line.

Back, long or sway-backed, indicating weakness over kidneys.

Barrel, small and round, drawn in the flank.

Hips, prominent and angular.

Dock, high and weak.

Hocks, standing close together, throwing the feet well out.

Limbs, knees, and hocks showing wind galls.

Pasterns, with scratches, cuts, or bruises.

Hoofs, "pigeontoed," high and narrow, and drawn at the frog, indicating the latter has lost vitality.

CHAPTER VII.

THE DALY APAREJO—SPECIFICATIONS FOR CONSTRUCTION.

SEC. 130. There are in general use the 62, 60, and 58 inch aparejos, i. e., measuring from end to end 62, 60, and 58 inches, respectively.

THE BODY OF THE APAREJO.

(1) The back piece, (2) the belly or body piece, (3) the boots, (4) the boot facings, (5) the front facing, (6) the center facing, (7) the carrier pieces, (8) the welts.

NOTE.—The first two items of the above are sometimes referred to as the "body pieces."

DETAILED SPECIFICATIONS.

Take a 60-inch aparejo as a standard—60 inches long and 24 inches wide throughout its entire length.

THE BODY.

(1) To be made of solid, black harness leather, tallow finish; sides to be of good spread, weighing for back piece, center facing, boot facings, and carriage pieces not less than 10 ounces to the square foot, and for the body piece, boot pieces, front facing, and welt to weigh not less than 12 ounces to the square foot. All leather must be free from cuts and other blemishes.

BACK PIECES.

To be cut 43 inches long and 24 inches wide.

BODY PIECES.

To be cut 45 inches long and 24 inches wide.

BOOT PIECES (TWO).

To be cut 24 inches long and 18 inches wide.

BOOT FACINGS (FOUR).

To be cut 18½ inches long and 12 inches wide; one side of each facing to have a semicircle cut on a radius of 6¾ inches to 7⅜ inches of opposite side; now commence on this opposite side and measure upward on each end 7¾ inches and describe a semicircle whose radius will be 2¾ inches, both semicircles meeting, the larger outward and the smaller inward. This provision leaves a straight edge of 5 inches on each end.

Now place two facings on each boot, semicircles meeting at center of boot and the outer ends on line of body pieces, facings to be sewed down with three seams, the first on the inner edge all around to top of boot, the second 3 inches from the outer and upper ends of boots circling to opposite ends, spaced 1¼ inches from outer edge of semicircles, the third to be spaced 5 inches from outer edge and 3 inches from the inner edge of semicircle.

FRONT FACING.

To be cut 43 inches long and 6½ inches wide, outer edge of facing to be flush with edge of back piece and sewed down with two seams measuring for the first 2¼ inches from the outer edge and 4 inches for the second. Now provide six ⅜-inch holes, to be punched 1 inch from inner edge, three holes on each side of center of facing, measuring 8½ inches for the first, 13 inches for the second, and 17½ inches for the third.

In placing the front facing on back piece place the heaviest side inward, as the holes receive the lacings of crupper. This facing forms the front of the aparejo.

CENTER FACING.

To be cut 24 inches long and 8 inches wide, placed at center of back piece, extending from front to rear; that is, 4 inches on each side of center of back piece, and to be sewed down with two seams one-half inch apart on each side, measuring one-fourth inch from the outer edges for the first and three-fourths inch from the outer edge for the second.

ASSEMBLING THE APAREJO

Lap the boots on to back and body pieces 1 inch on outside; in lapping, the "fleshy" side of the body piece must face outward; to be sewed down with two seams spaced one-half inch apart, the first one-fourth inch from edge and the second three-fourths of an inch from the outer edge.

In closing up the body, care should be taken to have the boots or ends doubled exactly alike, so that the top of the boot of body piece will just meet the end of back piece. The center seam to be sewed down to body and back pieces, and must positively be in the center of the aparejo.

The body piece will have a "handhole" 5½ inches long and 5 inches wide, cut out in center of body piece 15 inches from center seam to center of hole.

Back piece to have a handhole of similar dimensions cut in center of back piece, 10 inches from center seam to center of hole, this handhole to be cut around to within 1 inch from either side of center at top. This forms a lid and is provided with one hole at center of lower end, one-fourth of an inch from edge, large enough to receive thong for lacing. A similar hole is provided on the body in line with this, one-fourth of an inch from edge; both holes facing up and down.

On back piece at rear a slit 12 inches long is provided; to be 2 inches from the outward or rear edge; commencing with 1 inch above the boot, running upward toward the center facing, and provided with 5 holes on either side of slit, spaced equally distant to receive lacings. These slits are for the purpose of introducing the inside frame or ribbing for aparejo.

The "handhole" on back piece is provided for guiding ribs to position in boot and saddle bars.

In front there must be a welt of good, solid leather, 1 inch wide, laid in between the body and back pieces, extending from end to end, to be sewed down with two seams, one-half an inch apart and one-fourth inch from edge.

In sewing along edge at front, a space of three-fourths of an inch must be omitted, counting $3\frac{1}{2}$ inches from center seam each way. This to permit "key bar" to pass through in locking ribs of inside frame.

Now punch two holes, three-fourths of an inch apart; the first at center of space corresponding to hole provided in brass "key bar," the second on the lower side, and provide thong 10 inches long to secure "key bar" to aparejo, both holes to be "up and down."

The rear has a similar welt 1 inch wide and 14 inches long, extending 7 inches each way from center seam.

Below this welt the "carrier" pieces are placed for the purpose of carrying the crupper, and is arranged by taking a piece of leather 4 by 8 inches, of half the thickness of the welt, folded the narrow way, slipped in exactly three-fourths of an inch, leaving the folded part out.

The extending part of the "carrier" pieces will have three sets of holes five-sixteenths of an inch in diameter, two holes at the upper end and three-fourths of an inch apart, the first hole to be 1 inch from end; two holes will be provided in similar manner at opposite end, and two holes at center in similar manner; the holes to be parallel with the length of "carrier" pieces.

Thongs for each "carrier" piece will be provided; and to be of latigo leather, 12 inches long and five-sixteenths of an inch wide.

From the "carriers" to the end of the aparejo there must be a welt similar to that described for the front; the whole to be sewed down with two seams in similar manner as described for the front.

The collar that shapes the aparejo for the withers must be 6 inches wide and 6 inches deep; that is to say, 6 inches along the front seam at center and 6 inches back toward rear, shaped in this manner: Three inches on each side of center stitch line of the aparejo, run back 4 inches parallel with center stitch line, then run 2 inches toward center stitch line, then back 2 inches parallel with center stitch line, then up to center stitch line.

The center seam, like center of collar, must positively be in the center of the aparejo and exactly straight across the body.

It is understood the collar is placed on the front as indicated by the front facing of the aparejo, and, like center seam, is sewed to back and body pieces.

Now punch two holes, one on each side of the center stitch line and to be three-fourths of an inch apart at front and rear, spaced equally distant from center stitch line. These holes to be provided between the two outward seams with thong 10 inches long for lacing, to secure aparejo cover to aparejo.

If using willow or other sticks, cut two slits 2 inches long, one on each side of center stitch line, running downward from center stitch line, slits to be in center of aparejo. In cutting slits be careful not to cut through center stitch line.

In the case of mountain batteries and machine gun troops, provide a chock plate and staple, to be placed at the center of the front and rear end of the aparejo. These to be positioned so as to correspond with slits of frame that carry the gun (parts) and ammunition.

NOTE.—For 62-inch aparejo the body pieces are cut 2 inches longer than that for a 60-inch aparejo.

For 58-inch aparejo the body pieces are cut the same length as that provided for the 60-inch, the boots being cut 24 inches long and 16 inches wide.

Of 50 aparejos, make twenty-five 60 inches long and 24 inches wide, thirteen, 62 inches long and 24 inches wide, and twelve, 58 inches long and 24 inches wide.

NOTE.—In ordering 50 aparejos, the proportion of sizes should be as noted above.

In width they must be uniformly 24 inches throughout their entire length; and collar with center seam must *positively* be in the *center of* the aparejo.

In a requisition for 56, 54, and 52 inch aparejo, a uniform width of 22 inches will be provided. For 56-inch aparejo, the back and body pieces are cut 41 and 43 inches long and 22 inches wide, respectively.

Boot pieces (two) are cut 22 inches long and 16 inches wide.

Boot facings (four) are cut 16 inches long and 11 inches wide.

Front facing, 41 inches long and 6¼ inches wide.

Center facing 22 inches long and 8 inches wide.

In assembling the aparejo, the same provision will be observed as provided for larger sizes, having due regard to width of 22 inches, the size of collar being the same for all aparejos. The front facing will have six ⅜-inch holes punched in similar manner as provided for a 60-inch aparejo, measuring for the first 7 inches on each side of center of facing, 11 inches for the second, and 15 inches for the third.

For 54-inch aparejo, the back and body pieces, the front and center facings are cut the same length as that for a 56-inch aparejo; the boot pieces being cut 22 inches long and 14 inches wide, and boot facings 14 inches long and 11 inches wide. For a 52-inch aparejo, the back and body pieces are cut 39 and 41 inches long and 22 inches wide, the boot pieces, boot facings, and center facing are cut the same as for 54-inch aparejo; the front facing being cut 39 inches long and 6½ inches wide.

The handholes on the body pieces for the 56, 54, and 52 inch aparejo are cut the same as provided for larger sizes measuring 13 inches from center seam to center of hole.

If using willow or other sticks, a slit on each side of center line is provided. If using the Daly ribbing, the back piece is provided with handholes and slits in similar manner as provided for a 60-inch aparejo; the saddle and boot bars are 2 inches less in width than for standard sizes of aparejos 24 inches wide.

In ordering a complete equipment for one pack train, section 87, page 148, will be followed. In an order for the aparejo "proper" and parts thereof, the number and size of the respective aparejo must be stated.

THE CRUPPER.

(2) To be of good solid black harness leather, in weight to be as provided for the body pieces of the aparejo. Standard size for crupper for 62, 60, and 58 inch aparejos, to be 78 inches long and 12 inches wide. Standard size for cruppers for 56, 54, and 52 inch aparejos to be 72 inches long and 10 inches wide. To form crupper for 62, 60, and 58 inch aparejo, cut two sections 39 inches long and 12 inches wide, shaped in this manner: On right-hand section on left

end, measure downward from corner 2⅞ inches and cut in 4 inches, to form the upper portion of dock; in doing so describe the segment of a circle, whose radius will be five-eighths of an inch; now measure 12 inches from upper and lower corners along sides, and on upper side describe the segment of a circle on a radius of 12 inches, commencing at inner and upper corner of dock; now measure downward 8 inches on same end and cut in 4 inches to form this lower portion and describe a half circle on a radius of 2 inches; now measure 8 inches from corner on lower side and 4 inches upward at right angle, and describe the segment of a circle on a radius of 4 inches, commencing at inner and lower corner of dock.

Half the crupper is thus shaped. Cut a corresponding one and lap both, allowing 4 inches for upper surface of dock, lap to be sewed down in center with two seams one-half of an inch apart; length of seams 4 inches; before lapping ends shave down the under surface at ends.

For top facing provide a strip of good, solid leather 30 inches long and 3 inches wide, shaped to extend around dock to within 24 inches of each end; cut two more strips same width 26 inches long, lap 2 inches and sew down with two seams one-fourth of an inch from each edge.

For bottom facing provide two strips of good, solid leather 37 inches long, conforming to the shape of lower edge of crupper; commencing at one end there must be a uniform width of 3 inches, extending 15 inches toward opposite end, then describe a cut, circling toward center of dock, greatest width to be 6 inches; to be sewed down three seams, outer seams to be one-fourth of an inch from outer edges, the third or center seam, to extend from dock to within 24 inches of opposite end.

To form cover for dock, take a piece of good, solid leather 10 inches long and 7 inches wide doubled in center the long way and at center of ends cut in 3 inches, at end of cut and in center, use a ⅜-inch hand punch so that it will fit down into the dock, soak well, draw snug and sew down; shave off the under edges so as to leave it smooth on the animal's hips.

Leave 1⅝ inches for dock and leave one or both ends open to introduce the stuffing. Deer or antelope hair is best for the purpose.

Stuff and form the dock while the leather is soft.

In shaping the dock rub it on top as the stuffing is introduced, at the same time bringing the ends of the crupper together and bending the ends of the dock upward so as to shape the dock to the animal's tail, and the butt of the crupper to the animal's hips.

Lining for crupper to be of 28-inch No. 10 cotton duck, extending from dock to within 19 inches of end each way; in cutting allow for lap of 1 inch all around; to be sewed down with slanting stitch spaced one-half inch on upper and under sides. When lining is in position the upper edge of the crupper on either side of dock, extending 10 inches each way, to be bound down with sheepskin.

In sewing the upper edge of top facing a space of 10 inches should be omitted to receive this binding, binding to be then sewed down in regular manner.

At each end of crupper four ⅜-inch holes are punched, the first and fourth to be in center of top and bottom facings, the rest spaced equally distant between the first and fourth and 1 inch from ends.

On top facing and in center four ⅜-inch holes are punched, measuring for the first 24 inches from center of dock, and spaced equally distant to last hole on end of top facing.

Lacing for crupper to be of best latigo leather one-half inch wide and 7 feet long.

Lacings to have a slit at heavy end 1½ inches long in center and three-fourths of an inch from end. These to be fastened at hole provided on end of top facing of crupper.

THE APAREJO COVER OR SOBRE-JALMA.

(3) To be made of No. 4, 22-inch cotton duck. The canvas is cut 4 inches shorter than the length of the body of the aparejo. It is faced on both sides with leather 4 inches wide from end to end and 5 inches wide across ends. These facings when put on must be allowed to extend over the sides and ends of canvas so as to make the cover three-eighths inch wider and longer than the aparejo; to be sewed with seam at each edge. The sewing on end or bottom facings must extend to ends of facing.

The protecting sticks or shoes to be 21 inches long, 2½ inches wide, and three-fourths of an inch thick, taper the ends on one side to half the thickness at ends, extending 5½ inches toward center from each end, and taper on edges from center to a width of 1 inch at ends; to be placed in center of facings across ends.

In tapering sticks do not allow a ridge in center. The protecting sticks or shoes to be faced at each end, facing to be placed so as to leave an exposed surface of 10 inches wide in center; to be sewed down with two seams one-half inch apart.

Now punch two holes three-fourths of an inch from edge of center, in front and rear, and three-fourths of an inch apart. This to secure aparejo cover to aparejo.

In the case of mountain batteries and machine gun troops, provide a slit in center at front and rear, these to receive the staples that hold the gun frame; now cut two strips of leather, one for each staple, to be 6 inches long and ⅝ inch wide. These to be sewed down in customary manner convenient to slit, so as to permit the opposite end of strip to pass through eye of staple.

THE APAREJO CINCHA.

(4) To be made of No. 4, 22-inch cotton duck. The canvas to be 8 inches longer than the aparejo for which intended, and folded so as to make two thicknesses 10 inches wide; the lap to be sewed together with two seams and to be considered the surface side. For mountain battery service the canvas will be cut 10 inches longer than the aparejo for which intended.

One end of the cincha to be supplied with a section of ⅜-inch gas pipe, flattened at ends and curved so as to take the place of a ring, to pass the latigo or tightening strap around; when shaped must be 1 inch less than the width of the cincha. Flattened ends to be provided with holes punched 1½ inches from ends, to receive No. 8 copper rivets to hold it in place. This iron is fastened to cincha by two pieces of good, solid leather, 11 inches long and 5½ inches wide and riveted to iron. Place one end of canvas between the folds of leather facing and sew down with three seams, two seams one-half inch apart on outer edge, and one seam around edge of hole. This hole to be 3 inches wide and 3½ inches long, shaped half oval. The shape half oval to be up and down. This for the latigo or tightening strap to pass through. The reverse end of cincha is faced with leather 8½ inches on outside and 1½ inches on inside, 10 inches wide and 10 inches long, cut conical shape on outside. Fold 1½ inches from square end and lay into this fold a $\frac{5}{16}$-inch iron rod 9 inches long; lay it over end of cincha and sew down with one seam across the end, so as to catch the short or under side of facing, and two seams one-half inch apart along the edge of conical facing. Care must be taken that the sewing extends to ends, so that the $\frac{5}{16}$-inch iron rod will not escape.

Fifteen inches from strap or rod end of cincha sew on a round piece of leather 3 inches in diameter on outside of cincha; punch two ⅜-inch holes, one inch apart in center. This to hold fastening, or finger loop, as it is termed, and should be of good, solid leather. Thong for fastening loop to be 12 inches long and one-half of an inch wide, of best latigo leather, secured underneath, allowing as much loop to extend on outside as possible. Its use is to hold end of latigo or tightening strap when the aparejo is cinched on the animal.

The latigo or tightening strap to be from 7 to 8 feet long; width, 1⅜ inches at heavy end and three-fourths of an inch at light end.

The rendering ring in heavy end of tightening or cincha strap to be of 3-inch breeching ring, dropped into a bight, lapped 2½ inches inward; drop into lap the 3-inch ring, double over so as to leave a space of three-fourths of an inch from end of strap to the inside of lap. This loop is for the lace string to pass through.

Rivet in center of folds and sew down two seams.

The lacing for fastening straps to cincha to be one-half inch wide and 6 feet long; to be of best latigo leather.

The conical facing to be provided with three ⅜-inch holes, two 6 inches apart and one-half inch from rod, the third in center and 1 inch from top.

To fasten cincha and latigo strap with lacing, bring the ends together and pass through hole at center from underneath, allowing a loop of one-half inch to remain underneath, separate ends, and pass down through holes at end.

Take the folds of latigo, ring up, and pass the right end of lacing through loop from right to left and into left-hand hole in cincha from above, pulling sufficient through to pass into the loop in center underneath, about 6 inches.

Take the left-hand lacing and pass through loop from left to right; continue and finish as before.

NOTE.—The irons of cincha will be dipped in asphaltum varnish and allowed to dry before being placed in the folds of leather.

THE CORONA.

(5) To be three thicknesses of blanket; the first or top blanket to be of first-class kersey material, free from shoddy or any impure material; to be of uniform color, gray preferred, and two thicknesses of fair quality, together equaling the strength of the first or top blanket. To be 2 inches wider and 10 inches shorter than the aparejo for which intended; to be faced through center from front to rear with

kersey material contrasting in color with body 14 inches wide; to be sewed down with one seam on edges and one seam through center to first thickness or top blanket.

Center of one side of top blanket is provided with a numeral, 8 inches high, numbers running from 1 to 50, sewed down to first thickness or top blanket. Good tanned sheepskin is required for the purpose. The two thicknesses of underpinning to be basted down to first thickness or top blanket.

Sweat cloth to be of No. 10, 32-inch, cotton duck, 3 inches wider on sides and ends, lapped over corona, 2 inches from the edge all around, to be sewed down (over all) with two seams, machine stitch, three-cord flax thread, six stitches to the inch, measuring three-sixteenths of an inch from the inner edge for the first and 1½ inches for the second. In folding corners bring the overlap at right angles and sew down in customary manner.

THE PACK BLANKET.

(6) *Size.*—To be not less than 8 feet long nor more than 6 feet wide finished.

Weight.—To weigh not less than 5 pounds.

Wool.—To be of pure long, staple wool, free from shoddy, reworked wool, cotton, or any impure material.

Strength.—To be capable of sustaining a tensile strength without breaking of 35 pounds to the inch warp ways and 40 pounds without breaking to the inch filling ways. To insure an even strain on threads, care must be taken that the material is placed in the jaws of the dynamometer at exactly right angles to the opposite system of threads.

Color.—To be a mixture of an olive drab shade as required by standard issue blanket, or may be gray in color.

Border.—An olive-brown border about 3 inches wide to extend across the blanket about 8 inches from each end; the woolen border to be of the same grade as the body of the blanket; to conform in shape to the border of standard issue blanket, and to withstand the official tests for permanency of color.

Brand.—Each blanket to have the letters "U. S., Q. M. C., P. T." not less than 4¾ inches high; the lettering to be worked through the blanket either by hand or machine, using a yarn composed of the same material, shade, and permanency of dye as that of the border, or the letters may be dyed with the best cochineals. Place lengthwise in center of blanket.

Each blanket to be manufactured in a thorough and workmanlike manner, the ends to be secured from raveling by gimp and elastic overlock stitch, as provided for standard-issue blanket.

HALTERS.

(7) To be made of solid black harness leather, regulation size, six ring halters, and provided with brow band and halter shank with swivel snap, size of eyebolt 1 inch, to be provided with a section of one-half inch rope, cut 8 feet long; lap 4 inches on eye and plait down in customary manner, the opposite end to be well wrapped or seized.

One head halter with shank and snap will be provided for each aparejo.

One head halter with shank and snap will be provided for each riding mule.

One head halter with shank and snap will be provided for each bell horse.

PACKERS' BLINDS.

(8) To make a cup blind take a piece of good, solid leather, 26 inches long and 6½ inches wide; cut and shape to leave it 3 inches wide at ends and center and 6½ inches midway between ends and center. Now leave a space of five-eighths of an inch at center of cup and cut out a piece on each side, V shape, 1½ inches at edges; on the under side channel cut and sew together to form cup.

Face edges with strap three-fourths of an inch wide and long enough to come within 2 inches of ends; shave ends to slope and sew down with two seams.

Punch two holes three-fourths of an inch apart and three-fourths of an inch from ends; cut out between for tail thongs to pass through. For thongs cut a strip of best latigo leather five-eighths of an inch wide and 5 feet long; shave ends to slope and pass through slit at ends.

For end facings take a piece of leather 6½ inches square, double and shape to end; punch two holes in center of double three-fourths of an inch apart and cut out between; soak well and slip thongs through slit; draw up snug and sew down with one seam on edges. Thongs to be sewed down through center 9 inches from each end of blind, thongs to be lapped and riveted at end of sewing.

For thumb piece take a piece of leather 12 inches long and 3½ inches wide; punch and slit in 1 inch from edge and 3 inches from ends on each side. Lap the sides inward, so as to catch edges, and sew down with one seam. Draw it well together and cut ends, so as to shape in between straps; place in center of crown and sew down with one seam on edge, and rivet on each side of crown.

For every five aparejos one packer's blind will be provided.

For each organized pack train of 50 pack mules, 14 packer's blinds will be provided.

PACK COVERS.

(9) Made of 72-inch No. 4 cotton duck, cut 6 feet long; allow 1 inch at either end for hemming, to be sewed down at ends with three-cord flax thread, machine stitch, six stitches to the inch. Two for each aparejo.

RIGGING COVERS.

(10) Made of 22-inch No. 2 cotton duck, cut two lengths 24 feet long; to be lapped and sewed along one side with three-cord flax thread, machine stitch, six stitches to the inch, ends to be hemmed. Five for each organized pack train.

CARGO COVERS.

(11) Made of 28-inch No. 10 cotton duck, cut five widths 12 feet long; lapped on border line and hemmed at ends; to be sewed down with flat seam, with six-cord yellow machine thread, machine stitch, six stitches to the inch. Five for each organized pack train.

FEED COVERS.

(12) Made of 44-inch No. 10 cotton duck; to be 24 feet long, hemmed at ends, to be sewed down with three-cord flax thread, machine stitch, six stitches to the inch. Five for each organized pack train.

LASH ROPE WITH CINCHA AND HOOK.

(13) Lash rope, standard size to be nine-sixteenths or one-half inch best hand-laid manila, 50 feet long, provided with an eye at one end to receive lacing of cincha, the opposite end to be well wrapped or seized.

For cincha provide a section of 28-inch No. 10 cotton duck 18 inches wide; fold so as to have a width of 6 inches sewed down with one seam one-fourth of an inch from each edge.

On each end provide a semicircular facing of leather, the same under as well as over, length of facing to be 5 inches; the straight edge of facing to be parallel or flush with end of cincha, one end to be provided with five holes three-eighths of an inch in diameter. The first two to be spaced equally distant three-fourths of an inch from end of cincha and 3½ inches apart; the second two to be spaced in similar manner 2¾ inches from end of cincha and 4½ inches apart; the third or center hole to be placed at center at top and three-fourths of an inch from center of semicircle. These to receive lacings of cincha; facings to be sewed down all around with two seams one-half of an inch apart and one-fourth of an inch from edge.

Lacings to be secured to eye on lash rope in customary manner.

Facings on opposite end to be sewed down on semicircle with two seams one-half of an inch apart and one-fourth of an inch from edge; on open end provide four holes to correspond with holes provided on cincha hook, introduce the hook between the folds of cincha, place in center, and rivet down with No. 8 copper rivets.

Cincha hook to be as per sample and model furnished Quartermaster General's Office, and to be 16 parts aluminum and 1 part copper. (Designed by H. W. Daly. Adopted December, 1909.) One lash rope will be provided for each aparejo.

SLING ROPES.

(14) To be made of ⅜-inch best hand-laid manila, wrapped or seized at each end, and to be 30 feet long. One for each aparejo.

LAIR ROPES.

(15) To be made of ⅜-inch best hand-laid manila; to be provided with an eye at one end, the opposite end to be well wrapped or seized, and to be 30 feet long. Two for each aparejo.

STAMPING.

(16) The body of the aparejo and crupper should have their length and maker's name stamped on them. The aparejo cover, cincha, and corona should have the length of the aparejo stenciled on them, so that it may be readily known what parts belong together without measuring. Care must be taken to stencil corona on sweat cloth.

RIBBING FOR DALY APAREJOS.

(17) The ribbing consists of the following:

Two saddle bars (wood), right and left.

Two boot bars (wood), right and left.

Eighteen hickory ribs, consisting of two half sets of nine each, equally alike, with 6 pounds of suitable soft hay for padding or filling for each aparejo.

Two locking bars for saddle bars 19⅝ inches long, 1¾ inches wide, gauge 16.

Key bars for locking bars to be 23 inches long, five-eighths of an inch wide, and three thirty-seconds of an inch thick.

Locking bar for boot bar to be 19⅝ inches long and 1 inch wide, gauge 16.

Sixty flathead brass screws three-fourths of an inch, No. 6.

Saddle bars.—Take two pieces of clear basswood, free of blemishes, 21 inches long, 7 inches wide, and 2 inches thick.

Saddle bars, right and left, to be cut in at one end with two offsets.

First offset to be cut at right angles, 3¼ inches at one end, one way, by 2⅞ inches from upper edge.

Second offset to be cut at right angles at same upper and front end 5⅜ inches, one way, by 1 inch from upper edge.

These offsets are cut and shaped to fit under the collar of the aparejos and are considered the forward or front end of saddle bars.

Now space off "gains" of nine equal parts, commencing at both ends to center of "gain," which must be 2$\frac{11}{16}$ inches; width of gains to be 1⅛ inches; length of gains, 3¾ inches; depth of gains to be three-fourths of an inch.

Now gain for brass key bar, three-fourths of an inch wide and three-sixteenths of an inch deep. Position of gain for key bar to be 3¾ inches from upper edge to center of gain, extending from front to rear.

Next gain for "locking bar," 1¾ inches wide and one-sixteenth of an inch deep, 19⅝ inches long, spaced equally distant from each end, center of locking bar over center of key bar.

Locking bar for saddle bar.—To be of sheet brass 19 inches long, 1¾ inches wide, and one-sixteenth of an inch thick (gauge 16).

Locking bar is spaced off into nine equal parts, allowing three-fourths of an inch to fit into gains. This portion will be turned at right angles so as to fit snugly against the wall of gain, and provided with 20 holes to receive flathead brass screws three-fourths of an inch, No. 6, and screwed down to saddle bar.

Key bar.—Key bar to be of spring brass 23 inches long, five-eighths of an inch wide, and three thirty-seconds of an inch thick, rounded and slightly tapered at one end; the reverse or opposite end to be rounded and provided with a hole three-eighths of an inch from end, this to receive leather thong; diameter of hole, three-sixteenths of an inch.

Saddle bars, right and left, to be shaped on both sides as per sample furnished.

(18) *Boot bars.*—Take two pieces of clear basswood free of blemishes 21 inches long, 6 inches wide, and 3 inches thick.

Now space off "gains" of nine equal parts exactly similar to those provided in saddle bars. Length of gains, 4¾ inches.

75927°—17——12

Now gain for "locking" bar, 1 inch wide and one-sixteenth of an inch deep, 19⅝ inches long, spaced equally distant from each end, exactly similar as that provided in locking bar for saddle bar.

Locking bar for boot bar.—To be of sheet brass 19 inches long, 1¼ inches wide, and one-sixteenth of an inch thick (gauge 16).

Locking bar for boot is spaced off in similar manner as that provided in locking bar for saddle bar and turned at right angles so as to fit snugly against the wall of gain. It will be noted that while the portion fitting into gains in saddle bar faces downward, that supplied in boot bar faces upward. This leaves a space or portion of three-fourths of an inch extending over gains the length of locking bar.

Now supply one hole at center of each space to receive flathead brass screws three-fourths of an inch, No. 6, and screw down to boot bar.

All holes on brassing must be countersunk to receive screws.

Boot bars to be shaped on both sides, right and left, as per sample furnished. (Designed by H. W. Daly.)

HICKORY RIBS.

(19) To be of sound second growth straight-grained hickory, free of knots or other blemishes; 23 inches long, 1 inch wide, and three-eighths of an inch thick for 60-inch aparejos; 24 inches long for 62-inch aparejos, and 22 inches long for 58-inch aparejos.

In a half set of nine ribs, the third has a taper of 8 inches at its upper end, thickness at end to be three-sixteenths of an inch; for the fourth, fifth, sixth, seventh, eighth, and ninth, successively, a gain of 2 inches in the taper is provided.

On one side at bottom and 2 inches therefrom, numerals indicating the size of the aparejo, with number of rib, will be stamped thereon, a hyphen or dash to be used in separating the number of ribs from the number of aparejo.

In numbering the set of nine ribs, commence with the two that are not tapered; these to be numbered 1 and 2 each.

Two half sets of nine ribs each comprise a complete set for one aparejo.

In lots of 50 sets, 25 to be 23 inches long; 13 to be 24 inches long, and 12 to be 22 inches long, respectively.

All work to be done in a first-class and accurate manner.

HAY.

(20) Hay to be free of joints, or what is known as "swamp" hay; that is, fine, soft, elastic hay, and for each aparejo 6 pounds will be considered sufficient.

ALUMINUM CASTINGS FOR BOOTS AND SADDLE BARS.

(21) In lieu of the spaces (wood) between gains on boot and saddle bars, the spaces or separators, wood may be removed, the gain extending from front to rear between shoulders on boots and saddle bars, depth of gain to be 1 inch, depth of gain on shoulders, for key bar of saddle bars to be three-fourths of an inch wide and one-fourth of an inch deep; this for the key bar to pass between slots as provided on aluminum castings for saddle bars; aluminum castings for boot and saddle bars are provided with nine spaces for ribs of frame.

To strengthen the aparejo an additional rib cut 1 inch shorter may be employed between the first and second ribs under the collar of the aparejo as provided on the boots and saddle bars, of castings, as per sample at Jeffersonville Depot, Indiana. For aparejos cut 22 inches wide, the frame and castings are 2 inches less in width, and carry one rib less than for aparejos cut 24 inches wide.

HICKORY RIBS FOR ALUMINUM CASTINGS.

(22) To be made of second-growth hickory, free from knots and blemishes. Ribs for 62-inch aparejos to be 20; to be cut 25 inches long, 1 inch wide and three-eighths inch thick; composed of two half sets of 10 ribs, each half set to be equally alike, and to be numbered serially from 1 to 10; numbers to be stamped parallel with length of stick placed 6 inches from butt end of stick. Each half set of 10 ribs to be tapered in the following manner: Nos. 1, 2, and 3 are for the collar of the aparejo and are not provided with taper; No. 2, however, is cut 1 inch shorter than Nos. 1 and 3. No. 4 will be provided with a taper on one side, commencing 15 inches from butt to opposite end at top of stick, thickness at top end to be three-sixteenths of an inch. This provides a taper of 10 inches for No. 4. Each successive rib will have an increase in taper of 1½ inches. Thus, No. 4 has 10 inches and No. 10 has 19 inches in length of taper; that is, 6 inches from butt end to top of rib.

No. 2, however, will have a taper on right edge of one-fourth of an inch, commencing 5 inches from top end of rib, holding numbered side up. This is to permit No. 2 to be placed in position in space between slots Nos. 1 and 2 of saddle bar, and slot 2, as provided in boot bar. For each complete set of ribs from a 62-inch to a 52-inch aparejo a successive decrease of 1 inch in length will be provided.

That is, from 25 inches in length for a 62-inch aparejo, to 20 inches in length for a 52-inch aparejo. However, for 56, 54, and 52 inch aparejo, a uniform width of 22 inches is provided. This provision gives a complete set of 18 ribs composed of two half sets of 9 ribs, to be tapered in similar manner as provided for a 62-inch aparejo from No. 4 to No. 9; that is, a successive gain of 10 inches for No. 4 to 17½ inches for No. 9. Aluminum castings for saddle and boot bars and key bars (brass), to be 2 inches shorter for aparejos 22 inches wide than for aparejos 24 inches wide, as per sample furnished. All work to be done in a first-class and accurate manner.

RIDING SADDLES (PACKERS'), QUARTERMASTER'S (STOCK) CORPS.

Specifications for full-rigged riding saddle.

(Figs 111, 112, 113.)

(1) SEC. 131. This saddle is furnished only for use of the personnel of pack trains and pack-train sections, wagon masters, and assistant wagon masters. (Design modified by H. W. Daly.)

1. *Tree.*—To be No. 1013, modified "Wild West" tree, from 15 to 16 inch seat, 5-inch fork, 2¾-inch oval head, steel fork, grooved bars, beef-hide cover.

2. *Rigging.*—Saddle to be full rigged, with two girths (cotton preferred) of 18 strands for the front and 24 strands for the rear girth, and to be of two bar girths, with connecting straps and buckle.

3. *Stirrups.*—Stirrup to be 2-inch wooden stirrup, 5-inch tread, 3-inch neck, 1-bolt stirrup, reenforced with galvanized iron or brass binding.

4. *Leather.*—To be of hemlock or best oak tan leather, firm and solid in texture, and capable of withstanding a strain of 100 pounds when a section 6 inches long and one-fourth of an inch wide is cut into on the side, and not tear apart under strain of 100 pounds pressure.

5. *Tan.*—To be russet or fair in color and fast in grain.

6. *Skirting.*—To be full size and sheepskin wool lined, and to be not less than 30 inches long, 15½ inches wide at rear, and 14 inches wide at front end.

7. *Quarter straps.*—To extend around cantle and pommel, 3 inches wide for the pommel and 2 inches wide for the cantle, with connecting strâp 1½ inches wide, and long enough so that when doubled the distance from end to end will be not less than 9 inches long, the double of strap to meet at center of its length and to be secured with lacing, holes of suitable size, two at each end of strap, and securely tied.

8. *Stirrup leather.*—To be of good solid leather 3 inches wide and long enough to permit of adjustment for 34-inch leg, as in customary manner.

9. *Stirrup fender.*—To be 18¼ inches long and 10¾ inches wide. Fender stays 19 inches long and 3 inches wide.

10. *Girth straps.*—To be 19 inches long and 1¾ inches wide.

11. *Tie straps.*—To be 5 feet 7 inches long and 1¾ inches wide.

12. *Seat.*—The reenforcings in forming the seat of the saddle when finished to be well rounded and bound on the front edge, and well glued down to seat with best "Days" dry paste; the seat and jockeys to be of one piece.

13. *Cantle.*—The cantle of saddle on rounded edge to be bound all around with similar leather in a neat and accurate manner, and provided with small leather pocket in rear of cantle, and provided with bellows 1 inch wide; the upper strings over cantle must pass through the center of quarter strap; care must be taken in passing string through sheepskin wool lining that the string is properly bedded in the wool, the space between holes to be not less than three-fourths of an inch.

14. *Housings.*—To be of full size at front and rear, and to receive the strings of saddle as in customary manner, all exposed leather to be creased with two-bar crease on edges, and light, but not elaborate, stamping on exposed leather is permitted.

15. Nails, tacks, and rivets are not permitted in rigging the saddle, except in the "gullet" where small round-head brass nails may be employed in the customary manner.

16. *Saddletree.*—To be as modified, on the under surface of the bars, as shown in sample saddle now at the general depot of the Quartermaster's Department, Jeffersonville, Ind., made January 23, 1909.

17. All work to be done in a first-class and accurate manner.

Specifications for skeleton-rigged riding saddle.

(Figs 112, 113.)

(2) This saddle is furnished for teamsters and mounted messengers and for all other persons in the military service requiring riding

saddles which under the existing regulations are not supplied by the Ordnance Department, nor provided with the full-rigged riding saddle.

1. *Tree.*—To be No. 1013, modified "Wild West" tree, from 15 to 16 inch seat, 5-inch fork, 2¾-inch oval head, steel horn, beef-hide cover. Tree to be covered with No. 1 "Fair" collar leather.

2. *Rigging.*—Saddle to be "skeleton" rigged in a similar manner as provided for the full-rigged saddle, with the exception that the skirting and housings are omitted.

3. In sewing the cover down to saddletree sufficient space must be omitted at top and bottom of grooves that receive the stirrup leathers, the top surface of saddle bars to be reenforced on each side of stirrup leathers, to permit of rounding up the seat; at beginning and ending of all stitching three full back stitches to be made.

4. *Stirrup leathers.*—To be provided with stirrup fenders as in full-rigged saddle.

5. *Stirrup.*—To be of similar make and finish as provided for full-rigged saddle.

6. *Leather.* To be hemlock or oak, tan finish, best quality, and subjected to similar test as provided for in the full-rigged saddle.

7. All work to be done in a first-class and accurate manner.

(Approved by the Quartermaster General of the Army, November 11, 1909.)

BRIDLES

(3) *Bridles.*—Regulation size and make and provided with bits short in branch and of strong make.

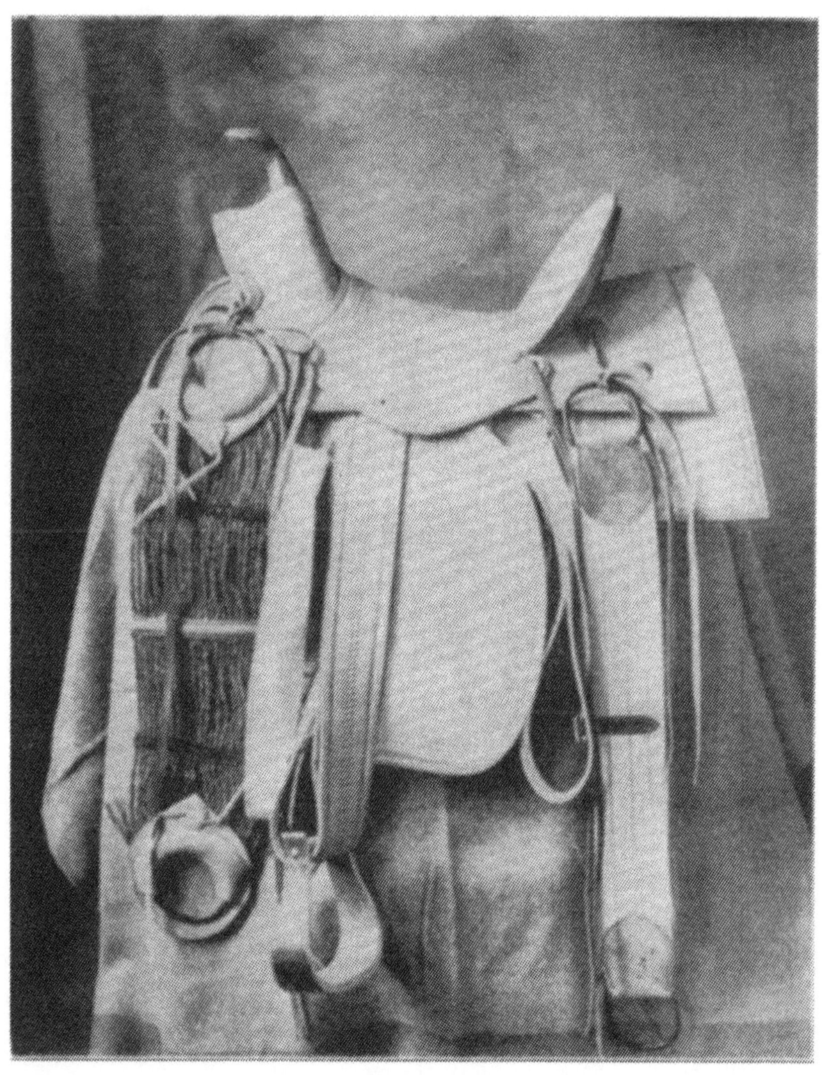

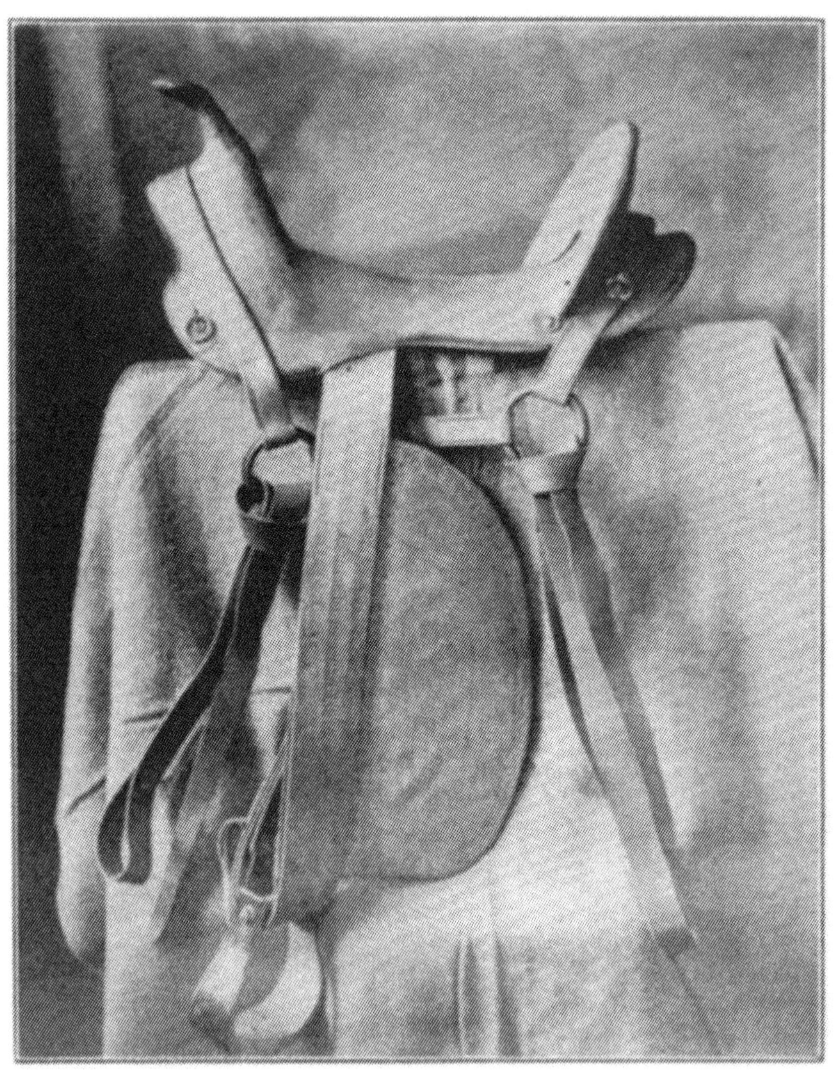

SEC. 132.—

Table showing weights of pack saddles and equipments.

THE APAREJO PROPER

	Weight	Total	
		Old method	New method
	Lbs. oz	*Lbs oz.*	*Lbs oz*
Body	18 0		
Crupper	7 0		
Cover	7 0		
Cincha	5 0		
Corona	5 0		
		42 0	42 0
Accessories:			
Lash rope with cincha and hook	6 0		
Sling rope	1 4		
Lair ropes (2)	2 4		
Pack covers (2)	11 0		
Pack blanket	5 0		
Head halter	2 8		
Blind	1 8		
		29 8	29 8
Set-up:			
Boot sticks (2)	2 0		
Sticks, willow (56)	7 0		
Hay	8 4		
		17 4	
Total, old method		88 12	
Daly aparejo set-up:			
Saddle bars (2)		6 0	
Boot bars (2)		6 0	
Ribs, hickory (18)		4 0	
Hay		6 0	
			22 0
Total, new method			93 8

THE CROSSTREE OR SAWBUCK

Saddle, Breeching, Breast strap	9 0		
Corona	5 0		
		14 0	
Accessories, same as aparejo		29 8	
Total			43 8

THE MOORE PACK SADDLE

Saddle	32 8		
Crupper	5 0		
Cincha	5 8		
Corona	5 0		
		48 0	
Accessories, same as aparejo		29 8	
Total			77 8

CHAPTER VIII.

SPECIAL DEVICES.

PACKING DEVICE (QUARTERMASTER CORPS).

(Figs 114, 115, 116, 117)

SEC. 133. This device consists of three parts—the frame, the platforms (2), the lashing. (Figs. 114, 115, 116, 117).

The packing device was designed to meet the requirements of men not skilled in the use of the diamond and other hitches to secure a load on the pack mule.

To assemble the pack device.—Place the frame on the aparejo so that its staple holes fit over the staples on the latter; and pass the straps on the sobre-jalma through the staples; pass the cincha over the side bars, finger loop up, and cincha strap to the left; double the cincha over the frame, strap inside; double or turn the crupper forward so that the dock piece rests on the cincha.

To place the aparejo on the mule, see Chapter III, sections 18 to 23, inclusive. The "frame" of the packing device being attached to the aparejo, two packers should assist in placing the aparejo on the mule, from rear to front, in proper position, and cinching in customary manner. The platforms are now placed in position, one on each side of the frame, the top and bottom rods resting on the hook plates or rests, spaced apart as may be required by the conditions of loading, as each platform is independent of the other, the "near" side platform may be carried higher on the hook plates, as the greater weight of the near side pack may require, so as to balance the load evenly on the pack mule; the locks or holdfasts are then adjusted, the hooks of the locks being pressed into the under openings of the hook plates or rests, thus holding the platforms rigidly in position; the side packs or top load, as conditions may be, are placed on the platforms and the load secured by its lashing. To place the "lashing" on the load, each packer will hold one-half of lashing, embracing three latigos, so as to keep the lash rods toward the body, then from rear to front elevate or swing the lashing so as to rest on top and center of load; the center latigo on each side is then made fast to the drop link at center of distance rod, observing the square of lashing is kept on center and top of load; this leaves a latigo fore and aft on each side of the load; now attach the ropes for lashing, one on each side, to the forward latigo, then bring the rope section under the boot of the aparejo, and attach the latigo at rear to the ring on end of section of rope, taking slack on latigos fore and aft, to securely tighten the load, always observing the section of rope is kept evenly divided fore and aft. It will be noticed that drop links are provided on the platforms fore and aft. The latigos may pass through these drop links before attaching to the rings on each end

of sections of rope, as may be required by the size of loading, usually to packages of small dimensions.

It is also important that the latigos engage over the upper corners of each side pack fore and aft, as is customary when securing the load with the diamond hitch method.

The platforms take the place of the "sling rope," the lashing takes the place of the diamond hitch. The hook plates of the frame are arranged so that the load may be balanced by raising or lowering the platforms as may be determined—as near an application of the diamond hitch method, the oldest and best, as may be provided.

THE DALY PACKING DEVICE.

SPECIFICATIONS

Standard size to be 54¾ inches from end to end and 19 inches wide throughout its entire length.

CONSTRUCTION

The device consists of three parts—(1) the frame, (2) the platforms, (3) the lashing.

(1) *The frame.*	
Hinges	2
Side plates	4
Hook plates	4
Distance plates	2
Distance shoes (wooden)	2
Reenforcing plates for shoes	2
Bolts for hinges	4
Rivets, iron	16
Rivets, copper	6

(2) *The platforms*	
Distance rods	6
Center plates for distance rods	2
Supports	4
Legs	4
Locks or holdfasts	4
Drop links	6
Staples for links	8
Distance boards for platforms	6
Reenforcing plates for boards	6
Rivets, iron	24
Rivets, copper	18

(3) *The lashing*	
Lash rods	2
D rings	10
Squares	2
Rings	4
Canvas	10 by 14
Facings for lashing (leather)	2
Straps for lashing (leather)	7
Latigos for lashing (leather)	6
Ropes for lashing	2

DETAILED SPECIFICATIONS

(1) *The frame.*

To be made of best spring steel 1½ inches wide and one-eighth of an inch thick.

For hinges (2), cut a section 13 inches long 2½ inches from each end, cut out a slot 1⅜ inches long and three-fourths of an inch wide; this to form eye for bolts. Circle section and weld both ends; then compress circle to a radius of seven-eighths of an inch diameter, leaving a space between the folds of hinge one-fourth of an inch diameter. A templet is good for the purpose; in shaping templet round each end and introduce between the folds of hinge when cold.

In introducing templets care must be taken that the ends of templet meet the center of slots, forming eye to receive side plates for hinge.

Side plates (4).—For side plates cut a section 32¼ inches long. At one end an opening is formed to carry the distance board of frame, opening for distance board to be 2½ inches long by three-fourths of an inch wide. In forming opening an extension is allowed on this end to form a hook on the outward face of opening, and is arranged in this manner:

Commence at end selected and measure off three-fourths of an inch and mark with punch on each edge; in similar manner mark off one-half of an inch, then 2½ inches, 3½ inches, and three-fourths of an inch. This gives 8 inches marked off on end, to form opening and hook on end of side plate, and will be considered the lower end of side plate.

In forming hook, it is well to commence at end. To do so, commence at the second line of markings 1¼ inches from end; turn this portion at right angles, and three-fourths of an inch from end turn again at right angles.

Now, on the space marked 2½ inches form a hook, depth of hook to be 1 inch; mouth of hook to be five-eighths of an inch wide. Now bend or compress sufficient of the space marked 3½ inches, so as to be flush with under and forward surface of hook; and at markings turn at right angles, and at last markings turn again at right angles. This forms the opening for the distance board, whose inside dimensions will be 2½ by three-fourths inches. This should leave the extension of side plate 24¼ inches long.

It will be noted, in the formation of opening for distance board, there is an angular opening on the under surface in the formation of the hook; the base of this opening should be not less than three-fourths of an inch.

In the formation of hooks on the hook plates, these openings are utilized by the locks or holdfasts provided on legs of platforms, to hold platforms securely.

Hook plates for side plates (4).—Hook plates to be 44 inches long and in their formation 7 hooks will be provided, arranged in the following manner:

Commencing at one end, space and mark off with punch on each edge, the following distances:

Three inches from end selected mark and punch; then 1⅜ inches further in similar manner; then 1½ inches; and then 6 spaces of 5¾ inches each; this leaves 3⅝ inches at opposite end for the outward portion of last hook on hook plate.

Now commence at first, or top end of hook plate, and at space whose distance is 1⅜ inches, cut out a section on each side of three-eighths of an inch wide; this leaves three-fourths of an inch at center. Now lap the end over at center of this space to form eye for bolt of hinge, diameter of eye to be one-fourth of an inch.

The 3-inch laps will be considered the under side of hook plate, and are to receive the distance plates of frame.

Now on the space of 1½ inches, form a hook whose depth will be three-fourths of an inch, mouth of hook to be five-eighths of an inch wide.

On the remaining six sections marked off, form hooks, whose depth will be 1 inch; mouth of hooks to be five-eighths of an inch wide. In the accurate formation of the hooks a templet is good for the purpose; hook plates to be as per sample furnished.

In assembling hook plates to side plates, the free end of side plates engages into the fold of hook plates, and to meet the shoulders of hinge; the opposite end of side plates engages into the free end of hook plates, this operation gives 8 hooks on the upper or face side of side plates; at the lower end of engagement one hole will be provided at center through hook plate and side plate, diameter of hole three-sixteenths of an inch, and riveted down. At the upper end between first and second hooks, two holes will be provided, in a diagonal line in similar manner; these holes to receive side plates of frame.

Both side plates and hook plates assembled must *positively* be in straight alignment, one with the other.

Distance plates.—To be 23 inches long, 3 inches wide, and one-eighth of an inch thick; at each end of distance plate provide a slot 1¼ inches long and five-sixteenths of an inch wide. Slot to be in center of distance plate and one-half of an inch from each end and to be parallel with length of distance plate. These slots or openings are to receive staples of chock plates that hold frame to aparejo.

In adjusting distance plates to side plates, measure 9½ inches each way from center of distance plate for side plates, from out to out. This leaves 2 inches at each end of distance plate, extending from side plate. The lower edge of distance plates to be flush with the lower edge of the 3-inch lap as provided on hook plates. Two holes will be provided at front and rear to correspond with those provided on hook and side plates, distance plates to be placed on the under side of 3-inch lap and riveted down.

Distance boards or shoes, wooden (2).—To be of good, sound hickory, free of knots and blemishes, and to be 19 inches long, 2½ inches wide, and eleven-sixteenths of an inch thick.

One and one-half inches from each end saw down to a depth of five-sixteenths of an inch on one side, portion between cuts to be "gained" out in a smooth and accurate manner, the upper and lower edges of "gained" surface to be rounded off.

Reenforced plates for shoes (2).—To be of band steel, gauge 14, and of dimensions similar to distance shoes. These to be placed on the under side of distance shoes. The flat surface of shoes will be considered the under side.

Reenforce plates to be secured to distance shoes by copper rivets, holes being provided on gained surface of distance shoes spaced equally distant, one at center and one at each end and 2 inches therefrom, holes will be provided on reenforce plates to correspond with distance shoe, diameter of holes to be three-sixteenths of an inch.

In assembling side plates and distance shoes it is well to introduce distance shoes first, care being taken to square the side plates when applying distance plates.

Now connect side plates with hinges, using 1⅞-inch bolts, oval head, and rivet down over nut.

At ends of side plates provide one hole at center three-fourths of an inch from end, hole to pass through metal and wood, secure rivets and rivet down on the under side.

(2) *The platforms.*

Platforms (2).—To be made of best Norway iron.

For distance rods cut three sections of ½-inch round iron.

The first section to be 22¼ inches long; the second or outward section to be 21½ inches long; the third section to be 20¾ inches long.

On the first and third distance rods provide an offset of three-fourths of an inch deep, length of offset to be 10 inches.

The second distance rod to be straight along its length.

Supports (*4*).—Cut a section of Norway flat iron 13¾ inches long, three-fourths of an inch wide and one-fourth of an inch thick. Provide an eye on each end of supports large enough to take one-half inch iron rod.

Legs (*4*).—To be of similar material, 15½ inches long, provided with eye on each end in similar manner.

In assembling legs to second distance rod leave a space of 15¾ inches from outside to outside, measuring distance from center of rod each way; now provide a three-sixteenths of an inch hole through legs and rod, and rivet down.

In assembling supports to second distance rod, engage the eyes of supports over each end of rod and leave a distance of 19¼ inches from inside to inside between supports, counting from center of rod each way. Now form a head on each end of rod one-fourth of an inch wide outside of head to be flush with eye of support.

In assembling the first distance rod to opposite end of supports introduce through eyes of supports, leaving a distance of 19¼ inches from inside to inside between supports, counting from center of rod both ways, and weld the eye of supports to distance rods. Now cut off whatever portion may remain on the outside and smooth down.

In assembling the third distance rod to the eye on opposite end of legs introduce rod through eye on legs and leave a distance of 19¼ inches from inside to inside between legs, counting from center of rod both ways, and rivet down in similar manner as at opposite end of legs. Now form a head on each end of rod one-fourth of an inch wide, outside of head to be flush with eye of support.

Center plates for distance rods (*2*).—To be of similar material as provided for side plates and to be 11 inches long. Form an eye on each end of plate, diameter of eye to be one-half of an inch; center plate to be engaged on first and second distance rods and center thereof.

Locks or holdfasts (*4*).—To be made of similar material as that provided for supports and legs, to be cut 11 inches long.

At one end and one-half of an inch therefrom provide a slot or opening whose length will be 1½ inches long and five-sixteenths of an inch wide; this to receive bolt for securing lock to legs of platform.

Now measure 6 inches from this end, turning section to an angle of 45°. Three inches from base of angle turn the remaining portion at right angles; diameter or distance from the under side of the right angled portion to base line of lock held horizontally to be 2⅛ inches. The portion turned at right angles or end of lock to be rounded; length to be not more than 1½ inches.

For each lock a 1-inch bolt, holding a wing nut, will be provided.

On each leg, counting 2½ inches from eye of leg on second distance rod a ¼-inch hole will be provided at center of leg; punch this hole square by metal punch.

Introduce a 1-inch bolt from outside of leg, and lay on to bolt the lock or holdfast as provided by slot or opening, and screw down with wing nut.

Locks to be right and left.

These locks or holdfasts engage into opening as provided on hook plates, as formed by the lapping of hook plates on side plates.

Drop links (*6*).—To be of ¼-inch round iron, cut 10 inches long; on each end of one section form an eye whose diameter will be three-eighths of an inch. Now, 1 inch from center of section both ways turn at right angles to form drop links.

Staples for links (*8*).—Cut a section of similar material 3 inches long; at center of section form semicircle over templet, templet to be of ½-inch round iron; diameter at base of semicircle to be 1 inch. One-half of an inch of each end to be flattened to a thickness of one-eighth of an inch; length of flattened surface to be not more than five-eighths of an inch and punch one hole at center of each end; diameter of hole to be three-sixteenths of an inch.

Now introduce a staple into each eye of drop link and place on the under surface of supports in such manner so that one rivet will engage the second and third distance boards and supports; the opposite end of staple will be riveted down to supports.

Distance boards for platforms (*6*).—To be of good, sound hickory, free of knots and blemishes. To be 20¾ inches long, 1½ inches wide, and one-half of an inch thick.

Reenforcing plates for distance boards (*6*).—To be of band steel, 1½ inches wide, gauge 18, length corresponding with length of distance boards.

In applying distance boards to supports space equally distant in such manner as to carry one rivet on the second and third distance boards at each end and center, this for the purpose of receiving one eye of staple holding drop link, the eye at opposite end of staple will be riveted down to support; at center of distance boards rivet down to center plates; in similar manner in center of space between ends and center plates, rivet reenforcing plates to distance boards.

The reenforcing plates will be considered the under side when applying distance boards to supports. All rivets between supports to be copper rivets; all rivets on supports to be iron rivets.

The remaining two drop links to be applied at center of second distance rod, engaging center plates between the eyes of drop links. All work to be done in a first-class and accurate manner.

(3) *The lashing.*

Rods for lashing (*2*).—To be of round iron $\frac{5}{16}$ of an inch diameter, to be cut 18 inches long; form eye on each end of rod, diameter of eye to be one-half of an inch.

Each eye of lash rods to carry a "D" ring. "D" rings to be of No. 326 X. C. D's.

For each lash rod a metal square will be provided, No. 1155 japanned square. These to be carried on fold of center strap of lashing.

Canvas for lashing.—To be of brown or khaki color, No. 4 cotton duck; to be cut 14 inches long and 10 inches wide.

On each end of canvas, the short way, lay a lash rod and fold over so as to leave a distance of 10 inches, and sew down with basting stitch.

Facings for lashing (*2*).—To be of good, solid, fair leather. Cut two sections 10 inches long and 7 inches wide; semicircle each section the long way, lay each section over distance rods in similar manner as described for canvas section, facings to meet in center of canvas; the semicircular portion to be considered the upper or outer side of lashing. Sew down semicircles with one seam one-fourth of an inch from edge.

Straps for lashing (7).—Cut one section 15 inches long and 2 inches wide; this strap to be applied over semicircular facings at center, carrying at each end a metal square as provided; the fold of leather holding metal square to be lapped under and the whole sewed down with one seam one-fourth of an inch from each edge.

Now cut six straps 22 inches long and 2 inches wide, double so as to have a length of 10 inches; on one end of each strap drop a 2-inch "D" ring; on opposite end lap strap over "D" portion of ring as provided on lash rods and sew down with one seam on each edge and one-fourth of an inch therefrom.

The remaining two straps will be lapped over square, held by center strap of lashing, the opposite end of strap holding "D" ring in similar manner, and sew down as before.

Latigos for lashing (6).—For each "D" ring on end of straps cut a strap of latigo leather 6 feet long and 1¼ inches wide; taper the lightest end of latigos.

Lap the heaviest end of latigos over "D" rings 3 inches and provide 3 holes for lacing, No. 8 punch. Two holes to be spaced equally distant apart in a horizontal line, the third to be at center of latigo and three-fourths of an inch therefrom.

Provide a lace string for each latigo wide enough to pass through holes provided thereon; finish lacing on hole at center.

Ropes for lashing (2).—Cut two sections of rope, best hand-laid manila, one-half inch diameter and 4 feet long; form an eye on each end of rope, each eye of rope to carry a 2-inch ring.

In assembling ring on each end of ropes connect the front and rear of first and third latigos with rings on ropes in such manner as in cinching a saddle.

In the application of the lashing, the lash rods or "form" of lashing rest on top and center of load, the latigos running downward over corners of side packs, and the rope sections under the boots of the aparejo at front and rear; the center latigo is secured to metal square at center of platforms, and the whole tied down as in cinching a saddle in customary manner. (Designed by H. W. Daly.)

Table showing weights of packing device

	Total.					
	Pounds.	Ounces.	Pounds.	Ounces.	Pounds.	Ounces.
Packing device for aparejo						
Frame	24					
Platforms	22					
Lashing	9					
Total	55					

TOOL POUCHES (ENGINEER CORPS).

(Figs 118, 119)

SEC. 134. The necessity for tool pouches has been the cause of the various troubles which the packer has had, from time to time, to provide suitable means to transport with safety the different tools employed by the Engineer Corps and afford proper protection for the body of the animal.

The assembly of the various tools, etc., so as to give ready access when needed, without the necessity of taking off the load, has been considered of vital importance to the rapid movements of detachments of the Engineer Corps under certain conditions.

To meet this contingency the tool pouches were designed.

The pouches are made of good, solid leather, about 60 inches long, 55 inches wide at ends, and 24 inches wide at center or middle, and carry two pockets on either side; the larger, at bottom, for such tools as short-handled shovels, axes, etc.; the smaller, at top or middle, for picks, augers, nails, sledge hammers, etc.

These pouches are secured to the aparejo by straps at front and rear, at the top, or middle, buckles being provided on the aparejo for this purpose, and at bottom of pouches by straps passing under the boots of the aparejo.

The pouches are further provided with a metallic device for carrying such tools as crowbars or implements of greater length than the lower pockets.

The device is attached to the pouches at top or middle by means of hinges with suitable provisions to retain crowbars in position.

PACK CHESTS (ENGINEER CORPS).

(Fig 120)

SEC. 135. These chests or boxes, like the tool pouches, were designed to be carried on the aparejo and may be used for carrying a small supply of prepared rations, or the interior of chests may be arranged for safely carrying explosive material or other supplies.

They are supplied on their exterior with metallic fasteners for securing chests on the aparejo so that the contents may be extracted without taking the boxes off the pack mule.

The following list of articles of engineer equipment and methods of packing them for the allowance of such equipments assigned to each squadron of cavalry and each troop of cavalry in the field has been approved by the Secretary of War:

Box No. 1. Outside dimensions 2 feet 8 inches by 12 by 12 inches, containing 1 box, match; 100 caps, detonating; 200 feet Bickford fuse; 200 feet instantaneous fuse; 50 pounds explosive. Weight, when packed, 85 pounds.

Box No. 2. Outside dimensions 4 feet 6 inches by 8 by 6¼ inches, containing 2 crowbars, 2 drills, double bitted; 2 hammers, drilling; 1 hammer, engineer; 1 pliers, 1 chisel, cold; 1 wrench, monkey; 1 spoon, drilling; 1 shoe, mule, set. Weight, when packed, 103 pounds.

For each troop outfit, 2 bundles, 5 shovels each, 60 pounds; 1 bundle, 5 shovels and 1 crowbar, 42 pounds.

Box No. 1. Outside dimensions 3 feet 7 inches by 11 by 8½ inches, containing 6 pliers, wire cutting; 5 pick mattocks, 1 auger, 2 rules. Weight, when packed, 80 pounds.

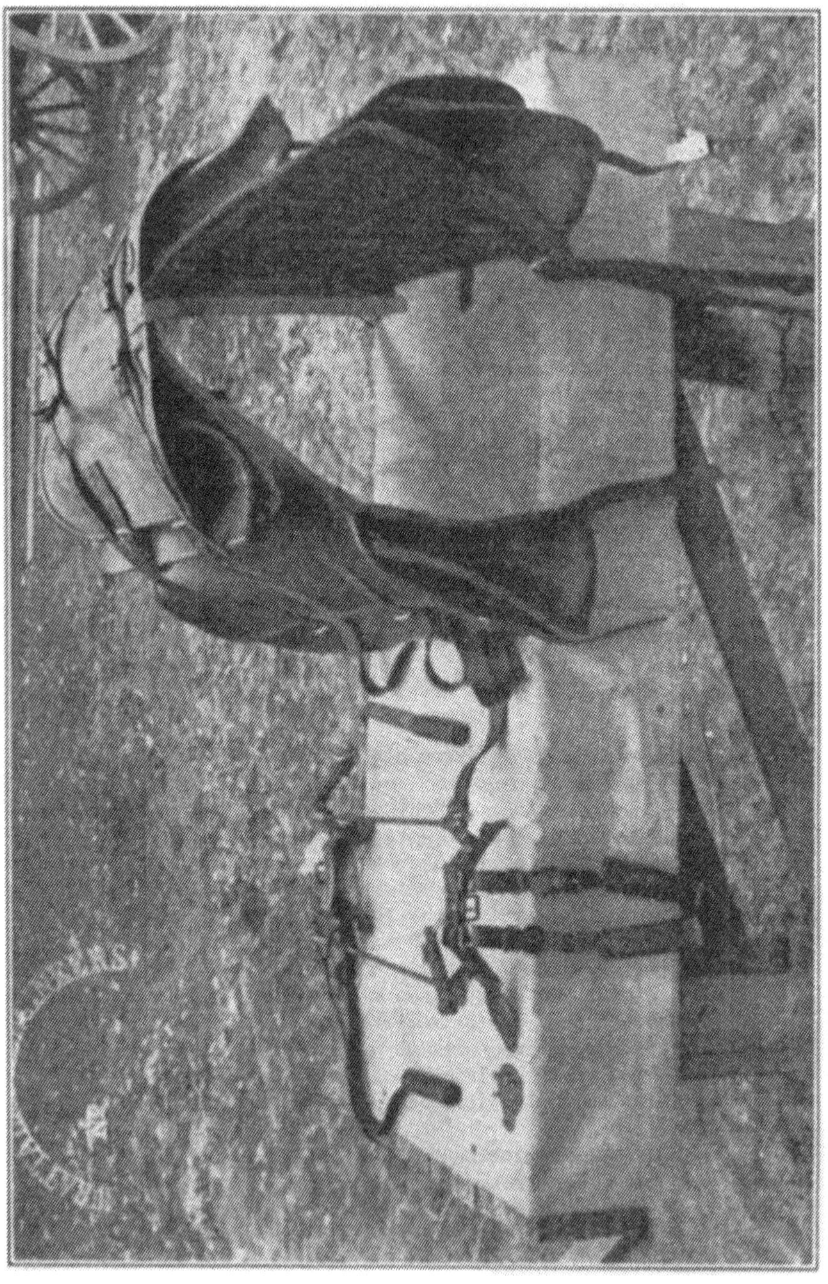

Box No. 2. Outside dimensicns 3 feet 8 inches by 11 by 7 inches, containing 4 hatchets, 4 axes, 1 saw, 5 pounds nails. Weight, when packed, 78 pounds.

Boxes to be made of $\frac{7}{8}$-inch dressed pine lumber, with lids screwed down when shipped, and to be hinged and provided with hasps and flat padlocks; cleats and partitions to be so placed in the boxes as to

prevent contents from being disarranged and injured by rough handling.

A list of the articles packed in each box should be fastened on the inside of the lid, and each box should be numbered and marked to show it contains engineer equipment for a troop or for a squadron. The word "explosive" should be plainly printed on all faces of Squadron Box No. 1.

PACK REEL (SIGNAL CORPS).

(Figs 121, 122.)

SEC. 136. The reel consists of the following: The platform, the turntable, the caging, and the saddle.

The platform consists of two side rails, two end rails for center boards for holding the gearing, and two brace rails connecting center boards and end rails. The platform rests on four strap-iron legs, braced at each end.

To the bottom of center boards is attached a metal plate, holding a vertical shaft and a provision for ball bearings; a horizontal shaft is supplied at the center of one side rail, holding a miter wheel at inner end.

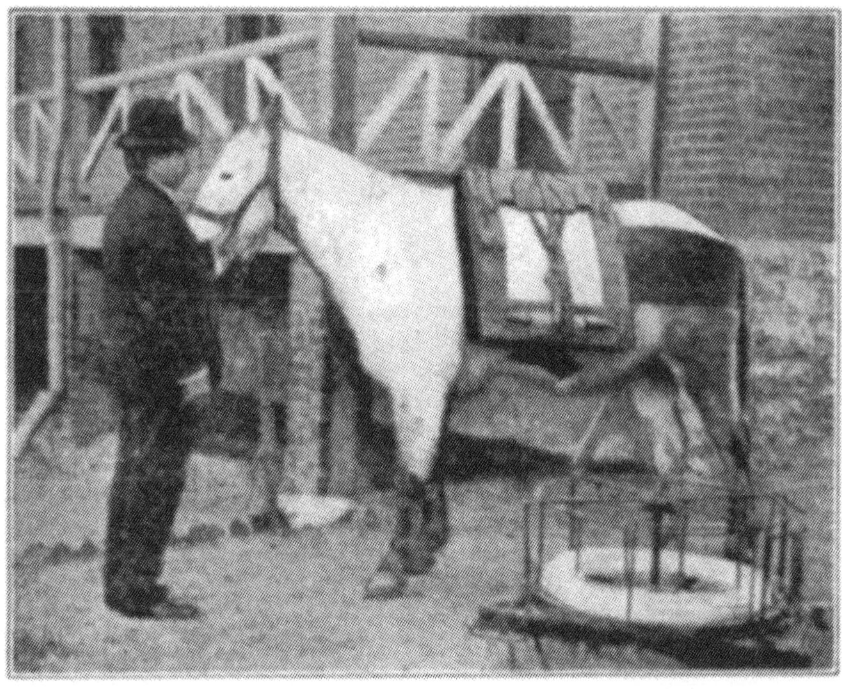

At the outer end of shaft a crank is supplied, by means of which the miter wheel may be turned.

On each side rail at ends a handle is supplied for lifting the pack reel to position on the saddle, as provided on the aparejo.

The turntable is composed of wooden crosspieces, holding at center and on under side a horizontal miter wheel. On its upper side a metallic cap is supplied with a hole through center of cap and crosspieces for the purpose of being engaged over the vertical shaft, as provided on platform. By this arrangement the miter wheel on turntable engages over its mate on platform and is rotated by means of the horizontal shaft, supplied with a crank or by engagement of the "pay-out" end of the coil of wire around a holdfast, the travel of the animal causing the turntable to rotate. On outer ends of crosspieces a circular metal band is supplied to hold the crosspieces rigid. On these crosspieces holes are provided to receive metal standards, around which is engaged the coil of wire.

At one end of platform a brake is supplied, carrying a section of light rope, by means of which the "unit" may apply the brake on the circular band, thus regulating the "pay out" of wire as may be determined. The brake as supplied on end rail is considered the front or forward end of pack reel.

For the purpose of holding the coil of wire within bounds when engaged around the standards a "caging" is supplied, composed of metallic cross arms that engage into slots near each end of side rails

of platform. At the center of the cross arms a metallic cap is provided at intersection of cross arms, a hole being provided at center of cap, which engages over the vertical shaft, holding the cross arms to place.

Two circular bands are provided, spaced about 12 inches apart by means of distance rods, the upper band being riveted to the horizontal portion of cross arms; the lower band is connected to the vertical portions of cross arms by means of short-distance plates. These horizontal distance plates connect with the vertical rods near point of engagement of the extremities of cross arms that engage on slots, as provided on platform, metal keys being supplied to hold extremities of cross arms rigidly in position to side rails of platform.

A third circular metal band of diameter equal to the outer holes, as provided on crosspieces, is provided, holes being spaced equally distant thereon, as provided on wooden crosspieces of turntable. This band is further supported at its extremity by sections of metal, shaped like the letter "L," attached to the horizontal portions of cross arms. When cage is in position the upper ends of standards on turntable engage into holes, as provided in metal crosspieces of this smaller circular band.

The connection of this smaller circular band, fitting over standards, causes them to be held rigidly in position, the turntable thus controlling rotation of this band, or, as may be said, in unison with it, the caging thus keeping the wire within due bounds when "paying out."

For "paying out" at rear two semicircular iron rods, holding two vertical rods, which travel from side to side, are supplied. These are attached to the vertical sections of cross arms at rear. Engaged between the vertical rods is supplied a device which travels up and down these vertical rods, a hole being provided at center of device through which the wire passes in "paying out" at rear. By this action the wire has liberty to keep in alignment in the "paying out," the vertical standards moving from side to side, and the device up or down, as may be controlled by the action of the wire, to relieve all possibility of a holdfast in the "pay out" of the wire.

For the purpose of carrying the pack reel a saddle is provided, fitting over the aparejo to which it is attached, at front and rear, and with suitable provisions to secure the legs of pack reel, and hold it securely in position. (Designed by H. W. Daly.)

PACK CHESTS (SIGNAL CORPS).

(Fig 123)

SEC. 137. These chests are constructed so as to hold the necessary apparatus for telephonic communication, as with the provisional field artillery.

The exterior of chests are supplied with metallic fasteners, latigos, and sections of rope, for securing the chests on the aparejo, in similar manner as provided for engineer-corps chests.

LITTER CARRIER (HOSPITAL CORPS).

(Figs 124, 125, 126)

SEC. 138. *The carrier.*—It consists of two hinges, four side plates—two at top and two at bottom or ends, reenforced by wooden shoes to strengthen same—four staples, two attached to each end, each staple carrying two tug loops.

Each tug loop is supplied with a side strap and quarter strap. The side strap holds a swivel clamp at opposite end and engages over the outer rail or bar of litter; the quarter strap is supplied with a distance strap at end, holding a ring on each end; these rings engage over the handles of litter at front and rear.

On each end of side plates swivel clamps are likewise provided that hold the inside rail or bar of litter. The swivel clamps on each end of side plates carry a strap, by means of which the litter, before using, is strapped to carrier.

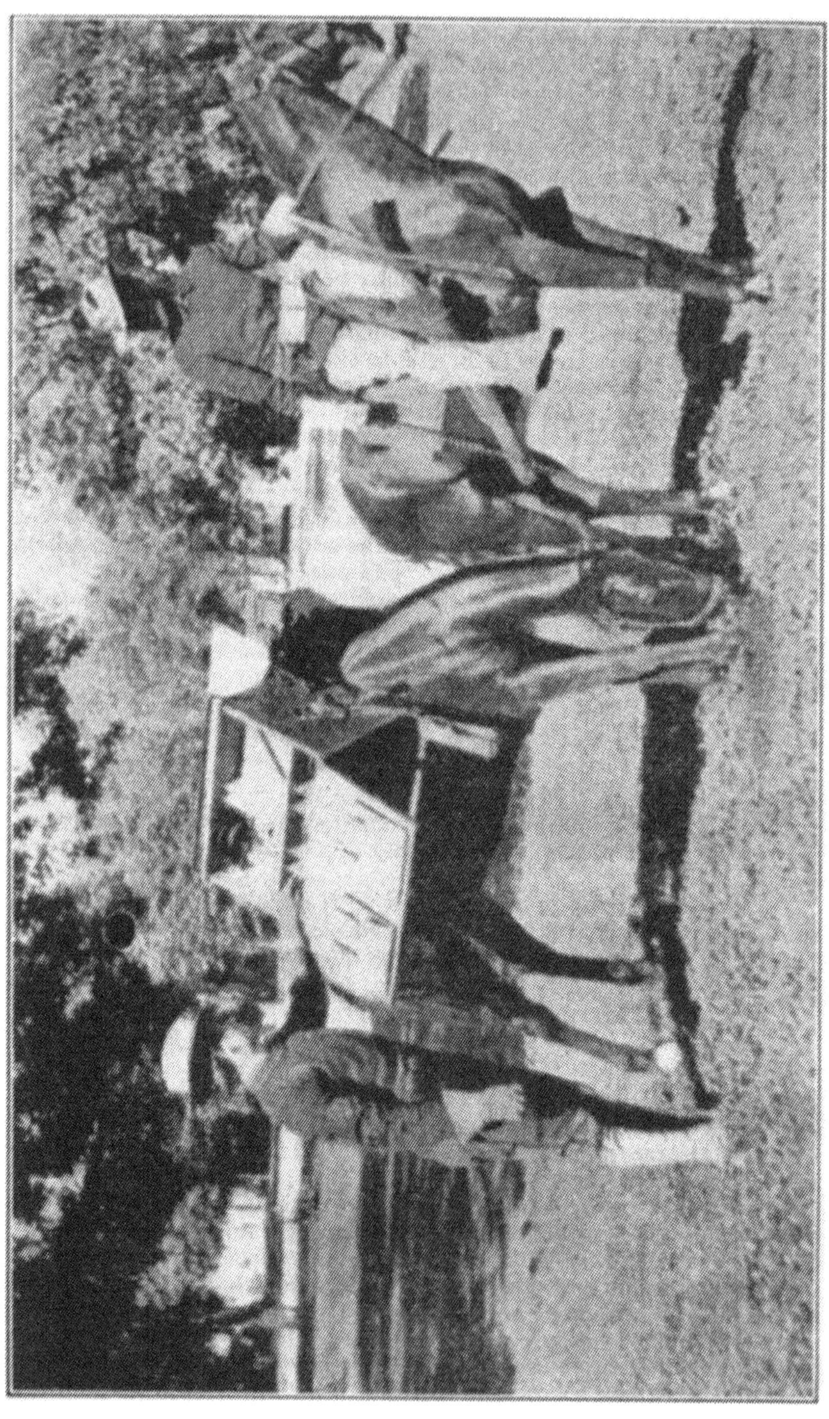

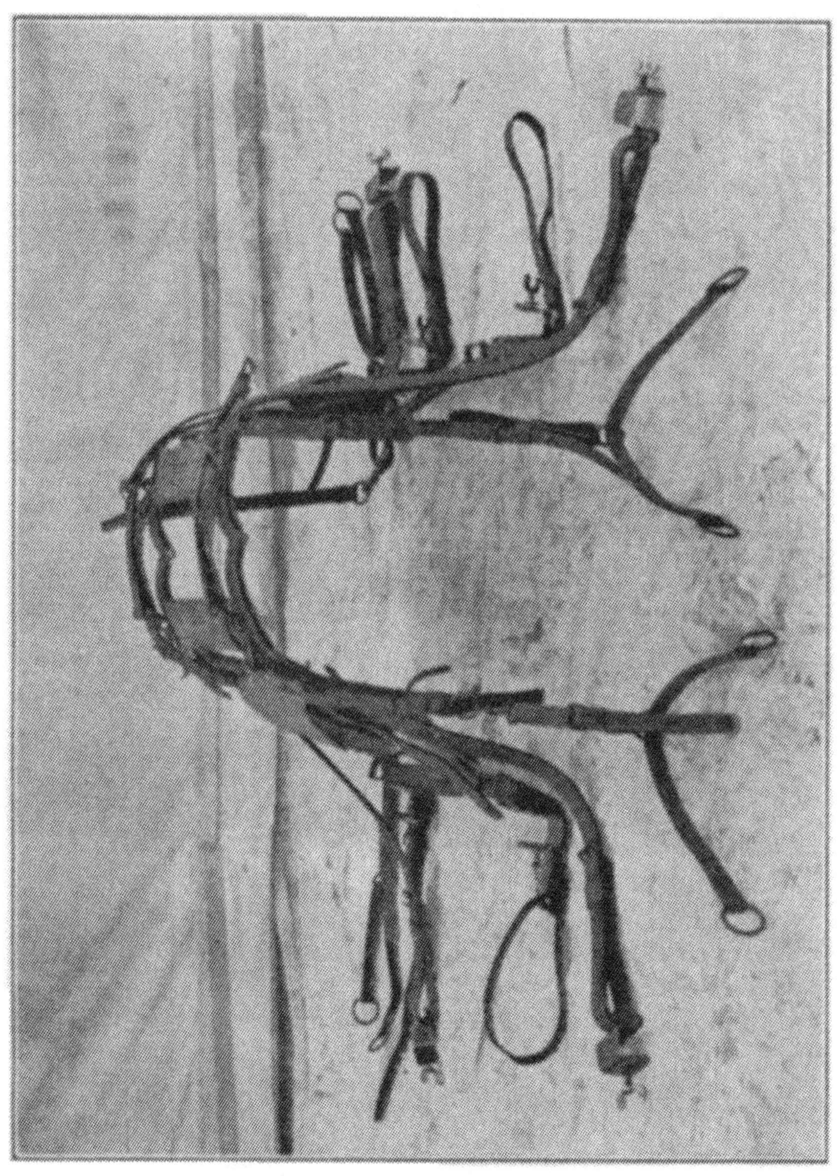

The side straps and quarter straps are adjustable, so that the litter may be carried at any desired incline when traveling up or down a mountain.

The swivel clamps carry set screws, by means of which the side rails or bars of litter are rigidly engaged.

Two leather bags or pockets are provided; these are attached between the top and bottom distance plates of carrier, and are used

for carrying bands to secure the wounded, when necessary, bandages, and medical supplies. Additional rings are supplied, to which may be attached canteens of water, etc.

A protection from sun and rain may be provided by the use of two shelter halves, always available.

Col. John Van R. Hoff, Medical Department United States Army, indorses the above, with the following report to the Surgeon-General, United States Army:

[First indorsement.]

FORT LEAVENWORTH, KANS., *March 15, 1905.*

Respectfully forwarded to the Surgeon-General, United States Army, Washington, D. C., recommending that the "Daly" litter frame be subjected to trial with view to its adoption by our service.

One mule with this appliance and 3 men could each day easily make 5 round trips of 3 miles each from battlefield to an aid station, carrying altogether 10 wounded. Assuming that 3 men alone could make 3 round trips, which would certainly be the limit, they would remove but 3 wounded; in other words, 3 men and a mule would do as much work, and do it better, than 10 men without a mule.

I have used the litter frame somewhat about the post and believe it to be a practical and valuable military appliance.

If it is desired to subject it to a trial in Washington, I have no doubt Mr. Daly, who is stationed here, would be glad to forward it or take the litter frame to Washington.

JOHN VAN R. HOFF,
Colonel, Assistant Surgeon-General, United States Army, Surgeon.

NOTE.—The litter carrier was designed to meet the necessity of the quick removal of the wounded from near the firing line to first-aid station in time of war. For this purpose gentle and easy-gaited mules should be used to carry the wounded.

While pack service is maintained in the Army there will always be a supply of suitable pack animals to draw from to carry the wounded, and much safer and better than by hand or ambulance; the possibility of jar as transmitted by the ambulance over ugly conditions of country is absolutely eliminated by the use of this device.

For single litter construction, see figs. 127, 128, 129, 130, 131.

SPECIFICATIONS FOR THE DALY LITTER CARRIER.

INDEX TO CONSTRUCTION.

Item	No.	Item	No.
1. Hinges	2	16. Quarter straps	4
2. Staples for hinges	4	17. Guy straps for quarter straps	4
3. Tug loops (triangular cockeyes)	8	18. Litter straps for swivel clamps	4
4. Coupling plates	4	19. Litter straps for hinges	4
5. Wooden stiffeners for coupling plates	4	20. Buckles, 2-inch	4
6. Side plates	4	21. Buckles, 1-inch	14
7. Staples for side plates	4	22. Buckles, ¾-inch	12
8. Swivel clamps	8	23. Rings, 1¾-inch	8
9. Bolts for swivel clamps	4	24. Rings, 1½-inch	4
10. Links or loops for swivel clamps	4	25. Rings, 1¼-inch	8
11. Staples for swivel clamps	4	26. Rings, 1-inch	8
12. Set screws for swivel clamps	8	27. Rings, ¾-inch	8
13. Box rod nuts for set screws	8	28. Snaps, double	4
14. Wing nuts for set screws	8	29. Snaps, single, "Trigger"	4
15. Side straps	4	30. Leather pockets or pouches	2

"DALY" LITTER CARRIER FOR APAREJO CONSTRUCTION.

DETAILED SPECIFICATION.

"Daly" litter frame.

1. *Hinges for frame (2).*—To be made of soft steel, when shaped to be 6⅝ inches long, from center of bolt at center of hinge to center of bolt at ends, each way, measuring horizontally.

Take a piece of soft steel 16 inches long, 2½ inches wide, and one-eighth of an inch thick (gauge 11), bevel each end, circle piece and weld.

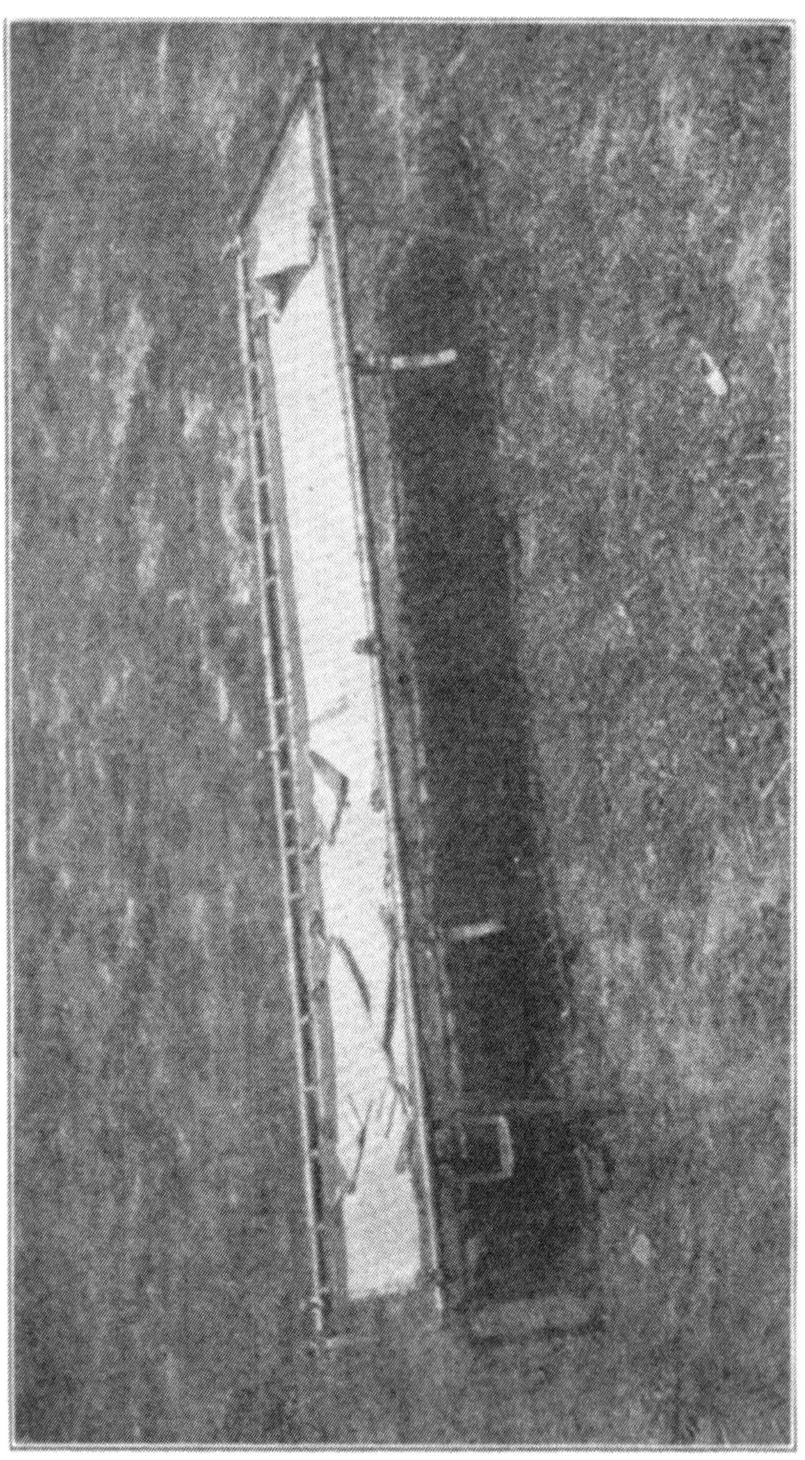

Now provide a "templet" 7½ inches long, 2½ inches wide, and five-sixteenths of an inch thick, rounded at each end.

Compress circled piece sufficient so as to introduce templet between its folds, and fit snug; keeping templet between folds, shape one-half of section, to form segment or portion of circle, whose diameter will measure 1⅞ inches (applied by square); remove "templet" and one-half of hinge is thus shaped, and provide a similar section. To do so, straighten "templet" and continue as before.

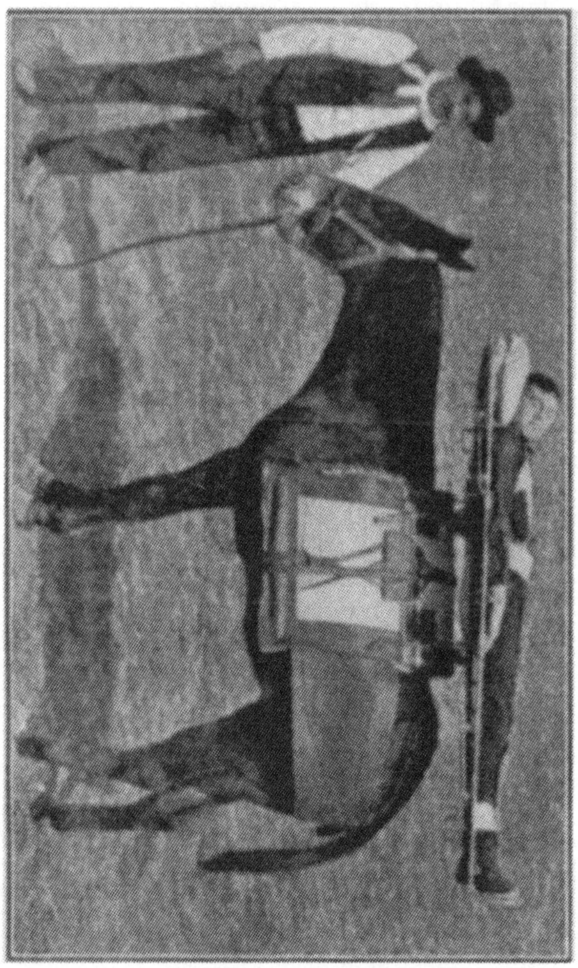

To connect sections, commence at circled ends to form hinge, for first section cut or saw out inward five-eighths of an inch on each edge and end to receive five-sixteenths of an inch bolt or rivet.

For second section, cut or saw out 1¼ inches at center of end, so as to receive first section and bolt described therefor. In cutting allow for filing so as to fit snug, bolt to be riveted on. The curved portion will be considered the center of hinge.

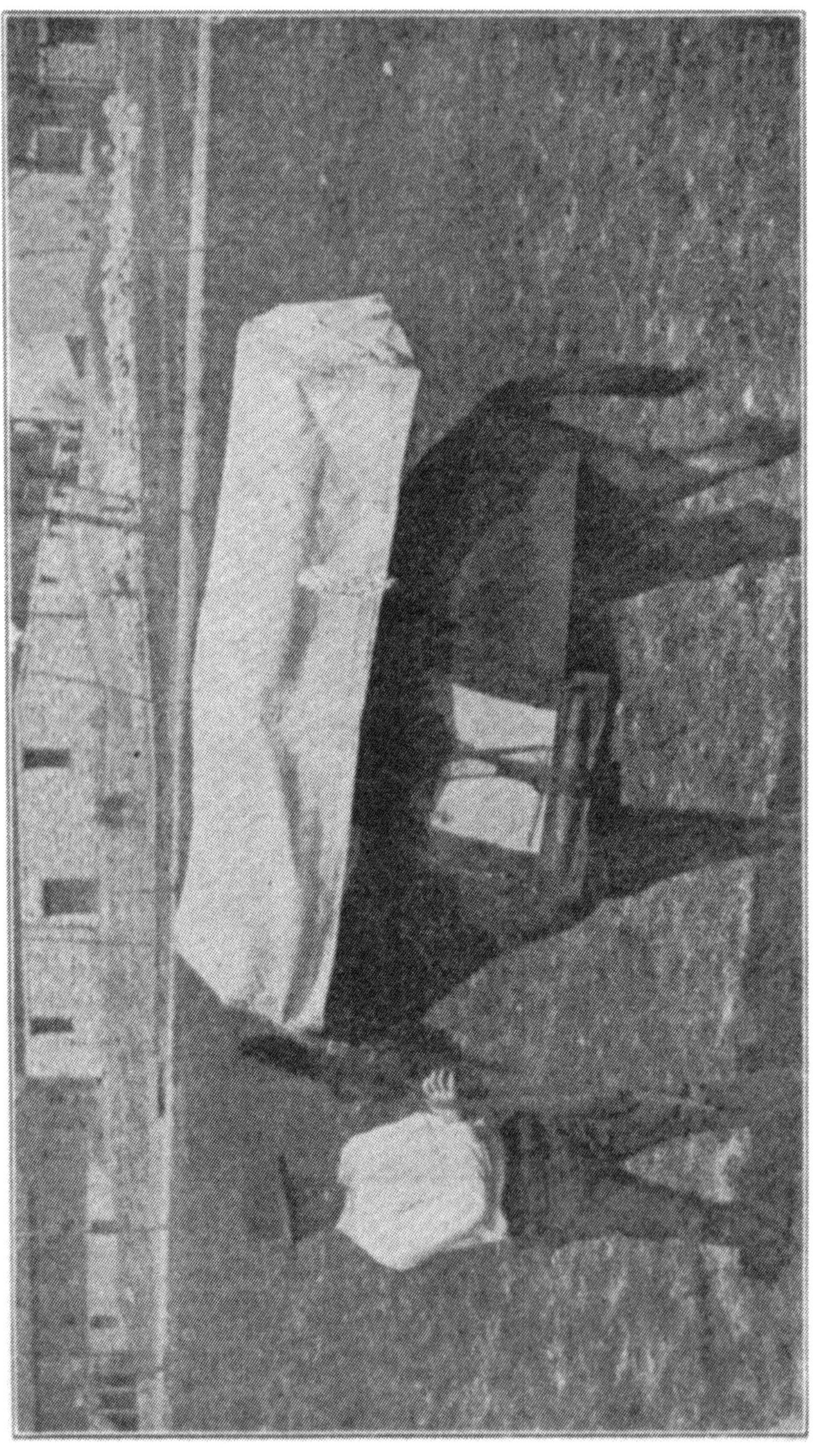

At each end of hinge, cut or saw out in entirely similar manner as that described for second section of hinge, similar bolts will be provided therefor. The ends of hinge to receive "side" plates of frame.

In cutting out for bolt, the aid of templet may be employed.

2. *Staples for hinge (2).*—Take a section of soft steel, 4 inches long, one-half of an inch wide, and one-fourth of an inch thick; allow a base of 1 inch at each end to rest on hinge, and form semicircle, distance between bases to be 1 inch; provide a $\frac{3}{16}$-inch hole at center of each base to receive rivets. The circled portion of staple will be rounded on under surface. These to receive two tug loops.

3. *Tug loops (triangular cockeyes) for hinge (4).*—Take a section of Norway round iron 7 inches long and five-sixteenths of an inch diameter, shaped in this manner: Two and one-half inches from each end turn at right angles so as to leave inside of base 2 inches wide; now $1\frac{3}{4}$ inches from ends turn at right angles parallel with bases, this leaves a perpendicular wall of three-fourths of an inch; now 1 inch from each end turn upward and form circle, and weld. Two tug loops will be provided for each staple. In applying staples to hinge, measure $2\frac{1}{2}$ inches from end of hinge to center of staple, the base of staple conforming to shape of hinge, placed exactly in center of hinge, the long way up and down. Now provide holes on hinge corresponding with those on staple and countersunk holes on under side of hinge.

In riveting staples to hinge, provide one nut for each rivet, thickness of nut to be five-sixteenths of an inch, diameter of hole in nut to be three-sixteenths of an inch. Place nut between the folds or plates of hinge so as to carry rivet; provide two tug loops for each staple, and rivet staples securely to hinge; rivet will be flush with under surface of hinge when riveted.

Staples holding tug loops on hinge will be considered the outward face thereof.

4. *Coupling or distance plates for hinges (2).*—To be of sheet steel, 22 inches long, 3 inches wide, and one-sixteenth of an inch thick (gauge 16), edges to be smoothed off. Now provide four holes at each end three-sixteenths of an inch diameter, spaced in this manner: At each end and one-half of an inch therefrom and one-half of an inch from the upper and the lower edge provide one hole; now 2 inches from ends provide two similar holes, these holes to be countersunk on one side of coupling plate.

In applying coupling plates to hinges, place plate on the under side of hinge and one-half of an inch from end, end of coupling plate to be flush with the outward edge of hinge, holes as countersunk on coupling plate will be considered the downward side.

Now provide corresponding holes on the lower plate only of hinge, and rivet down securely.

Now provide 10 similar holes on coupling plate, between hinges, 5 holes on the upper side and 5 holes on the lower side of plate, spaced in this manner: Four inches from each end of coupling plate, and three-fourths of an inch from the upper and the lower edge provide 1 hole, and between these, on the upper and lower side, provide 3 holes, spaced equally distant, these holes to be countersunk on the under side, in similar manner. These to receive rivets and screws for wooden stiffeners.

5. *Metal squares for coupling plates of hinges (4).*—For squares provide four ¾-inch brown japanned buckles, and remove the tongues; now supply four sections of sheet steel same gauge as coupling plate, 2 inches long and three-fourths of an inch wide; fold each section so that ends will meet, and lay into fold the metal square; provide one hole in the center of each section, and three-fourths of an inch from bar of square held in fold of section, diameter of hole, three-sixteenths of an inch; now introduce the folds of section on the downward edge of coupling plate, flush with the bar of square, and 1 inch from the inward edge of hinge to center of square, provide a corresponding hole on coupling plate and rivet down securely.

These to receive straps of leather bags of frame.

6. *Wooden stiffeners for coupling plates of hinges (2).*—To be of sound hickory, free from knots or other blemishes, 17 inches long, 3 inches wide, and seven-eighths of an inch thick, shaped in this manner: Three and three-eighths inches from each end saw down on one side three-eighths of an inch, and "gain" out this portion, between cuts. This leaves one-half of an inch in thickness on the bottom side of stiffener, the gained surface to be smoothed off, and the upper and the lower edges to be well rounded. This to receive cincha of aparejo (pack saddle).

Now place stiffener on the upper side of coupling plate, between hinges, keeping their edges flush, and provide two holes, through stiffener, at each end, corresponding with those on coupling plate, and secure rivets and burrs (malleable iron). Introduce rivet and burr from upper side of stiffener and rivet down on under side of coupling plate.

Now provide 6 screws, one-half of an inch, No. 6, and screw down to stiffener as provided.

Stiffener holding plate to be covered with fair leather, and sewed down with one seam, 6 stitches to the inch, seam to be flush with lower edge of coupling plate.

7. *Side plates for hinges (4).*—To be made of sheet steel, 30 inches long, 2½ inches wide, and three thirty-seconds of an inch thick (gauge 14), shaped in this manner: At one end, and 1½ inches therefrom, fold this portion back, so as to take a $\frac{5}{16}$-inch bolt, and secure with two rivets; for rivets provide two holes three-sixteenths of an inch diameter, one-half of an inch from each edge, and three-fourths of an inch from end of folded portion, countersink holes on under side of plate, and rivet down. Now cut or saw out in entirely similar manner as that described for first section of hinge, provide bolt, and rivet down to end of hinge. Now measure 20 inches on the free end of side plate, counting from center of bolt on end of hinge, and turn at right angles. Next provide a "templet," shaped in this manner: Take a section of flat iron 3 inches long, 2½ inches wide, and 1¼ inches thick. On one side at end bevel or taper to a thickness of five-eighths of an inch, the beveled end will be considered the bottom, and the tapered side the outer face of templet.

Now place templet on the angle formed on the free end of side plate, and secure templet to side plate, and fold the free end around templet, lapping the remaining portion upward on side plate. Next provide two holes, three-sixteenths of an inch diameter, one-half of an inch from each edge, and free end of side plate, holes to be countersunk on under side of side plate. These holes to receive staples for side plates.

8. *Staples for side plates* (*4*).—To be made of Norway flat iron 6 inches long, one-half inch wide, and three-sixteenths of an inch thick, shaped in this manner: One and five-eighths inches from each end turn at right angles; this will leave the outward or front side of staple 2½ inches from out to out. Now three-fourths of an inch from each end turn inwardly at right angles, parallel with outward or front side of staple. Now provide two holes on basis of staple corresponding with those on end of side plate. Two 1-inch rings will be provided for each staple and rivet down securely. Its use is to receive litter straps attached to "swivel clamp" of side plate.

9. *Coupling plates for side plates* (*2*).—To be similar as those described for coupling plates for hinges. In attaching coupling plates to side plates, they will fit flush with ends and outward edge of side plates; corresponding holes will be provided on the bottom portion of side plate and countersunk on its upper side. When riveted down, rivets will be flush with upper and under surface of plates. The loop so formed on end of side plate by "templet" is to receive wooden stiffener.

10. *Wooden stiffeners for coupling plates of side plates* (*2*).—To be of sound hickory, free from knots or other blemishes, 22 inches long, 3 inches wide, and 1¼ inches thick, shaped in this manner: Five and seven-eighths inches from each end saw down on one side three-fourths of an inch deep, and "gain" out portion between cuts. This leaves one-half of an inch thickness on bottom or under side of stiffener; now 2½ inches from each end on same side saw down one-half of an inch and "gain" out between cuts. This leaves an offset 3⅜ inches long and three-fourths of an inch thick. Next each outward portion of 2½ inches will be beveled or tapered on same side to a thickness of five-eighths of an inch on one end, and will be considered the downward side of stiffener. This portion will fit exactly in form shaped by "templet" on the end of side plates and stiffener will ride flush with the upper and lower edges of coupling plate. Stiffener will be provided with bolts and screws in similar manner as that described for stiffener on coupling plate of hinges.

11. *Swivel clamps for side plates* (*4*).—To be made of soft steel, 7 inches long, 2½ inches wide, and one-eighth of an inch thick (gauge 11), shaped in this manner: Bevel one end and form circle or turn as close as can be had, so as to form a rounded surface on end. Now measure 1⅞ inches from this end and turn at right angles, the end of circle outward; now 1½ inches from inside of angle, turn again at right angles parallel with first portion, the base formed between parallel sides to be level and fully 1½ inches in the clear, the angles or corners of free end to be rounded. In shaping base the angles or corners should be slightly rounded; the aid of a templet should be employed for this purpose. This to receive the pole or side bar of "litter." Now provide two holes whose diameter shall be one-half of an inch; the first on free end of clamp, whose center shall be equally distant from each edge and 1 inch from free end of clamp; the second on outward side or portion first formed, likewise equally distant from each edge and 1 inch from rounded end.

The first hole on free end to receive swivel bolt for clamp, the second hole on outward side of first portion to receive box-rod nut with set screw and to be considered the front of swivel clamp.

12. *Swivel bolts for clamps* (*4*).—To be of malleable iron, length 2 inches, diameter one-half of an inch, head of bolt or rivet to be three-fourths of an inch diameter, shaped in this manner: One and thirteen-sixteenths inches from end of bolt turn down to three-eighths of an inch diameter, head of bolt to be reduced in thickness to three-sixteenths of an inch diameter, rim of head to be beveled on its upper or outer surface. Head of bolt to be inclined at such slope so as to fit flat against the face of clamp when clamp is applied to end of side plate on form as made by "templet." In applying clamps on end of side plate the free end of clamp will ride flush with upper end of form, the edges of clamp flush with the edges of side plate.

Now provide three-eighths of an inch hole horizontally through form and stiffener, whose center is indicated by center of half-inch hole on clamp. This to secure clamp to side plate by means of bolt as provided.

13. *Box-rod nuts for swivel clamps* (*4*).—To be 2½ inches long, diameter of hole three-eighths of an inch, and provided with thread for set screw; now provide one hole at each end of box-rod nut, diameter of hole to be three-sixteenths of an inch, hole to be one-half of an inch from each end and in center. These to secure box-rod nut to the outward face of clamp.

14. *Set screws for swivel clamps* (*4*).—To be 1 inch long and three-eighths of an inch diameter, thread on screw to correspond with that on box-rod nut, and provided with wing nut on one end; this end will be squared to receive wing nut hole in center of wing nut, to correspond with the squared end of set screw, so as to fit snug, and to be countersunk on the outward side and rivet down securely. Now introduce set screw through box-rod nut from the front side, and bevel end of set screw oval shape, giving sufficient head on end of set screw to prevent extraction.

Now place box-rod nut on the outward face of clamp, set screw in center of half-inch hole, ends of box-rod nut to be equally distant from the upper end of clamp, provide corresponding holes in clamp, holes in clamp to be countersunk on the inner side, and rivet down securely; rivets on the inner side of clamp will be smoothed off flush with the inner side.

15. *Staples for swivel clamps* (*4*).—To be made of "Norway" flat iron 3½ inches long, one-half of an inch wide, and three-sixteenths of an inch thick, shaped in this manner: One and one-fourth inches from each end turn at right angles so as to leave the portion between sides 1 inch in the clear. Now five-eighths of an inch from each end turn outwardly at right angles, parallel with first portion; this for base of staple. In center of each base each way provide a $\frac{3}{16}$-inch hole for rivets. Now place staple on the under side of swivel clamp at base, the long way, with the width of clamp, the ends equally distant on base; provide corresponding holes on clamp; holes to be countersunk on the inner side on base of clamp, and rivet down securely; rivets will be smoothed off on the inner side of swivel clamp, so as to be flush with base.

Staple on swivel clamp to receive litter strap, these to attach closed litter to "frame" by means of staple on side plate as provided. In securing swivel clamp to end of side plate, on form as provided, the shorter side of clamp will be outward, and provide washer for swivel bolt, diameter of hole to be one-half of an inch; introduce bolt through half-inch hole on free end of clamp and apply washer over bolt; thickness of washer must not exceed what is not covered for swivel portion, so as to permit clamp to swing freely when riveted on the clamp swivels on the shoulder formed on bolt, the washer acting as an aid to clamp to swing or swivel freely. Now introduce bolt through hole on form on end of side plate, and rivet down securely on under side of side plate.

16. *Swivel clamps for side straps* (*4*).—To be made in similar manner as that described for swivel clamps for side plates of frame, with the following exception: The free end of clamp to be rolled outwardly to receive link or loop, whose diameter will be five-sixteenths of an inch.

17. *Links for swivel clamps for side straps* (*4*).—To be of "Norway" round iron, 6½ inches long and five-sixteenths of an inch diameter, shaped in this manner: Two inches from each end turn at right angles; this leaves a base of 2½ inches to be engaged by roll on free end of clamp. Now 1 inch from each end turn again at right angles and weld; this leaves a base of 2 inches wide to receive side strap; diameter of link to be three-fourths of an inch between bases. In engaging the lower base in roll provided on clamp, allow sufficient play in roll for link to work freely, roll on free end of clamp to be turned outwardly and link engaged securely; the upper base or portion of link to receive side strap of frame, width of side strap to be 2 inches.

18. *Side straps for litter frame* (*4*).—To be made of good solid harness leather, one-eighth of an inch thick. Cut two straps 5 feet long and 2 inches wide, shave each end of straps, and fold, keeping the "grained" side of each strap outward; this gives a doubled thickness for side strap. In folding allow an extension of 3 inches on one strap; this gives a similar extension at opposite end. Now provide two sections, each 6 inches long and 2 inches wide, and shave ends. Lay the first section on one end between the folds of strap, so as to extend to end. Now fold over extension and section, so as to receive the ends of section between the folds of strap, and lap the free end of strap on outer side of folds; this gives a doubled thickness at center of fold. Next punch opening at center of end to receive a 2-inch japanned buckle. Introduce buckle receiving section and extension and fold back ends as indicated. Now provide keeper for strap, to be placed on the upper side and 2 inches from buckle, width of section for keeper to be 2 inches. Sew down both sections of side strap to within 4 inches of opposite end and one-fourth of an inch from edges. Provide six holes, spaced 2 inches apart, large enough to freely admit tongue of buckle, first hole to be 9 inches from buckle end of strap. Now provide a swivel clamp for side strap and introduce the free end of strap through the link of clamp and through keeper and buckle; engage buckle on free end of strap so as to leave a loop of about 9 inches long. The back of clamp will correspond with back of buckle.

Now place the "second" section on the free end of side strap and pass this end through both tug loops or cockeyes, on one side of hinge as provided, from underneath, and engage around first or upper tug loop on opposite side of hinge; the section and extension of strap on free end to be folded in similar manner as described for opposite end and sewed down.

In applying side strap with swivel clamp for opposite side of hinge, pass the free end of strap through the lower tug loop from underneath, and engage around the first or upper tug loop on opposite side in similar manner and sew down.

It will be noted the side straps overlap or cross over each other, causing tension on strap to come from opposite side of hinge.

Proceed in similar manner in applying side straps for second hinge.

19. *Quarter straps for litter frame* (*4*).—To be made of good solid harness leather, one-eighth of an inch thick. The first two to be known as the "front" quarter straps, the second two the "rear" quarter straps. Each quarter strap to have three sections, to be designated as the first or upper, the second or lower, and the third the guy or distance strap.

First section.—For the front quarter straps cut two sections 30 inches long and 1 inch wide, shave one end of each strap, and fold 2½ inches and punch for buckle; provide a 1-inch japanned buckle and engage onto strap. Next provide two keepers, width of keeper to be 1 inch, the first cr upper to be 1 inch from buckle, the second or lower to be 2 inches therefrom and sewed down one-eighth of an inch from each edge, the opposite end of strap to be rounded or tapered on edges. Now provide 15 holes punched No. 8 punch, counting 3 inches on the free end of strap for the first, and spaced 1 inch apart. Now provide one 1¼-inch japanned ring and one double snap; engage ring on the buckle end of strap and the double snap onto ring. The opposite end of snap will be engaged onto the lower tug loop on side of hinge, and to be known as the front hinge or front of frame. The free end of strap will be provided with similar ring and engaged thereon, this to receive second section of quarter strap.

Second section.—For second section provide two similar straps; on the buckle end engage a 1½-inch japanned ring; on the free or opposite end engage a single snap (trigger snap preferred).

The single snap on second section will be engaged onto ring on first section. The ring on opposite end of second section to receive the "guy" or distance strap (or third section).

Third section.—For third section provide two straps, cut 30 inches long and 1 inch wide; shave each end of strap and fold each end so as to leave a length of 24 inches; provide two 1¾-inch japanned rings; drop one ring into the fold of straps at one end and sew down. Now pass the free end of guy strap through the ring on second section, and drop the second ring into fold on free end and sew down in similar manner as described for first section.

For the rear quarter straps, first section, cut two straps 48 inches long and 1 inch wide, and provide in similar manner as that described for first section of "front" quarter straps, each strap to have a running or free keeper engaged about center of strap. First section will be engaged onto lower tug loop on hinge at rear, as described for the front.

For the second section provide two similar straps as that described for second section of front quarter straps, to be engaged in similar manner.

For third section provide in similar manner as that described for the front quarter straps. It will be noted the ring on end of second sections at front and rear hooks freely on the "guy" straps, being engaged on strap between rings at each end. The rings at each end of guy strap engage over handles of litter.

20. *Litter straps for swivel clamps* (*4*).—To be 36 inches long and 1 inch wide, provided with japanned buckle and two keepers. Straps to be engaged on staples on the bottom or under side of swivel clamps on side plates. These to secure closed litter when traveling to the firing line.

21. *Litter straps for hinges* (*4*).—To be made in two sections, and designated as the buckle piece and tongue piece.

First section.—For buckle piece cut a strap of leather 12 inches long and 1 inch wide, shave each end, and supply a 1-inch japanned buckle for one end, lap 2½ inches, drop buckle into lap in the usual manner, provide keeper on upper side, and sew down. The opposite end to be engaged on lower tug loop on one side of hinge, lapped 2½ inches and sewed down.

Second section.—For tongue piece cut a strap 18 inches long and 1 inch wide, shave one end, and lap 2½ inches, and point the opposite end. The shaved end will be engaged on lower tug loop on opposite side of hinge, lap 2½ inches, and sew down. Tongue piece to be provided with 9 holes punched No. 8 punch, spaced 1 inch apart, commencing for the first 3 inches from pointed end.

The second hinge will be provided in similar manner. The tongue piece on each hinge will not be on the same side.

22. *Leather bags for frame* (*2*).—To be made of good solid bag leather, fair preferred, shaped in this manner: Cut one piece 15 inches long and 15 inches wide, allow 9 inches for back, and 6 inches turn over for lid, for front piece; cut a section 15 inches long and 9 inches wide or deep. For bellows cut one piece 33 inches long and 4½ inches wide, round the four corners of back piece and two corners of front piece to correspond with the bottom portion of back piece, hemstitch bellows to back and front piece and provide binding same material cut 1½ inches wide, two pieces; first piece to be long enough to extend around the back piece, the second piece long enough to extend around the front piece; shave binding sufficient to lap over edges freely, and sew down, six stitches to the inch, four cord, Barbour's No. 12 waxed with best fair wax. Now cut two pieces 12 inches long and three-fourths of an inch wide for back piece, shave ends and supply four ¾-inch rings, lap 1½ inches at each end, drop rings into lap, and sew down.

In applying ring pieces to back piece, measure 2½ inches from each end to center of strap, and sew down to back piece, the long way of strap to be up and down.

Buckle piece for ring pieces of back piece (*4*).—Cut two straps for upper rings, 10 inches long and three-fourths of an inch wide, supply buckle and two keepers for each piece, and sew down in usual manner.

These to be engaged onto upper rings on back piece and strapped down to squares as supplied on the lower edge of coupling plate.

For the lower rings of back piece cut two straps 20 inches long and three-fourths of an inch wide, provide in similar manner as that described for the upper straps, and engage onto lower rings on back piece, these to be strapped down to rings as provided on staple of side plates.

For lid provide two tongue pieces cut 8 inches long and three-fourths of an inch wide shave one end of each strap and point opposite end, space tongue pieces on lid as provided for ring pieces on back piece, and sew down 1½ inches from end of lid. Now provide two buckle pieces for tongue pieces on face of front pieces, to be spaced in similar manner as provided for tongue pieces. Supply buckle and keeper in usual manner and sew down on face piece, buckle piece when finished not to exceed 3 inches long, the end of buckle piece on end of face piece, tongue pieces to have holes spaced one-half of an inch apart the length of tongue piece, commencing for the first 1 inch from end of tongue piece.

These to receive flexible band (webbing) to secure wounded to litter, medicine supplies, etc. [Designed by H. W. Daly.]

AMMUNITION BOXES—ORDNANCE DEPARTMENT.

SEC. 139. During the Spanish-American war (1898) the necessity for a rapid ammunition supply, by the aid of suitable ammunition boxes, without the necessity of removing the boxes from the pack animal, forced itself upon the writer, from the fact that many ropes were lost or left at point of delivery when exposed in the zone of fire; also owing to the fact that ammunition deteriorated by exposure to dampness, a hermetically-sealed tin case was provided, inclosed in the wooden box. (Figs. 132, 133.)

For the purpose of rapid delivery, two wooden boxes of equal dimensions were provided, the inside dimensions having a greater depth and length than the metallic case. A lid was provided on one side, acting on hinges; a band of iron passed along the front of the lid lengthwise and running upwardly on each end of box at an acute angle with the lid of box, the ends of bands being secured by a bolt passing through from inside of box and secured over band on outside.

This arrangement allowed the band to be raised over top of box and the lid to open out and down; to retain the band when in position over lid, a spring was supplied at center that engaged the band, holding band firmly in place.

On the inside of box, against the top at rear, a cleat was supplied, taking up the extra space between the tin case and top of box, or nearly so.

On the front side and bottom of box an iron roller, about one-fourth of an inch in diameter was attached, and in front of roller a wooden cleat was supplied as a guard for roller in introducing the tin case. To add to the easy introduction of the tin case, strips of tin were supplied, adjusted along the bottom and ends of box, and for the easy action of the roller, a strip was supplied under roller and properly secured.

This arrangement left a space of about 1¼ inches between the tin case and lid of box; to take up this play or space and hold the tin case in position behind its roller, a short wooden cleat is attached at the center of lid, so that when lid was closed it abutted against the side of tin case, holding it in place.

On the outside of box metallic fasteners, fitting over the corners at rear and bottom of box, were supplied. The device or fastener on right-hand corner of each box held a hook, working on a hinge and pivot; the left-hand corner of each box being provided with an angle iron holding five buttons, over which the hook engaged when the boxes were in position on the aparejo, the number of buttons per-

mitting the raising or lowering of either box to equalize the load should the contents of one box be lighter than its mate.

Each box by this arrangement has a right-hand hook and a left-hand angle iron, holding buttons, thus making boxes interchangeable. Each box is then supplied with a "D" ring on each end of box to receive the "lashing."

For lashing two sections of rope about 4 feet long, standard size, holding a ring on each end, and attached to each ring a latigo of suitable length is attached; the rope portion is held under the boot of the aparejo and latigos engage on to "D" rings on ends of box, and secured as in cinching a saddle.

For the purpose of delivering ammunition at or near the firing line, as may be desired, the metal band on front of each box is released and passed over the top of box. Both hands then grip the wooden box, the thumbs raising the metallic case inside of box so as to free the roller at bottom; this action causes the tin box to fall on roller, forcing the case out instantly, the angle at which the boxes are held on the pack mule giving impetus to the delivery of metallic cases by their weight when raised above the roller.

The lid is then closed and the band, by quick action, takes position over spring, retaining the band securely, and the animal is ready to return to the supply depot for another load of ammunition and deliver as before.

By the aid of these wooden boxes and metallic cases, a rapid and systematic ammunition supply can be maintained along the extent of firing line by pack mules; on the basis of 1,000 rounds to the metallic case, 100,000 rounds of ammunition can be delivered at any point on the firing line in from two to three minutes, with proper assistance on reaching the firing line, with a train of 50 pack mules. (Designed by H. W. Daly.)

PACK OUTFIT, AMERICAN MODEL, FOR MAXIM AUTOMATIC MACHINE GUN, CALIBER 30, MODEL OF 1904.

(Figs 134-135)

Sec. 140. A complete outfit for one gun comprises five packs—one for the gun and tripod, one for carrying six boxes of ammunition loading machine, and box of tools and accessories, and three each carrying six boxes of ammunition and two water boxes.

The following is a list of the parts common to all the packs: (1) Halter bridle, (2) blinders, (3) corona, (4) aparejo, (5) crupper, (6) sobre-jalma, (7) pack frame, (8) aparejo cincha, (9) belly cincha, (10) load cincha.

To complete the ammunition and belt-filling machine pack, add to the above ammunition hangers six ammunition boxes, one belt-filling machine and box, and one box of tools and accessories. To complete the ammunition and water box packs, add to the above: The ammunition hangers, six boxes of ammunition, and two water boxes. On one of these packs is carried (1) the filling cup with its straps.

To complete the gun pack, add: (1) Gun hanger and gun, (2) tripod hanger and tripod, (3) barrel case and spare barrel, (4) ammunition boxes.

The packs are practically identical in all details, except the design of the hangers, these being especially adapted to the loads they are to carry.

APAREJO, PROPER.

The aparejo, proper, includes the body, crupper, sobre-jalma, cincha, and corona.

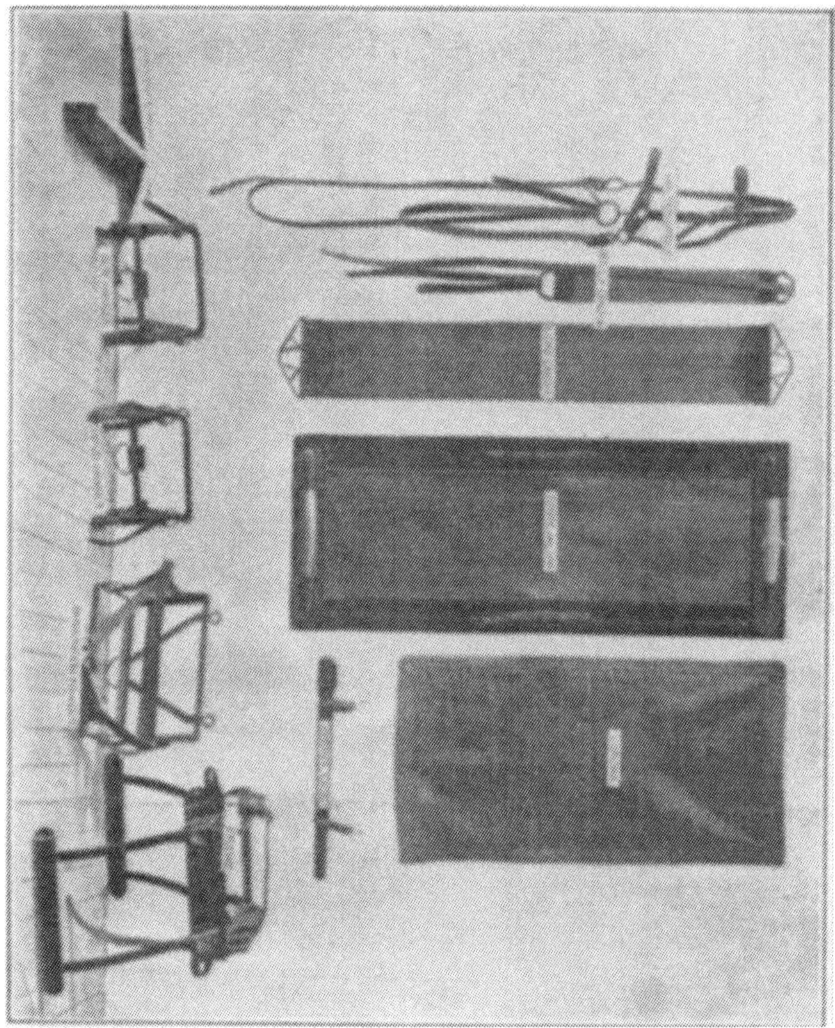

THE PACK FRAME.

The frame is identical for all packs. It consists of two bronze arches connected longitudinally by steel angles. To the projecting ends of the arches are riveted four steel hoops or ribs, which hang downward and partly embrace the body of the animal. The framework thus formed is strengthened by four steel plates riveted fore and

75927°—17——15

aft, two to the under side of the ends of the arches and two to the floating ends of the ribs. Strips of wood are attached to these steel plates, which serve to stiffen them. The upper strips of wood are gained to form a seat for the aparejo cincha. These, and also the lower strips, serve to distribute the pressure of the cincha and the load. To the ends of the bronze arches hooks are attached for holding the hangers.

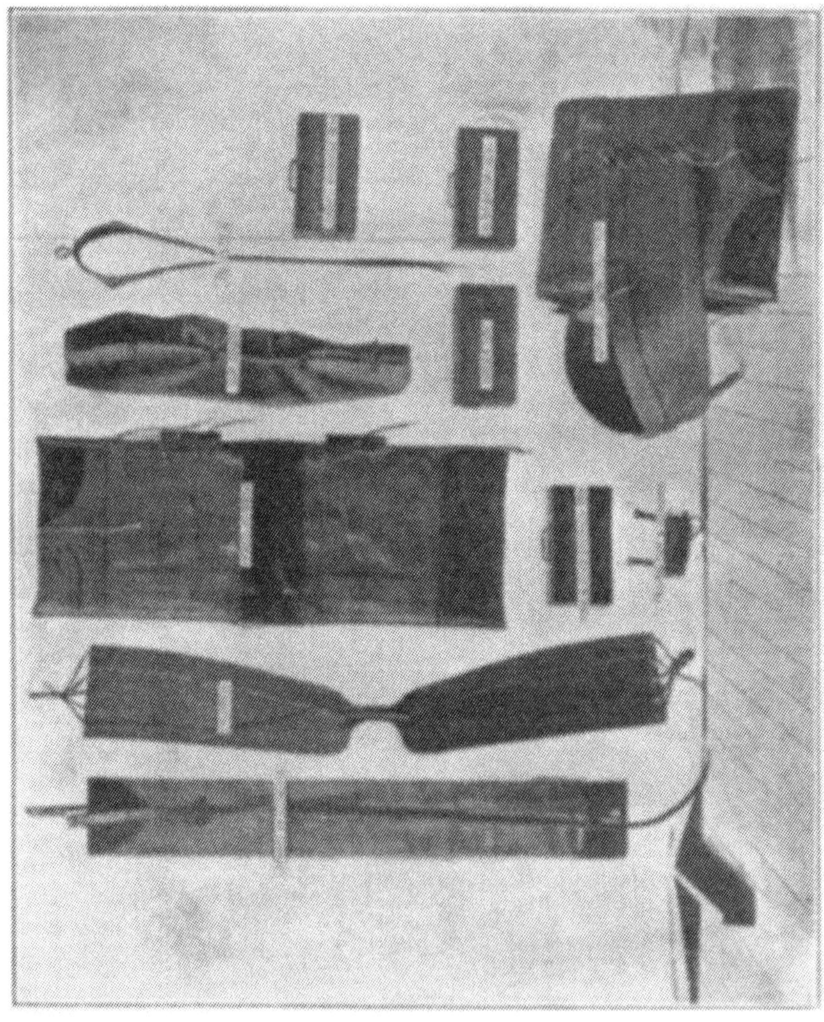

There are three different designs, viz, the gun hanger, the tripod hanger, and the ammunition hanger.

The ammunition hanger consists of a rear frame made of angle steel, to the lower side of which is riveted the bottom frame, made also of angle steel, but with the webbing cut away from the ends of the frame. The top of the rear frame and of the outer corners of the bottom frame are connected by side braces. The rear frame has a rear top brace riveted to its upper ends; also two inclined braces riveted each with one end to the middle of the lower bar of the frame, the other end to the rear top brace near its ends. To these latter braces are riveted the hanger eyes. To the back of the rear frame and about 3 inches from its lower edge is riveted the rear bottom

brace. This brace rests against the ribs hanging from the pack frame.

The hangers for gun and tripod consist of two hooks bent to suit the load, and are made of steel. They are provided with eyes for attachment to the hooks on the arch frame, and are fitted with distance pieces, which rest on the ribs hanging from the pack frame, thus keeping the load away from the sides of the animal.

THE GUN COVER, SPARE BARREL, AND FILLING CUP.

The gun cover is made of heavy olive-drab duck and protects the gun from dust and rain.

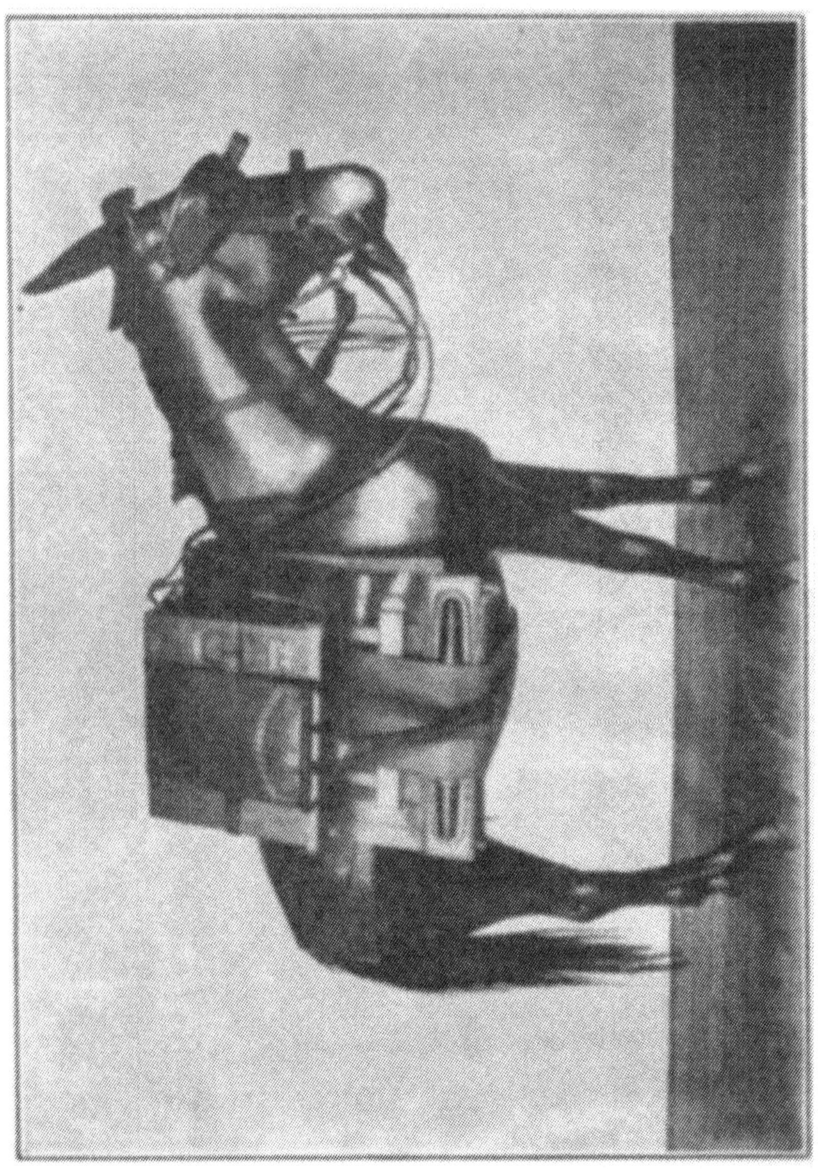

The spare barrel is carried in a russet-leather case strapped to the pack frame under the hanger on the gun side of the pack.

The filling cup for filling water jacket is carried strapped to the pack frame of one of the ammunition and water packs.

The various parts of the pack are shown separately in Figs. 134 and 135.

The weights of the loads are as follows:

Gun and tripod pack

	Pounds.
Blinder	1
Halter bridle	5
Aparejo proper	53 75
Belly cincha	2. 2
Load cincha	5
Gun with water jacket filled	74. 5
Pouch for rear sight carriage	18
Tripod	77. 5
Hanger of gun, with cover	10
Hanger of tripod	9
Spare barrel and case	7. 5
Pack frame	29
Pack cover, 78″ x 36″ 5	3 25
Total	278. 35

Ammunition and belt filling machine pack

	Pounds.
Blinder	1
Halter bridle	5
Aparejo, proper	53 75
Belt-filling machine and box	23 38
Ammunition hangers (2)	22
Ammunition boxes, empty (6)	30 96
Belly cincha	2 2
Load cincha	5
1,500 rounds of ammunition	96
Box with tools and accessories	20
Pack frame	29
Pack cover, 78″ x 36″ 5	3 25
Total	291. 54

Ammunition and water box pack

Blinder	1
Halter bridle	5
Aparejo, proper	53. 75
Ammunition hangers (2)	22
Ammunition boxes, empty (6)	31
Belly cincha	2 2
Load cincha	5
Water boxes, filled (2)	37 25
1,500 rounds of ammunition	96
Filling cup and straps[a]	1. 75
Pack frame	29
Pack cover, 78″ x 36″.5	3. 25
Total	287. 20

The top of the pack frame is so constructed that it may in emergencies be used as a seat, on which to pack from one to three standard-sized boxes of ammunition or other contents. For ordinary service, however, these packs are sufficiently heavy without such a top load.

[a] On one pack only.

TO PREPARE AND LOAD THE PACKS.

The animal being bridled and blinded, the pack is placed in position as follows:

The corona is first put on, the canvas side next the animal and the edge with circular stitching just over the withers.

The crupper, sobre-jalma, and pack frame are all bound to the aparejo body. The crupper is first attached by the leather thongs provided for the purpose. The sobre-jalma is then placed in position over the aparejo body, the slits near its center being passed over the staples projecting from the aparejo body. Next comes the pack frame, which is placed over all, the staples mentioned above passing through slots in the projecting ends of the flat steel pieces riveted to the bronze arches. The whole is fastened together by leather billets sewed to the sobre-jalma, the ends of which pass through the eyes of the staples.

The parts thus assembled are placed on the animal over the corona and bound in place by the aparejo cincha. The cincha is placed in position by passing the gas pipe end (seam side up) through the pack frame from the near side and bringing it up under the animal's belly. It is bound by simply passing the cincha strap several times through its seat in the end of the cincha and a ring fastened to the cincha strap near its fast end.

The pressure of the folds one upon another prevents slipping of the cincha strap. The loose end of the cincha strap is passed through a loop sewed to the cincha.

The hangers, gun, and tripod, or ammunition, are next placed in position and secured to the belly cinchas. The loads are then placed in position and fastened by straps attached to the various hangers.

The load cincha is now put on and lashed in place by the straps in the ends of the belly cincha. These straps also pass through D rings attached to the hangers, thus binding the various parts of the load firmly together.

CARE AND PRESERVATION OF LEATHER EQUIPMENTS.

These equipments are made of russet leather containing enough oil to materially improve the quality and increase the life of the leather, but not enough to soil the clothing if the equipment is properly cared for.

The leather is pure oak tanned, of No. 1 tannage and finish, hand stuffed, with a light dubbing made of pure tallow and cod liver oil to preserve the leather, the dubbing being so sparingly used that the oil will not exude.

The following directions for cleaning and preserving the leather equipment should be carefully followed:

To preserve the life of russet leather equipments they should be cleaned whenever dirt, grit, or dust has collected on them or when they have become saturated with the sweat of a horse. In cleaning them the parts should first be separated and each part sponged, using a lather of castile soap and warm water. When nearly dry a lather of Crown soap and warm water should be used. If the equipment is cared for frequently this method is sufficient; but if the leather has become hard and dry a little neat's-foot oil should be applied after washing with castile soap. When the oil is dry the equipments should be sponged lightly with Crown soap and water, which will remove the surplus remaining on the surface. If a polish is desired a thin coat of russet-leather polish issued by the Ordnance Department should be applied and rubbed briskly with a dry cloth.

Particular care should be taken not to use too much Crown soap or water, as the result will be detrimental to the life of the leather. *In no case should leather be dipped in water or be placed in the sun to dry.*

Weights.

Weight of gun, water jacket empty	pounds..	61.5
Weight of gun, water jacket filled	do....	74.5
Capacity of water jacket	pints..	13
Weight of tripod, complete, with cleaning rod	pounds..	78
Weight of wheeled mount, without equipment	do....	235
Weight of one ammunition box, with belt containing 250 cartridges	do....	21.16
Weight of tool box, filled	do....	20
Weight of water box	do....	18.62
Weight of belt-filling machine box, filled	do....	21

This short description or portion is taken from No. 1770, Handbook of the Maxim automatic machine gun, caliber 30. Revised January 7, 1908.

NOTE.—For improved method of carrying the Maxim automatic machine gun, caliber 30, see figs. 138 to 142. (Designed by H. W. Daly.)

PACK OUTFIT, AMERICAN MODEL, FOR 2.95-INCH VICKERS-MAXIM MOUNTAIN GUN.

(Figs. 143 to 149).

SEC. 141. Experience in the Philippines demonstrated that the English outfit is not entirely satisfactory, and a new pack, based on American practice, has been designed. The component parts per unit (one gun) of the American outfit are as follows: (See footnote.)

13 halter bridles.
13 aparejos—three 58-inch, seven 60-inch, and three 62-inch.
13 coronas—three 48-inch, seven 50-inch, and three 52-inch.
13 sobre-jalmas—three 59-inch, seven 61-inch, and three 63-inch.
13 aparejo cinchas.
10 belly cinchas.
13 cruppers 12 by 8 by 78 inches.
2 drag ropes.
2 wheel hangers.
1 pad for trail.
1 tool case, with inside pockets.
1 tool case, with inside straps.
4 lifting rods.
3 load cinchas
9 ammunition cinchas.
13 blinders.
1 sponge brush and sponge rod.
1 cleaning brush.
2 tubular oil cans
1 tubular oil-can carrier, with straps.
2 piston-rod protectors.
1 cradle cleaner.
1 set of tompions for cradle.
1 front-sight cover.
1 breech cover.
1 tangent-sight cover.
1 muzzle cover.
1 gunner's pouch.
6 lash ropes.
3 implement straps.
13 pack frames.
12 combined packing cases and ammunition hangers (12½-pound shell)
6 combined packing cases and ammunition hangers (18-pound shell).

NOTES.—(1) The above provides necessary equipment for one mule for gun, one mule for trail, one mule for cradle, one mule for wheels and accessories, and nine mules for ammunition. (2) A complete outfit for a four-gun battery would be obtained by multiplying the number of each of the articles above enumerated by four.

The pack frame placed on the aparejo is identical for all packs, and consists of two cast-bronze arches connected by bronze side bars, the frame thus formed is riveted to two steel hoops or ribs, which are connected fore and aft by four steel plates stiffened by flat pieces of wood, the lower ones supporting and distributing the effects of side loads when hangers are used.

The arrangement of the packs remains the same as in the English system, and while the weights of the loads with packs are greater they are closer to the mule's back, lessening the tendency to shift, are more securely lashed, and the weight is better distributed by the greater bearing surface of the aparejo. The method of lashing is shown in figs. 143 to 149, inclusive.

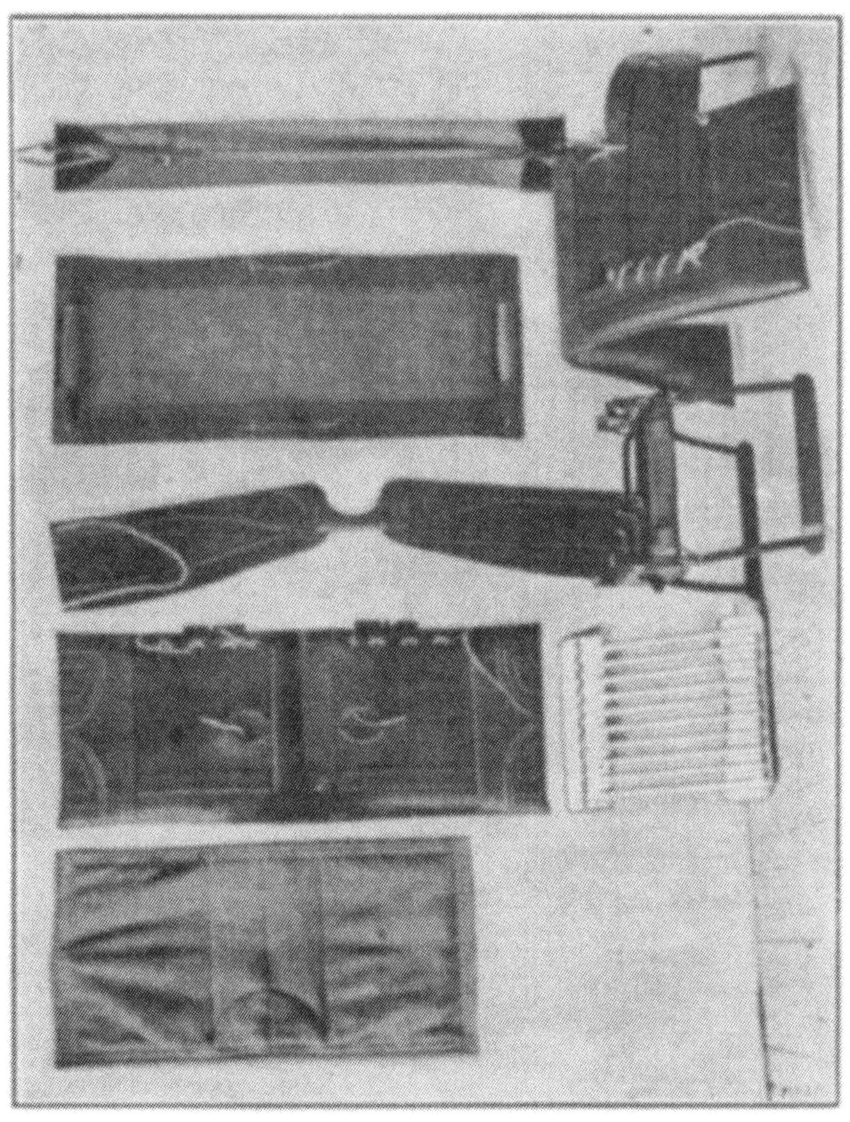

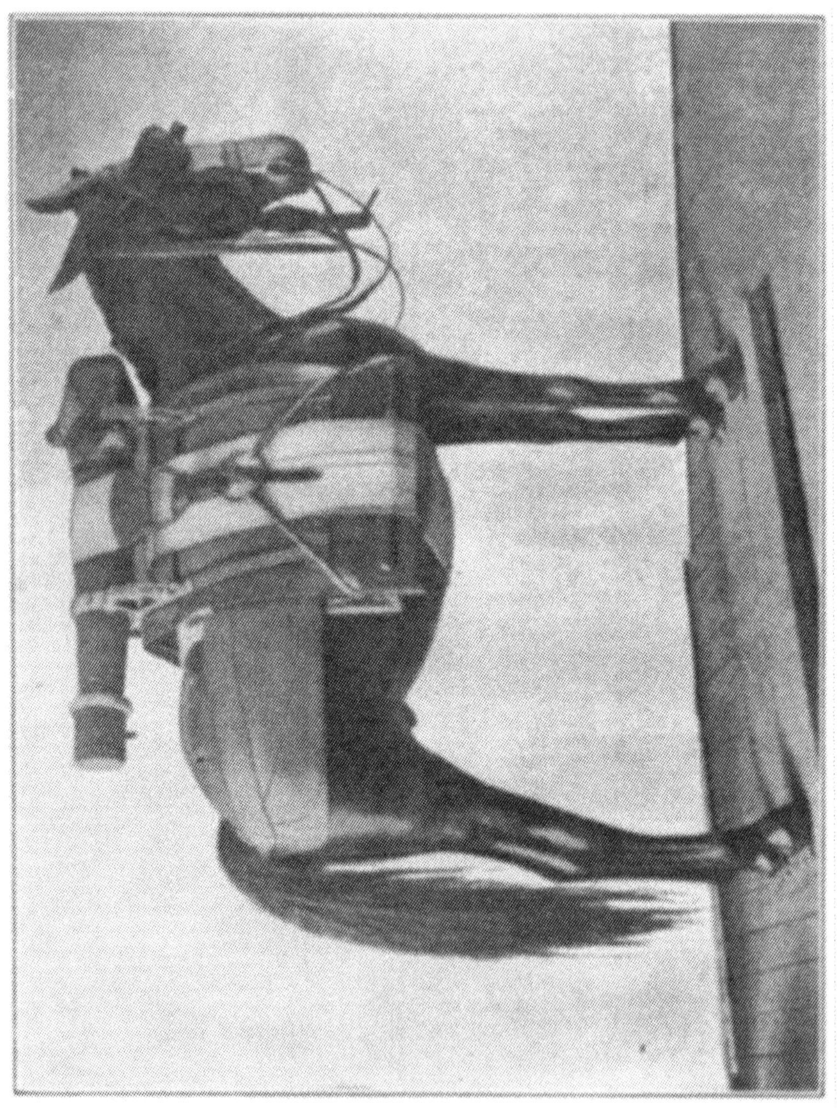

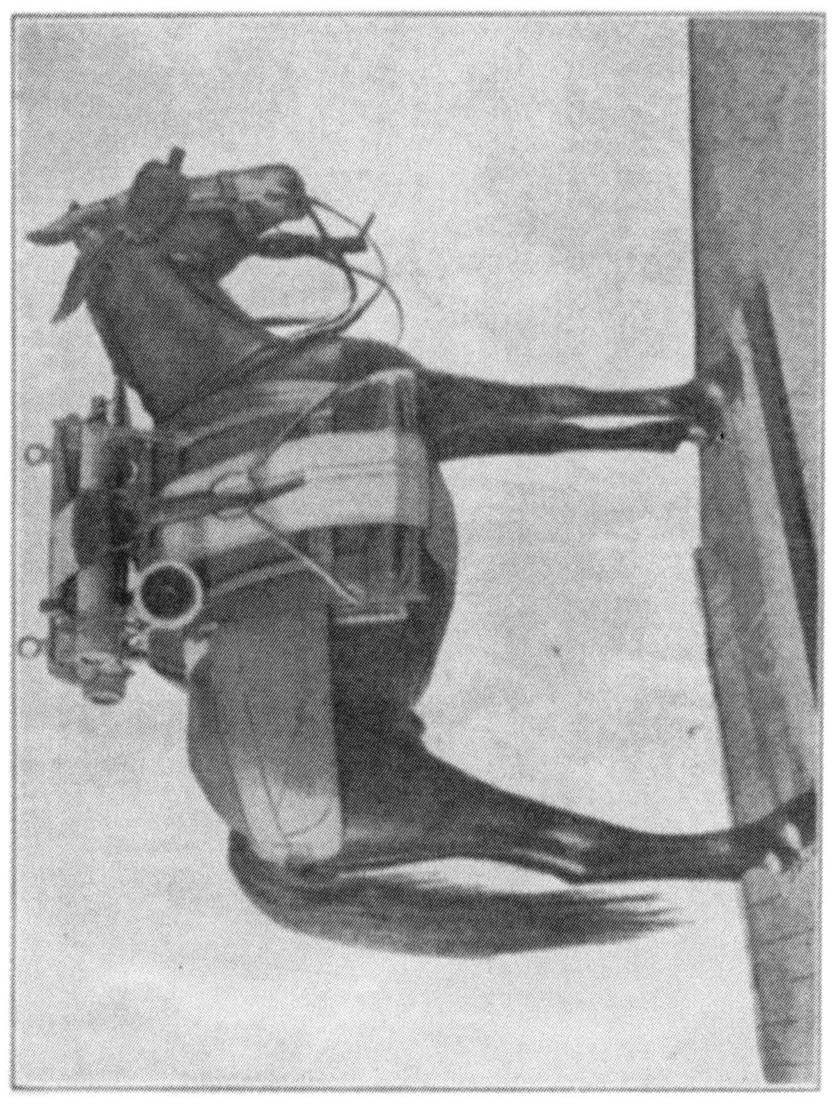

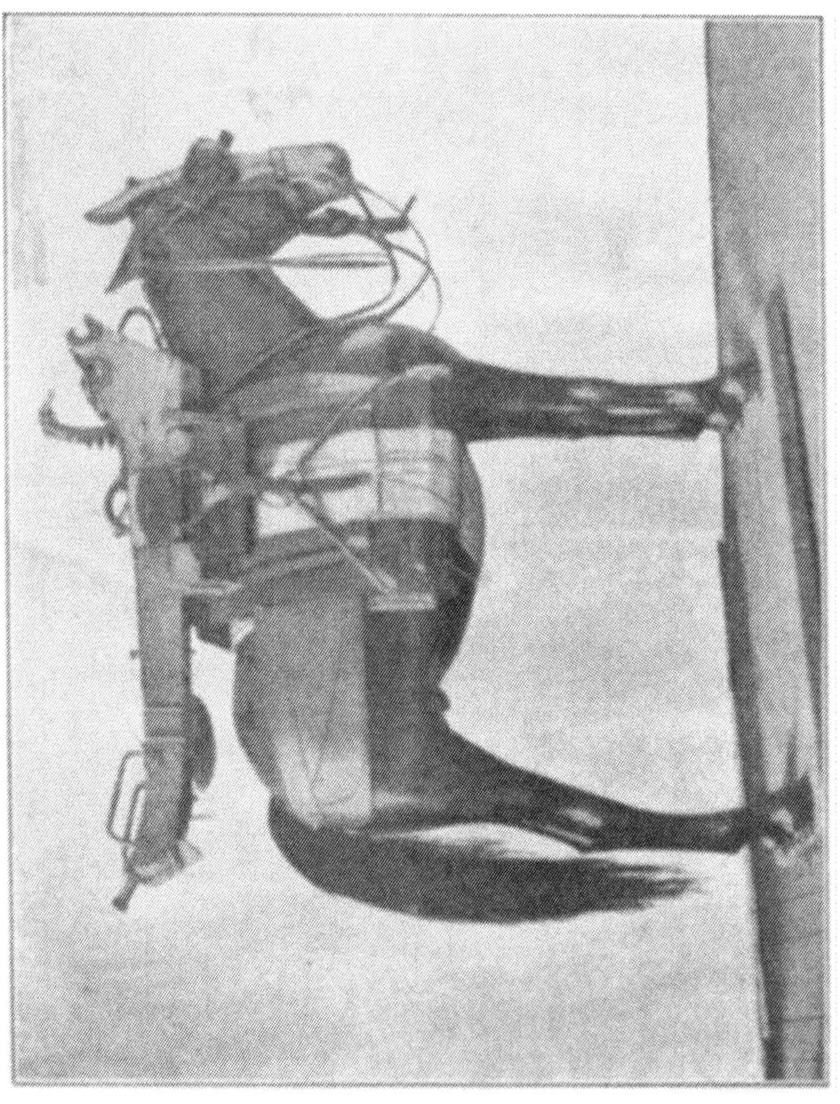

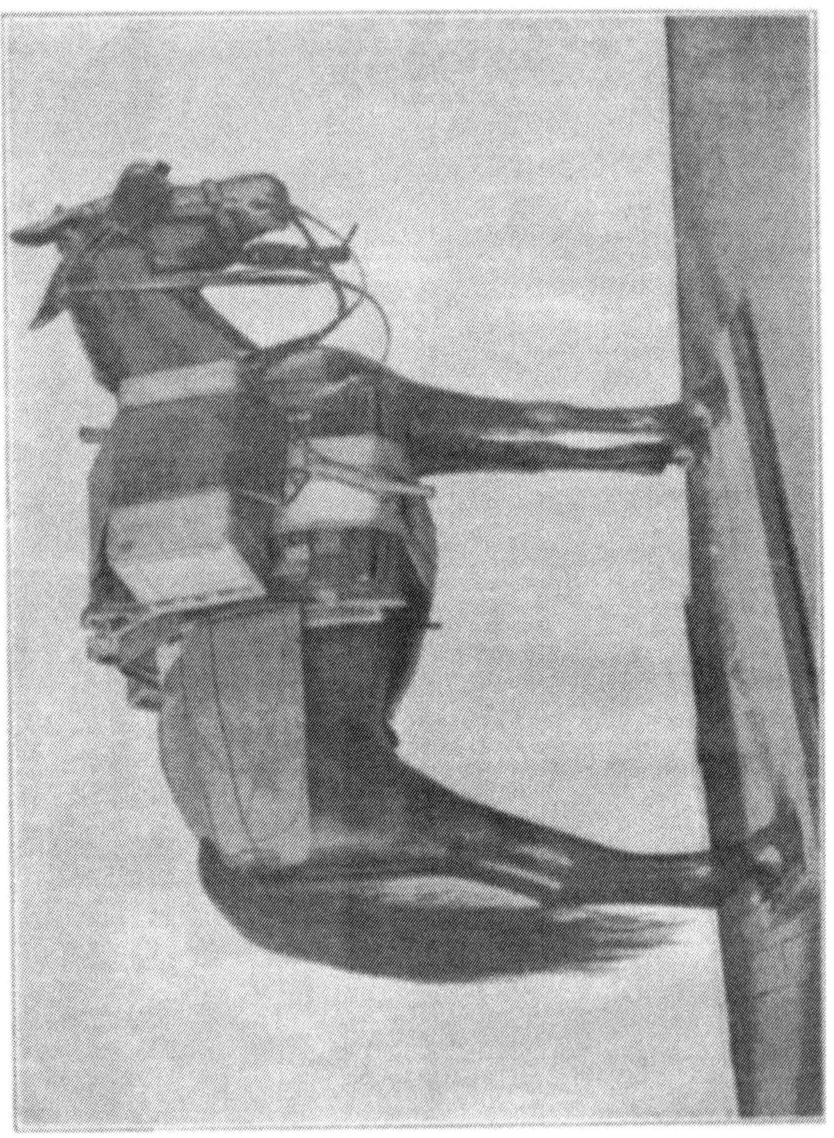

No of mule.	Description of load.	Weight.
		Pounds.
1	Gun, complete, with mechanism	236
	Breech and muzzle covers	2
	Load cincha	4
	Lash ropes	2
	Gunner's pouch	1
	Pack, complete—bridle, aparejo, crupper, cinchas, coronas, sobre-jalma and frame	90
	Total	335
2	Cradle, with buffers filled with oil	194
	Load cincha and lash loops	6
	Cradle cleaner and tompions	4
	Tool boxes, with tools	12
	Pack, complete	90
	Total	306
3	Trail with elevating gear	238
	Trail pad, lash loops, and load cincha	8
	Pack, complete	90
	Total	336
4	Wheels (2)	131
	One axle, with linchpin and washers	48
	Hangers	20
	Dragropes (2), brake ropes (2)	18
	Handspike, lifting bars, sponge brush and rod	25
	Implement straps and belly cincha	5
	Pack, complete	90
	Total	337
5	Ammunition-box hangers (2)	44
	Rounds, complete (12)	180
	Ammunition and belly cinchas	7
	Tubular oil can (filled)	12
	Pack, complete	90
	Total	333
6	Ammunition-box hangers	42
	Rounds, complete (10, double common shells)	205
	Cinchas	7
	Pack, complete	90
	Total	344

www.ingramcontent.com/pod-product-compliance
Lightning Source LLC
Chambersburg PA
CBHW031832090426
42741CB00005B/212
9781589634534